Procreative Man

Procreative Man

William Marsiglio

NEW YORK UNIVERSITY PRESS
New York and London

NEW YORK UNIVERSITY PRESS
New York and London

Copyright © 1998 by New York Univeristy
All rights reserved

Library of Congress Cataloging-in-Publication Data
Marsiglio, William.
Procreative man / William Marsiglio.
p. cm.
Includes bibliographical references and index.
ISBN 0-8147-5578-X (clothbound : acid-free paper).
ISBN 0-8147-5579-8 (paperbound : acid-free paper).
1. Fatherhood. 2. Men—Psychology. 3. Men—Sexual behavior.
4. Human reproduction—Social aspects. I. Title
HQ756.M345 1997
306.874'2—DC21   97-21089
                  CIP

New York University Press books are printed on acid-free paper,
and their binding materials are chosen for strength and durability.

Manufactured in the United States of America

10 9 8 7 6 5 4 3 2 1

Contents

Preface

It was more than twenty years ago, on an early Wednesday morning in June. The hallway doors near the hospital's delivery room swung open with a thud, startling me to consciousness. I rose from the linoleum floor, sleep deprived, exhausted, and anxious to hear the doctor's voice. "Congratulations, you're a father. It's a boy," he calmly remarked as his outstretched hand found my own. After thanking him, and asking about my wife, I was overcome by the thought that I was really a father now, yes, a dad. It seemed so peculiar to me; I was only eighteen. Buried among my muddled thoughts and inexperience, I imagined that eighteen-year-olds were sons and daughters, not parents. But here I was, a proud father of a little baby boy named Scott. Life was strange.

Riding my emotional high, I spent the next several hours basking in the afterglow of this momentous occasion, my rite of passage to manhood complete. I phoned my father in search of his approval. Unfortunately, his devotion to his own image of the good "family man" kept him from leaving his job at a local factory to share my euphoria in person. He would anoint my entry into manhood with a handshake later that afternoon. My mother was nearby in the hospital, as was my older sister and several other relatives. Despite their enthusiasm, this was ultimately my moment. I was in many respects alone with my thoughts. Although I had relentlessly executed my coaching role during my wife's twenty-seven hours of strenuous labor, the physician had denied me access to the delivery room because he had induced my wife's labor. My son was born while I waited prone on the hallway floor.

My identity as a father would come into focus when I first saw Scott snuggled safely in his mother's arms a few hours after the doctor's message. Throughout the months leading up to this day, I had wrestled with vague images of myself as a father. Seeing my son, and then holding him in my arms, brought to life my new identity as a father. I was apprehensive about this transition to fatherhood, but it was at least beginning to make sense to me. I had struggled to think of myself as a "father-in-waiting" during the pregnancy. The childbirth preparation course may have helped a bit, but the transition was still difficult. Prior to my girlfriend's pregnancy, I had never thought of myself as a father; it did not jibe with my plans for the immediate future. I found no comfort either in the fact that thousands of teenagers throughout the country were also walking in my shoes; in fact, I was unaware of these demographic patterns. None of my close friends were parents. As I recall, my limited view of fatherhood was based on my own father's relationship to me; my generational focus took aim at the past not the future. I had not thought about what it would be like to have my own child, at least not prior to learning that my girlfriend, soon to be my wife, was probably pregnant. I suppose I was too busy honing my jumpshot and dreaming foolishly of the NBA—a working-class kid hooked on sports.

My own imagery of being a father first surfaced on a Saturday afternoon in February when an unknown hospital counselor, cloaked in secrecy, whispered the unforgettable news to my girlfriend and me as we sat restlessly on the designated bench adjacent to the bird cage at the local mall, "Your test was positive; you're four months pregnant." Those words numbed us both. Our denial had been shattered, and our ignorance and sense of invulnerability could no longer protect us from the harsh reality. We were going to be parents; our families would not be pleased!

During the months that followed, I began to feel as though I had proven my manhood, without intending to do so, by impregnating my girlfriend. In the process of eventually becoming the father of a child, I had prematurely advanced myself along the life course in a way quite different from my peers. Within the year I was pondering how I could hold my baby without breaking him while my former high school buddies plotted ways to get their underage hands on a case of beer. This unique identity as a young father would continue to distinguish me from my peers throughout my college years. In the tradition of humanistic sociology, my appreciation for men as procreative beings and fathers is shaped at least in part by my personal experiences during those formative years over two decades ago. Other personal experiences since then have no doubt modified my understanding of men as persons capable of creating and fathering human life.

My personal views about such matters have also been fashioned by my scholarly endeavors. Throughout my career as a sociologist, I have been consumed by my desire to understand the rhythms of men's thoughts, feelings, and behaviors in this sphere of life. I have also been fascinated with the institutional forces and social conventions that structure men's experiences as procreative beings.

Ironically, a series of serendipitous events provided the impetus for my scholarly calling. I fondly remember giving the humorous and well-received speech on men and sperm banks in a speech communications course that gave me the confidence to pursue a career in the academy. I had repeatedly postponed taking this required course until the final term of my senior year in college. As luck would have it, the topic of this semi-risqué speech was greeted with curiosity because most people at the time had not yet heard of the emerging commercialized sperm bank industry. No doubt my detailed and tantalizing description of the sperm collection procedures captured my fellow students' attention.

From there I went on to complete a master's thesis that examined husbands' and wives' willingness to use a reliable male birth control pill if it were marketed to the public. This topic evolved out of a group project I completed for a graduate seminar in consumer behavior. Students were required to develop an elaborate marketing research plan for a new product; my group choose to market a male birth control pill. While the world still anxiously awaits the development and distribution of a safe and effective male hormonal contraceptive, the scientific community inches closer to what will undoubtedly be a revolutionary moment in contraceptive history.

I soon thereafter landed a graduate research position at the Center for Human Resource Research at Ohio State, where I was given the opportunity to use national survey data to write a book chapter on teenage fathers. Being an opportunistic graduate student, I turned my work on that chapter into a dissertation project and collected other survey data from local high school students, asking them to share their views on how they would deal with an unplanned pregnancy at this point in their lives. During my graduate school days, I also completed a class assignment by conducting a needs assessment study targeted at men who accompanied their partner to a local abortion clinic.

Since those early years of my career, I have continued to explore a variety of issues related to my initial studies. Most notable among these have been men's attitudes about fathering children and their subsequent conduct with them, men's attitudes about sex and condoms as well as their behaviors in these areas, men's attitudes about pregnancy resolution and abortion, men's concerns about using asexual reproductive technologies, and men's perceptions about fatherhood. Thus *Procreative Man* clearly represents one of those books that has informally been in progress for many years. My personal testimony about the joys and struggles I experienced as a young man reveal the longstanding affinity I have had with the meaning of fatherhood, especially for those young men who assume this status unexpectedly. Meanwhile, my more academic scholarship on a range of topics dealing with men's sexual, procreative, and paternal experiences demonstrates my concern with the big picture of how men experience their multifaceted lives as procreative beings. In the pages to follow, I develop an analytic synthesis of my diverse interests in this area. In so doing, I try to integrate the relevant interdisciplinary literatures in this broad area to provide an overview of men's procreative lives with an eye toward the past, present, and future. The conceptual framework I introduce provides a general scheme for viewing men's varied experiences. I supplement this framework by using a gender lens to organize much of my thinking about specific topics. A basic premise of my approach is that the world of reproduction is a highly gendered domain.

The title I've chosen for this book clearly alludes to my interest in exploring men's gender-based experiences with reproductive issues. My decision to opt for a simple and stylistically appealing title deserves comment, though, since it may suggest, especially to those sensitive to the ongoing theoretical debates about the varied masculinities that give meaning to men's lives today, that I intend to portray a singular figure—a universal "procreative man." Men obviously have varied experiences as procreative beings as a result of the types of romantic relationships they maintain as well as their family and cultural background, religious beliefs, health status, life course stage, and age. While I highlight these differences where the scholarly literature permits, the available data in some cases are either quite thin or absent. Moreover, because I explore how reproductive physiology as well as social and cultural factors help shape the different contexts within which men and women experience themselves as reproductive beings, much of my discussion focuses on men collectively, as a separate gender category. Thus, the paucity of data on some of the topics I cover limits my ability to explore procreative experiences for different categories of men, many of whom are affected by different types of masculinities. My principal contribution, then, is to develop new ways of thinking about men's diverse procreative experiences and to generate future research avenues.

Given the centrality of the gender perspective to my work, I am indebted to Scott Coltrane, Michael Kimmel, and Joseph Pleck for paving the way for me to tackle a project that deals with men and masculinity issues. They have each provided me with guidance, collegial support, and inspiration over the years as I sought to make a contribution to the growing literature on men. Likewise, I would like to thank Frank Furstenberg and John Scanzoni for helping me to appreciate more fully various dimensions to the study of fatherhood and social families that I have woven into this book. Elizabeth Menaghan and Frank Mott each deserve my recognition for their unwavering faith in my ability to undertake and complete my unconventional projects on men during the early phases of my career, and their subsequent support as I expanded my vision of men as procreative beings.

I draw extensively on some of my previous writings to organize several sections of this book. Two of these papers were coauthored with Elizabeth Menaghan and another with Constance Shehan. I am grateful for their contribution to my work on issues associated with married men's attitudes toward using a male birth control pill and young men's views about the various options for resolving pregnancies, most notably abortion. I also appreciate two attorney friends, Michael Barbarette and Thomas Edwards, who shared their insights with me about the legal consequences associated with my controversial proposal that deals with men, abortion, and child support issues. I might add that they were not very optimistic that my proposal was practical from a legal standpoint.

A number of undergraduate and graduate students provided me with invaluable research assistance and critiques of my work during the past three years, including Doug Diekow, Neil Drake, Rahil Jammani, Christine Kudisch, Cristina Lizarazu, Goldie MacDonald, Kevin McLain, Janet McNellis, Scott Melzer, Tina Shah, Bradley Tripp, and Jeremy Walker. I appreciate their assistance and interest in my work. Likewise, I appreciate Jeff Musick's valuable editorial advise. Finally, I am fortunate to have had Tim Bartlett serve as my NYU Press editor. Tim's enthusiastic support and insightful guidance were invaluable as he challenged me to make this book accessible to a diverse audience of scholars and other interested readers.

Now, with the faint echo of the hospital doors reminding me of this project's lengthy journey, I dedicate this book to my son, Scott Michael.

1

Men and Procreation

While the social and biological aspects of contraception, pregnancy, and childbearing have been, and continue to be, the principal province of women, men have begun in recent years to play a more prominent role in activities associated with reproduction and fatherhood. In the United States and other western societies, social expectations surrounding men's involvement in these areas during the past few decades have shifted in response to changing gender roles, women's increased participation in the labor market, child poverty and concerns about children's general well-being, fears of excessive population growth, the HIV/AIDS epidemic, and the introduction of new technologies related to reproduction and contraception. As a result, the general public, as well as social policymakers, family planning personnel, and academics have deepened their desire to understand and promote men's positive involvement in areas associated with reproduction and fatherhood.[1]

This burgeoning interest in men's involvement in reproductive and fatherhood activities has evolved alongside the public discourses about women's and children's well-being specifically and about family issues more generally. Some of the most controversial public and scholarly debates in recent years have dealt with issues related to reproduction and the care of children. Confrontations over the basic meaning of the term "family," fueled largely by interest group politics, and over the relative rights and obligations of family members to one another distinguish these ongoing discussions. The participants in these high-profile debates have included advocates of liberal or "progressive" family ideologies and others who are guided by more conservative and, oftentimes, religiously oriented views. Technological advances (e.g., in-vitro fertilization techniques) and biosocial innovations (e.g., sperm banks, surrogate pregnancy) have also pushed the meaning of familial relations into unchartered territory. These changes have raised a variety of questions relevant to men's and women's reproductive experiences.[2]

Concerns about the comparative importance of biological versus social fatherhood are central to some of these discussions and are directly relevant to my analysis of men as procreative beings. While the debates in question are equally germane to biological, gestational, and birth mothers,[3] I limit my discussion to fathers. Legal disputes in this area have been waged to determine when, if ever, birth parents' rights supersede those of adoptive parents. Several landmark cases in the 1990s, such as the "Baby Jessica" case,[4] have brought these issues to the public's attention while highlighting men's paternity interests in the process.

The Baby Jessica case and others like it reflect a larger social trend toward paying greater attention to men's diverse roles in reproduction. These roles refer to men's activities prior to conception, during gestation, and after birth. Men's parenting roles have received the most notice as images of "new age" and "androgynous" fathers, juxtaposed against images of "bad dads" and "deadbeat dads," have inundated popular culture. As a result, men who live with their children are increasingly thought to be involved in the hands-on tasks of parenting and, presumably, thinking more than ever before about what it means to be a father. This emerging interest in men's procreative and paternal roles in the U.S. and other western societies coincides with individuals' attempts to wrestle with shifting demographic patterns associated with marriage, divorce, remarriage, and childbearing. Likewise, this interest is fueled by individuals' varying perceptions of family life and their sense of gender equity as it relates to reproductive issues.

The Study of Procreative Men

In the 1980s, the first concerted, large-scale effort was made to accentuate men's potential roles and responsibilities in the areas of family planning and fatherhood. Some of the major initiatives and reports during this period included the awarding of small grants to twenty agencies in 1984 by the Office of Family Planning in the Department of Health and Human Services to develop male involvement programs, the National Urban League's Adolescent Male Responsibility Program begun in 1986, the National Academy of Sciences' 1987 Panel on Adolescent Pregnancy and Childbearing (which argued that it was counterproductive to view adolescent pregnancy and childbearing as simply a female problem), and the 1988 Children's Defense Fund report, *What about the Boys?*

This trend has continued unabated throughout the 1990s, with no signs that it will be reversed anytime soon. Indeed, it may actually be picking up steam. In policy circles, the emerging sentiment is that the cornerstone to national and local efforts to promote responsible fatherhood involves a better understanding of the male role in pregnancy prevention.[5] Along these lines, one of the principle objectives of the National Campaign to Prevent Teen Pregnancy is to target teenage and young adult men. One important step in this direction included the roundtable of scholars and social service providers who were assembled in Washington, D.C., in February 1997 to discuss how pregnancy prevention programs could be improved by focusing more attention on men's sexual and procreative roles.

Efforts to promote research and policy initiatives that focus specifically on fathers are very much in vogue as well.[6] These activities have been aided by the new research and policy-oriented centers located around the country that address fatherhood issues.[7] The main objective of these organizations is to understand and promote fathers' positive involvement in their children's lives. In addition, fatherhood issues have come under scrutiny by social movement groups such as fathers' rights groups[8] and the Promise Keepers,[9] as well as many community-based groups like the Responsive Fathers Program in Philadelphia, the National Institute of Responsible Fatherhood and Family Revitalization in Cleveland, and the forty or so affiliates of MAD DADS (Men Against Destruction–Defending Against Drugs and Social Disorder) in the United States.[10] Finally, policymakers' efforts to improve the rate at which paternity is established for children, and to increase the collection of child support payments from nonresident fathers, have also played a major role in drawing attention to fatherhood issues.[11]

Events including the National Science Foundation's sponsorship of the America's Fathers and Public Policy conference in 1993,[12] the series of seven roundtable meetings in 1995 and 1996 sponsored by the National Center on Fathers and Families at the University of Pennsylvania, and the National Symposium on Men in Families sponsored by the Pennsylvania State University in the fall of 1996 have all helped to perpetuate scholars' interest in fatherhood. Perhaps the most significant event occurred in 1995 when the White House launched the Fatherhood Initiative. The major objective of this initiative, directed by the Domestic Policy Council and the vice president's National Performance Review, is to promote fathers' positive involvement in their children's lives, even when they do not live together. Federal agencies have been charged by the Clinton administration to do everything they can to promote research on fatherhood issues by improving data sources on male fertility and fatherhood. This initiative has resulted in a series of multidisciplinary conferences and workshops, culminating in the Conference on Fathering and Male Fertility: Improving Data and Research held in Washington, D.C., in March 1997.[13]

The preceding list of activities reflects scholars' and policymakers' keen interest in men's sexual, procreative, and familial roles. This attention, which is consistent with the general public's curiosity about these topics, has generated a fairly extensive body of scholarly work. Although there is still plenty to learn, particularly about men from different socioeconomic and racial backgrounds, we know much more about men's lives as procreative beings than we did twenty years ago.[14]

One of the major shortcomings of this literature, in my view, is the absence of a conceptual model that articulates and synthesizes the common threads to the various aspects of men's lives as procreative beings.[15] The scholarship in this area focuses on various topics, including men's sexual behavior and condom use, abortion views, feelings about using assisted reproductive techniques (ART), involvement with partners during their pregnancy, and responses to siring a child out of wedlock.[16] It makes sense, though, both theoretically and from a social policy perspective, to examine men's lives as procreative beings in a more holistic fashion. Much can be gained by not only studying men's specific types of experiences as procreative beings, but clarifying how these experiences are also part of a larger procreative domain. My basic objective in this book, then, is to provide a fresh conceptual scheme for viewing men's diverse thoughts and actions as procreative beings. I strive to be comprehensive in presenting a theoretically informed overview of men's experiences as they encounter the variegated question of procreation.[17]

Presenting a nuanced portrait of men's lives as procreative beings necessitates an appreciation for the larger sociohistorical context within which men think, feel, and act. Men's experiences as procreative beings have been transformed throughout history by cultural, social, and scientific developments. While it is not my intent to provide an elaborate historical analysis of men's lives in this area, I briefly discuss some of the more significant developments, particularly those that have occurred in recent decades.

Future innovations will surely provide men with additional opportunities to experience their procreative lives in new ways. For example, dramatic changes may occur because of technological advances in male contraception and ART. Other changes will result from policymakers, social service providers, educators, and other involved citizens joining in a cooperative effort to take men into account when they develop public policies and programs that deal with reproductive issues. Some of these efforts will be designed to encourage male responsibility prior to conception, others will deal with men during the pregnancy process, and some will focus on men after their children are born. Thus, in addition to exploring how recent social developments have altered the context for contemporary men's procreative experiences, I speculate on how new developments are likely to affect men's procreative lives in the next century.

Throughout this book, I explore aspects of men's lives in America and other western industrialized societies that are expressed within what I alternatively refer to as the *reproductive realm* or *procreative realm*.[18] These terms represent my shorthand way of identifying individuals' personal and social experiences related to reproduction. In theory, the reproductive and procreative terms can be used interchangeably. However, I use the reproductive label to refer to the domain of reproductive issues that incorporates both women's and men's perspectives and the procreative label to signify reproductive issues from the "male" perspective. I revisit this distinction later in this chapter when defining the concept *procreative consciousness*. The procreative realm is comprised of issues dealing with conception, contraception, abortion, assisted reproductive technologies, gestation, childbearing, adoption, and stepfatherhood. Whereas adoption and stepfatherhood issues technically pertain to the domain of parenting rather than reproduction per se, I focus on them here because they serve as alternative pathways to procreation and fatherhood. Lastly, I briefly discuss child support and child care issues as they relate to the procreative realm.

Men as Procreative Beings

Among the factors that affect how men think about themselves and experience their lives in the procreative realm are what students of culture term "symbolic forms."[19] In an abstract sense, these cultural elements represent the ways social life is organized or the "stuff" of specific cultures. People can use different types of symbolic forms to experience and express themselves as members of a particular culture and to manage their lives in relation to others. Two symbolic forms central to the present discussion are labeled "ways of forming social bonds" and "ritual practices." Each of these cultural elements provide individuals with opportunities to experience and express their meaning as reproductive beings. Ways of forming social bonds refers to social processes that enable people to establish formal or informal ties with one another (e.g., marriage, adoption, signing paternity papers, fraternity or sorority initiations). Ritual practices include activities that enable people to express their needs, moods, motivations, sentiments, and feelings, many of them with a ceremonial dimension (e.g., weddings, gift giving, and competitive games). These two symbolic forms are sometimes related because a ritual practice may take place as part of the process of forming a particular type of social bond.

Establishing a paternal identity is one of the most basic and significant images men have of themselves within the procreative realm. Although there are several paths for establishing paternity—and the social bonds that unite fathers and their children as well—a paternal identity in its crudest form represents men's recognition that they see themselves as being someone's father. Possessing a paternal identity does not guarantee, however, that men will necessarily behave in a particular way, and men's resolve to be a "responsible" father figure varies considerably. Paternal identities are ultimately expressed in a personal or psychological fashion, while the various paths to establish paternity involve some combination of legal, social, and medical circumstances. The legal process of signing paternity papers establishes in a formal sense that men accept the legal responsibilities of being fathers for particular children—even though in some cases they may not be the biological fathers, a fact that they may or may not know.[20]

The informal social aspects of developing paternal bonds are most commonly associated with men's involvement in the labor and delivery process. The most significant moment is likely to occur shortly after labor and delivery. Fathers who are motivated and permitted to be involved have the opportunity to hold their children for the first time. The initial, and subsequent, father-child interaction represents the basic social gesture for establishing a paternal social bond and father-child attachment. For many men today, this bonding process actually begins during the gestation process when they recognize that their partners' body is changing and/or they are exposed to the fetus through modern technologies such as ultrasound.

The social paternal gesture may be expressed differently among men who formally adopt children (either as an adoptive parent or stepparent to a partner's biological child) compared to stepfathers who informally assume paternal roles without claiming legal paternal rights and obligations toward "their" children. In the latter case, there is unlikely to be a specific gesture or defining moment when the fatherlike identity emerges. Nonetheless, some of these stepfathers over time develop an image of themselves as a father figure.

Another example of an alternative path to fatherhood involves those men who become social fathers through the use of donor semen. Their efforts to form a bond with their children may parallel those of biological fathers who are actively involved with their infants, although some men who rely on donor semen may do much less in the way of forming a social bond or becoming attached to their children during the prenatal period. Instead, they may rely on their interaction with their children once they are born.

While few rituals are available to men in the United States that enable them to develop and solidify their paternal identity, prepared childbirth classes do present one significant ritual. Over the past several decades, these classes have become an exciting forum within which men learn to appreciate more fully their father-in-waiting[21] status. They also serve the purpose of giving men the chance to strengthen the connection between their paternal and partner identities as they and their partner jointly learn about the pregnancy and childbirth processes.

Men's experiences in the procreative realm, when considered collectively, can also affect the larger cultural and social milieu that shapes how procreative issues for men are defined. One timely example involves men's participation in the gestation process. Over time, as more and more men have begun to participate in prepared childbirth classes as well as labor and delivery procedures, their participation has apparently modified some of the popular images associated with fatherhood. My general impression is that images of fatherhood have evolved, especially for committed couples, to include men's roles in the prenatal period. People increasingly view men as fulfilling a paternal role when they are actively engaged in their partner's pregnancy prior to the actual birth of their child. Pregnant women continue to receive more attention than fathers-in-waiting, but prospective fathers are at least acknowledged more readily than in the past; some even have baby showers organized for them or are included in a "couples' shower." In the future, men's involvement in the pregnancy and childbirth processes is likely to become even more institutionalized in response to changing gender roles as well as changing policies within the medical community.

Other examples of how men's activities may alter the cultural landscape involve men's recent exposure to modern forms of reproductive technology and the forthcoming improvements in male birth control technology. As I discuss in subsequent chapters, these technologies will alter individuals' perceptions of paternity and change the decision-making dynamics between couples contemplating birth control. In the future, as individuals directly or indirectly incorporate these innovations into their understanding of men's experiences, they are likely to alter cultural expectations for men as procreative beings.

Guiding Theoretical Themes

My analysis of men as procreative beings draws primarily on three interrelated theoretical approaches used by sociologists and other social scientists: *symbolic interactionism*, the *scripting perspective*, and *identity theory*. To a lesser extent, the phenomenological and developmental perspectives sharpen my analysis of men's lives in this area.

In the following pages, I sketch some of the basic theoretical themes that guide my analysis. My objectives in this regard are modest; I do not attempt a grand synthesis of these perspectives, rather I use them selectively to direct my discussion. While these themes emphasize men's ability to control the way they think and act as procreative beings, I highlight how men's experiences are structured by larger social forces.

Symbolic Interactionism

My view of men's experiences in the procreative realm is shaped most profoundly by the symbolic interactionist perspective. A basic tenet of this perspective is that the way individuals come to define objects, situations, and experiences emerges out of their social interactions.[22] The specific definitions and meanings that are associated with men's procreative roles and feelings at any one point in time are not intrinsic or inherent to men. Men are not born with these definitions and meanings in their minds, rather they form their ideas about abortion, contraception, paternity, and other related issues through their socialization and personal experiences.

Thus cultural and social factors play an important role in shaping the meanings surrounding procreative issues. Men of different ages and those from various racial, social class, religious, and other social backgrounds may view these meanings quite differently.[23] Cross-cultural differences in men's lives as procreative beings, though generally beyond the scope of this book, are quite dramatic as well.

The symbolic interactionist perspective points out that individuals continually negotiate and renegotiate these definitions as they go about their everyday life activities. Thus these definitions and meanings are subject to change over time, especially in response to men's developmental stages and life course experiences.

Some of these themes are illustrated by an ethnographic study of economically disadvantaged teenage and young adult men in Brooklyn, New York, during the 1980s. This study revealed that some respondents felt that they were too young and not sufficiently mature to impregnate their partner. Some "referred to their ejaculate as 'dog water' or said that they thought they were 'shooting blanks'" (p. 3), although the majority were aware that sex could lead to pregnancy.[24] The young men in this study were not born with these perceptions, they learned these "street" ideas, as well as the appropriate vernacular to share their thoughts about them, during a developmental period in their lives that took place in a specific subcultural and socioeconomic environment. As these teenage boys became adult men, they probably grew more knowledgeable about their ability to sire children and in the process developed different images of themselves as procreative beings—particularly in those instances where they learned that they had sired a child.

We must not forget, as we consider the insights of the symbolic interactionist perspective, that men's perceptions and attempts at negotiating definitions of themselves as well as situations are imbedded within specific community contexts. For poor, minority, inner-city young men, this means that they will often be exposed to a subculture of despair, limited economic opportunities, minimal supervision, and peer groups who thrive on taking risks.[25] White middle-class men, on the other hand, are likely to be immersed in social networks and communities where employment opportunities are relatively plentiful and a favorable view of marriage and responsible fatherhood is more pervasive.

My discussion of how men interpret and feel about their experiences in the procreative realm also emphasizes the symbolic interactionist perspective because it highlights the connection between men's relationships with others and how they define themselves. The way men see themselves as procreative beings is thus affected by the way others interact with them and, more importantly, how these men interpret others' behaviors and perceptions. Men's procreative lives consist of a multitude of activities (e.g., contraception, attempts to conceive, abortion, prepared childbirth classes, visits to a fertility clinic, attendance during labor and delivery) that have both symbolic and practical significance for men. Interpersonal and situational factors affect how men perceive and experience these activities. For instance, men who are in committed relationships and are prospective fathers are likely to perceive their procreative experiences differently than men who are not romantically committed to their partners. In the former situation, men are probably much more likely to perceive their partner and paternal identities as being interrelated. The feelings and perceptions they have in relation to one identity can therefore affect their other identity.

The significance of situational factors is most clearly revealed by considering men who are trying to impregnate their partner through sexual intercourse but have been unable to so. Men typically have little reason to question their procreative potential unless they are frustrated by their inability to sire children with their partners. Most men simply assume they are able to sire children; they tend not to worry about their ability to procreate until they encounter some type of difficulty. Once men experience difficulty—especially if they are personally diagnosed as having a fertility problem—some may feel as if their masculinity is threatened and agonize over their inability to fulfill their paternal and partner roles.

The way men interpret and feel about situations in the procreative realm are affected by their awareness of, and response to, prevailing social expectations. Consider for a moment middle-age men who have not yet fathered children. Some are affected by pronatalist norms and feel social pressure to have children. Their reaction may be complicated further if they are affected by societal norms that disapprove of out-of-wedlock paternity. Some unmarried middle-age men may therefore feel compelled to consider more seriously the possibility of getting married and having children if they feel a need to fulfill what they perceive to be their adult and masculine roles. Meanwhile, those men who are already involved in a relationship but unable to impregnate their partner may feel anxious or inadequate because of the social stigma associated with male infertility.

Scripting Perspective

The scripting perspective provides a related approach for theorizing about the connection between social expectations and individual men's personal experiences in the procreative realm.[26] It views much of social life as being expressed on three distinct but interrelated levels: *cultural scenarios, interpersonal scripting,* and *intrapsychic scripting.*[27] It also recognizes how the patterned aspects of the social world, including social norms, can affect people's behavior. At the same time, it takes into account the notion that people are autonomous beings. Individuals are free to create their own idiosyncratic ways of thinking about themselves and interacting with others.

The most general level of this model refers to the cultural and subcultural scenarios[28] associated with the expression of particular roles. These scenarios include the basic ideas and normative guidelines that clarify how individuals should think, feel, and act within the context of specific roles, or in some instances according to particular social attributes they may possess (e.g., gender).[29] In their most general form, cultural scenarios also include social expectations about how others should think, feel, and act toward persons who are expressing themselves through a role. In addition to this normative emphasis, cultural scenarios can be viewed as including general knowledge, ideal images, and stereotypes about specific roles.[30] These scenarios, whether they are of the more general or subcultural variety, are sustained by ongoing formal and informal social processes that are susceptible to the whims of social change as people's attitudes and beliefs shift over time. Moreover, being aware of these roles and cultural scenarios does not mean that people will adhere to them at all times, or at any time for that matter.

While the scripting perspective views men as autonomous beings, it underscores the idea that men's behavior is affected to some extent by the cultural scenarios that touch their lives. The cultural scenarios and roles most important for the aspects of social life that I examine in this book include those associated with being a romantic partner, father, and masculine man.[31]

Men's experiences in the procreative realm are often affected by cultural scenarios that combine aspects of specific interpersonal roles such as being a father with expectations associated with more general images of masculinity. For instance, mainstream cultural images of manhood in the United States tend to encourage men to take financial responsibility for children they beget.[32] These images address men's interpersonal fatherhood roles, the "good-provider" role in particular, as well as their more general role as masculine men. The norms associated with men's father and partner roles encourage men to support their families financially and to express their masculinity through paid labor.[33]

Cultural scenarios also provide men with a set of general guidelines for how they should view themselves as men and how they should behave in areas of life not directly related to procreative issues. Many of these expectations differ considerably according to individuals' age, race/ethnicity, socioeconomic status, and religious background. Those norms that indicate how men should generally treat their intimate female partner are especially relevant to my analysis because they can indirectly affect the way men interact with their partner in the procreative realm. If men are exposed to and adopt the view that they should communicate with their partners and share various responsibilities with them, then they may be more likely to accompany their partners for doctor visits and prepared childbirth classes or to discuss contraception with them.

Individuals typically interpret these scenarios, given their abstract and general nature, and then use them as crude guidelines for developing and managing their interactions with others in specific situations. Interpersonal scripting, as the second level of the scripting model, highlights how other individuals (including partners) often play a significant role in shaping men's actual experiences and orientation toward their roles. Men's partners often find themselves capable of affecting the way men think about and behave with regard to procreative issues.

The interpersonal scripting process is sometimes restricted by circumstances largely beyond an individual's control (e.g., poor health status that has produced a man's impotence, a partner's infertility, a partner's unwillingness to discuss her decision regarding the resolution of her pregnancy, limited job opportunities in a particular locale). The net result is that, from a practical standpoint, some men may be unable to live their lives according to their preferred ideals. Hence, the institutional and structural context within which interpersonal scripting takes place must be acknowledged.

The third level of this perspective, intrapsychic scripting, conveys the notion that men will at times privately construct images of how they want to present themselves as partners, fathers, and masculine men. Intrapsychic scripting acknowledges the impact that psychological and social psychological processes have in shaping men's behavior. Imagine, for instance, individuals having conversations with themselves in which they contemplate how they want to see themselves and have others see them, too. These introspective conversations might take one of the following forms: Do I want others to see me as someone who has profeminist values, and if so, can I achieve this by offering to use condoms or pay for her contraceptives as a way of sharing the responsibility of contraception with my partner? Can I present myself as a loving, supportive partner by offering to accompany my partner for an abortion? Or can I impart the image of being a responsible adult male by doing the "right" thing and offering to marry my pregnant partner? While some men may think carefully about these kinds of issues at times, especially during a crisis situation (e.g., an out-of-wedlock, unplanned pregnancy), some may spend little if any time pondering the types of images they project in these areas.[34] Nevertheless, even men's passing thoughts about these issues presumably can affect how they act.[35]

Identity Theory

Role identity theory is useful for my purposes because it sheds light on how fathers, or men contemplating paternity, organize aspects of their "self," especially those roles related to their procreative attitudes and experiences.[36] According to identity theory, individuals typically possess numerous role identities, which represent particular types of conceptions and definitions they have of themselves. These self-conceptions are tied to individuals' involvement in structured, ongoing relationships with others. Individuals possess a role identity by virtue of having a status or position relative to others (e.g., to be a father requires that this person has a child). The multiple role identities that individuals possess can be ranked into a type of hierarchy reflecting the relative probability that one of these identities will be expressed often and in different situations.[37] A role identity's standing in this hierarchy can be used to predict how conflicts between identities are resolved.

For individual men, some role identities may be much more important than others. A man's paternal identity may be more or less significant than his other identities, such as athlete, employee, gang member, or romantic partner. His paternal identity may also have numerous roles associated with it, such as breadwinner, playmate, nurturer, moral teacher, protector, and disciplinarian, that may also be ranked in a hierarchial fashion. Those identities that are the most salient for individual men should have the greatest influence on them psychologically and emotionally.[38]

The commitment concept is a key feature of identity theory and is the basis for determining an identity's degree of importance to an individual man.[39] A father's commitment to his paternal identity, and to the particular role relationships related to it, is a function of at least two factors: the extent to which a father must be a particular kind of father in order to maintain specific role relationships with his partner and/or children, and the strength of a father's conviction to sustain these relationships.

Given the growing diversity of opinions about how fathers should behave, and the increasing permutations of fathers' roles, it is reasonable to assume that fathers today, compared to their earlier counterparts, are more likely to vacillate in their commitment to their paternal role identity and experience shifts in how their identities are ranked.[40] This is likely to occur because the familial context within which contemporary fathers experience their paternal roles is more likely to change during their tenure as a father. Men may marry, divorce, remarry, discontinue living with biological children, or begin to live with stepchildren, and so forth. As a consequence, their need to be recognized as a father, or a particular type of father, is also likely to change. Many men therefore experience a number of transitional periods where their perceptions about their paternal role identity are in flux.

The commitment concept takes into account the dynamic and negotiated nature of how individuals organize their lives. Their level of commitment to particular identities sometimes changes over time; men's level of commitment to their paternal identity, for instance, may fluctuate as a function of their procreative experiences (e.g., pregnancy, birth, fertility testing, abortion) or other events unrelated to the procreative realm (e.g., anxieties about work or the aging process). Their level of commitment may either increase or decrease depending upon how they feel about their experiences. Men's involvement or lack of involvement in romantic relationships may also affect how they view particular procreative issues.

Another version of identity theory suggests that salient identities and commitment tend to operate in a manner similar to a cybernetic control system, that is, a machine-like device that processes complex calculations.[41] Individuals create identity standards or settings for themselves and then evaluate their performance based on their perception of how others respond to them. If individuals perceive that others' reactions to them are inconsistent with their own identity standards, they are likely to experience distress. When this occurs, they are likely to employ techniques to reduce the dissonance so that the meanings associated with others' reactions to them are consistent with how they define their own identity. When identity salience is defined in relation to the likelihood that the identity will be used in a variety of situations, identity theory predicts that salient identities will tend to lead to role-congruent behavior unless structural conditions preclude this from happening.

Using role identity theory, attention can be given to how the self is organized and is affected by social factors and how this self structure is, in turn, related to men's conduct in the procreative realm. This theory is also helpful in studying how individuals attempt to reorganize the structure of their self over time as they adjust to life course events or personal experiences and engage in negotiations with others, especially current romantic partners.[42]

A Conceptual Model

In the subsequent pages, I introduce a conceptual framework for organizing men's dynamic, multifaceted experiences in the procreative realm. As alluded to earlier, the procreative realm label represents a convenient way of referring collectively to the various physiological, social-psychological, and interpersonal phenomena associated with birth control, pregnancy, and procreation. When applied to men, for example, the procreative realm includes such things as men's perceptions about begetting or not being able to beget children, their contraceptive attitudes and behaviors, their thoughts about and their actual involvement in their partner's pregnancy, their reactions to various permutations of in-vitro fertilization and artificial insemination, men's sense of obligation to their offspring prior to and after their birth, and the symbolic meaning that men associate with begetting and raising children.

While there are many ways to focus on men's procreative roles and experiences, I organize my discussion around two loosely defined social psychological concepts or themes (*procreative consciousness* and *procreative responsibility*), as well as several other basic ideas.[43] My interest lies with the subjective dimensions to these two concepts and their connection to men's partner, father, and gender role identities.

Procreative Consciousness

I introduce the first concept, procreative consciousness,[44] to accentuate some of the key phenomenological dimensions to men's procreative roles and experiences. This concept captures men's ideas, perceptions, feelings, and impressions of themselves as they pertain to various aspects of procreation. In some instances, men may not be fully cognizant of their emotions in this area. Nonetheless, men's experiential sensations may affect their outlook and actions. Furthermore, I use the concept to highlight how men's experiences in the procreative realm relate to their romantic partner, father, and gender role identities. Men's views about their procreative potential and their actual paternity are essential in this respect.

My reliance on the term "consciousness" warrants further comment because this concept has been discussed at length and in unique ways by other scholars. The philosopher-sociologist Alfred Schutz used the term consciousness to refer to an individual's awareness of, or attentiveness to, his or her experiences at a given point in time.[45] Generally speaking, consciousness implies a state of being where an individual reflects upon something or attends to it, even if this process occurs somewhat superficially. Schutz developed an elaborate theoretical system to describe why and how objects come into an individual's field of attention. He stressed the concept "relevance" to convey the notion that an individual develops and attaches meanings to his or her experiences throughout life. These interrelated relevances are the cornerstone to how an individual develops knowledge about particular situations and his or her relationship to them. Phenomenologists emphasize this point because an understanding of human motivation must be built on a clear sense of how individuals acquire knowledge.[46]

While I am indebted to Schutz's work on consciousness, my approach differs from his in significant ways. Whereas he theorized about the stream of consciousness, the process by which consciousness unfolds moment to moment, I focus on the more enduring features of men's awareness and experience of themselves as procreative beings. This does not mean that I am not interested in the dynamic aspects of how men experience their procreative consciousness, quite the contrary. I am less concerned than Schutz, though, with the decidedly ephemeral aspects of consciousness.

From my perspective, men's procreative consciousness has both a temporal and a more enduring quality. I use the phrase *situational procreative consciousness* to identify those relatively short-lived occasions when men are actively attending to procreative issues during a specific activity (e.g., thinking about their contraceptive role as they buy or use a condom). Men are also likely to be influenced by a relatively stable, albeit a frequently fuzzy, set of thoughts and feelings that represent how they see themselves as procreative beings. I label this broader type of awareness *global procreative consciousness*. This kind of awareness is probably most distinctive during prolonged and identifiable phases of men's lives and will be affected by their previous experiences with contraception, abortion, pregnancy, infertility, and childbirth. Identifiable periods might include, say, the period of time between learning about a pregnancy and having an abortion, or the entire gestation period for a pregnancy that is brought to term, or the treatment period associated with attempts to become a father using ART. Men's global procreative consciousness is built upon and shaped by their various situational experiences.

Men's perceptions about their past experiences are likely to affect their thoughts and feelings about procreation in specific situations or on a more general level. In many instances, men have recourse to personal thoughts and feelings that stem from their earlier experiences in the procreative realm. At times, men may be inattentive to these experiences. In fact, many of these former perceptions have probably had little effect on men's consciousness for a considerable period of time. However, everyday life events sometimes trigger these past experiences so that they once again become relevant. Men may therefore recall previously meaningful experiences when they confront a suitable relevance structure—the set of circumstances or symbols that alert a person to view an aspect of reality in a particular fashion.[47]

Take, for example, a man whose partner is pregnant with their unplanned fetus. He is likely to experience a range of thoughts and emotions that tap into his sense of being a procreative man and a father-in-waiting. During this time, when he is keenly aware of his predicament, aspects of his procreative consciousness may dramatically influence the way he experiences his everyday life. The intrapsychic scripting process described earlier is often significant under these circumstances because the prospective father may be consumed by fantasies related to procreative roles. During this time, he may draw upon his previous experiences in the procreative realm, if he has any, in order to make sense of his current situation. He may recall, for instance, the emotional trauma he experienced a number of years ago when his girlfriend at the time informed him that she was pregnant. This recollection may arouse a flood of memories about the agonizing questions he struggled with years ago: "Should we abort the pregnancy? Should we have the baby and raise the child together? Should we get married?" He may also compare his situation to those of friends and family members who have had similar experiences. In Schutz's framework, these processes of men reflecting on past experiences can be viewed as examples of individuals making use of previously established relevance structures.

Interpersonal scripting also shapes a prospective father's experiences if he finds himself negotiating different ways of resolving a pregnancy with his partner or family members. He is likely to be more engrossed in the procreative realm if he is absorbed in an in-depth conversation about related issues. While a man's procreative consciousness would be stimulated and remain highly pertinent in this situation, his intense experience in this area could dissipate quickly if his partner were to have an abortion, particularly if he no longer maintained contact with her. He may quickly "forget" about these experiences, at least for the time being. Memories of his negotiations and this experience more generally may be relegated to his "inactive" procreative consciousness. The man, in effect, might unknowingly file away his emotions and thoughts about this experience in his long-term memory or suppress them in his subconscious. These memories can be thought of as deactivated or stored relevances that may once again become significant given the appropriate circumstances.

Men do not necessarily develop a specific level of awareness of or sensitivity to their procreative experiences, either in a given situation or in relation to their more permanent sense of self, their global procreative consciousness. Some men have a keener sense than others of their procreative self when they are engaged in one of the many practical activities and situations associated with this realm (e.g., purchasing and/or using birth control, abortion decision making, fertility testing, attending prepared childbirth classes). On occasion, men may also react differently to similar activities at various points in their own lives.[48] Because men sometimes feel that the procreative realm is not relevant to them, they spend little if any time thinking about procreative issues. Sixteen-year-old boys may spend no time whatsoever thinking about their potential to beget a child, even those who are sexually active. Likewise, fifty-five-year-old men whose wives are past their childbearing years may have lit-tle personal interest in procreative issues.[49]

In some instances, though, men's situational or global procreative con-sciousness may be highly focused. Men's procreative awareness is likely to be sharpest during those periods when they are trying to plan for and conceive children with their partners. Men may express a similar level of awareness when they desperately want to avoid impregnating someone. Take, for instance, Darryl, a twenty-eight-year-old, college-educated African American man, who told one group of researchers in the early 1980s, after he had experienced multiple abortions,

> My main view, maybe a way of not dealing with the issue, and my new feel-ings, is to just *not* get a woman pregnant. It's a cautious viewpoint. Now, I don't want to go through an abortion again. . . .
>
> I've concluded I have potent sperm, since it's happened with birth con-trol. I guess I've begun to feel my seed was important and I didn't want to waste it on just anyone. I feel equally responsible in any case. . . .
>
> . . . The whole abortion experience has made this [raising children] more important to me. It's made me think about kids, and parenthood, about effort and time.[50]

How do men typically organize their global procreative conscious-ness? Few men are distinctly aware of all of their procreative ideas and feelings, and fewer still possess a unified sense of themselves as a procre-ative being. Men's emotions and thoughts about aspects of the procre-ative realm are likely to be short-lived and diffuse. Consequently, men's experiences are probably most frequently tied to men's situational pro-creative consciousness rather than being expressed as part of a coherent package of experiences, ideas, or specific perspective. This means that men's global procreative consciousness, with its myriad aspects, is prob-ably more dynamic and fragmented in character than, say, men's per-sonal sense of health and fitness or the perception that Fundamentalist Christian men may have of themselves.

At different points in their lives, some men may actually be quite con-scious of their views and feelings in relation to the procreative realm. They may even be aware of how their respective roles in the procreative realm are interrelated. Men are probably most likely to possess this type of procreative consciousness or self-awareness when they also subscribe to a profeminist, a men's rights, or a Fundamentalist Christian ideology about interpersonal issues and attempt to think about their sexuality and procreative roles from one of these three perspectives. When guided by these types of ideologies, men are likely to interpret experiences within the procreative realm by drawing upon a cohesive set of ideas, rather than relying on a medley of disjointed beliefs and attitudes.

An important distinction can be made between men who have vague and fragmented procreative feelings and thoughts, and men who have a clear sense of how they feel about various procreative issues. In the former case, men's procreative consciousness is often not central or relevant to the way they happen to be experiencing their lives at a particular point in time. This does not mean, though, that individual men are unable to develop a heightened sense of awareness about procreative issues. As mentioned above, men's inactive thoughts and feelings can surface rather quickly if the right situation arises. However, men may or may not experience these thoughts and feelings as being part of a coherent orientation toward the procreative realm once they revisit them.[51]

A combination of social and personal factors influence how men perceive and express their procreative consciousness in their everyday lives. As procreative beings, men's perceptions are shaped most immediately by their interpersonal relationships, which provide them opportunities to demonstrate how a particular kind of romantic partner, father, and masculine male should behave. The identities men possess in connection with these relationships are, in turn, shaped by larger social forces.

Men in the United States are repeatedly exposed to traditional and emerging definitions of masculinity through the educational, family, legal, media, and religious institutions. The media's influence in particular has grown tremendously throughout the late twentieth century. Individuals, young and old, are exposed to countless cultural images that depict gender roles that are either directly or indirectly related to men's activities in the procreative realm. During the past several decades, Hollywood movies and television shows have at times portrayed men as loving, devoted fathers interested in their children's daily lives. Some advertising campaigns have also begun to emphasize the need for men to demonstrate sexual and paternal responsibility. However, many forms of entertainment continue to glorify male actors' sexual prowess while omitting scenes where these same actors deal with the consequences such actions may bring. Whether media messages have significantly influenced how men view themselves as procreative beings is unclear.

We do know that the shift in recent decades from a manufacturing-based economy to one that is service based has, along with the general displacement of working-class jobs from urban areas, reduced men's income adjusted for inflation.[52] For some categories of men, the lack of job opportunities in general has limited their ability to make a significant financial contribution to their children's support. Taken together, these recent economic developments have decreased the proportion of men who can realistically occupy or hope to occupy the breadwinner role commonly associated with fatherhood. Despite these developments, other factors, including the prevailing gender-segregated labor market, ensure that men on average continue to have higher-paying positions than their female counterparts. Thus, despite financial difficulties of many, men are still more likely than women to associate the provider role with their gender and parental identities.

In addition to these economic factors, social policies may influence men's lives in the procreative realm. During the past decade, there has been a groundswell of support for policies and programs designed to increase the proportion of children for whom paternity is established and child support received. To date, these initiatives in many states have been only moderately successful. However, some states have made considerable progress in this area.[53] To the extent that these initiatives eventually prove to be successful, growing numbers of men are likely to think about and experience their procreative consciousness and sense of responsibility in new ways.

At the micro level, men will exhibit varying levels of commitment to their role identities and individual men may alter their commitment to each of their identities throughout their life course. When men shift their level of commitment to a particular identity, it may be in part the result of, or produce comparable shifts in, aspects of their procreative consciousness (and sense of procreative responsibility in particular). Men who are compulsive about their work or leisure roles may change their lifestyle by becoming more involved partners as well as more devoted fathers. These changes might be fostered by the way men personally experience a pregnancy, childbirth, or postnatal period. Some men become sentimental during these times as they muse about the remarkable aspects of procreation and possibly coparenting. While it is unclear to what extent these experiences affect men's future attitudes and behavior, they are likely to have some effect. On occasion, some men's experiences might even lead them to reprioritize their identities to reflect their increased commitment to their identities as partners and fathers. Unfortunately, not all men have experiences that lead them to develop a stronger commitment to these identities. Some might discover, for example, that they have an extremely low sperm count and are unable to impregnate their partner. This news may encourage them to reorganize how they rank their identities. They may de-emphasize their partner and prospective father identities, while increasing their commitment to their work or leisure activities. Thus, just as specific role identities may be more or less central to a person's life at a given point in time, fertility-related concerns may be more or less pivotal to the enactment of these identities.

As the previous example suggests, men's fecundity and paternity status will be closely linked to their partner, father, and gender role identities. Most teenage and young adult men, about 90 percent, report a desire to have children at some point in the future.[54] Men seem to differ, though, in their level of curiosity, sense of confidence, and anxiety about their ability to sire children. These differences are probably due to cultural and subcultural values as well as familial and personal experiences. Men's perception of their ability to procreate (and their actual paternity status) can have a dramatic impact on their definition of self. In part, this may reflect their perception of whether they have lived up to what they perceive to be the prevailing expectations others have of them as a partner and man. Men's perceptions may therefore affect their subsequent behavior, especially if they or others associate procreative prowess with masculinity—a practice that has been observed extensively in other cultures.[55] Although we know little about the strength of this relationship in the United States at present, it is likely that restricted access to the conventional cultural status symbols associated with employment may encourage economically disadvantaged males (including those from racial and ethnic minority groups) to perceive paternity (and sexual prowess) as an alternative means to establish their masculinity and enhance their status within their class/subcultural environment.[56] Some research has found that after young men learn that they are responsible for impregnating a partner, they are more likely to report higher levels of sexual intercourse and lower levels of condom use.[57] Presumably these young men engage in risky sexual behavior because they perceive that few negative consequences are associated with their previous pregnancy experience, and this experience made them feel more masculine while generating support from their male peer group.

Along these lines, some evidence suggests that young unmarried men living in poor neighborhoods, when compared to their more affluent peers, are more likely to report that impregnating a young woman now would make them feel like a "real man" and that they would be less upset by the event.[58] When asked if this event would make them feel like a real man, 45 percent of those living in the poorest neighborhoods chose "not at all," whereas 65 percent of those living in the most affluent neighborhoods provided this answer. With socioeconomic and other background factors controlled, black young men—but not Hispanics—are more likely than white men to report that siring a child now would enhance their sense of masculinity. Thus, some young men living in disadvantaged environments may be inclined to see paternity as a source of prestige, especially if they do not have long-term educational and employment goals.[59] They may even feel as though women's access to abortion threatens one of their potential sources of self-esteem.

For those males responsible for a pregnancy, the significance of becoming a father, and the connection between their paternal and partner identities, is evidenced by some men's physiological reactions to their partner's pregnancy. Research conducted in the 1980s[60] is consistent with earlier cross-cultural accounts[61] in suggesting that expectant males in the United States, especially those involved in committed relationships, sometimes experience pregnancy-like symptoms during their partner's pregnancy and labor/delivery. Anthropologists have labeled this phenomenon the "couvade syndrome." Estimates for how many men experience their partner's pregnancy and their own childbirth role symbolically range widely from 11 percent to 65 percent of expectant fathers.[62] I discuss this phenomena more fully in chapter 6.[63]

Procreative Responsibility

In addition to showing how the procreative consciousness concept can be used to organize men's experiences, insights can also be derived by highlighting one particular dimension to this concept, which I label procreative responsibility. It, too, addresses issues that deal with men's awareness of and attention to specific procreative issues.[64] More specifically, this concept refers to men's beliefs about their obligations as well as their involvement in areas related to contraception and conception, processes using ART, discussions about how a pregnancy should be resolved, childbearing, and, to some extent, paternal activities. Thus this concept not only emphasizes men's views about their options for acting "responsibly" in the context of different events related to procreation, it includes their actions in this area as well. The procreative responsibility concept deserves separate attention because it has important implications for social policy.

Procreative responsibility encompasses two closely related yet conceptually distinct areas of activity involving men's perceptions and interactions with others. These domains include: (a) men's perceived level of obligation to their social father roles, and (b) the practical aspects of the sequence of procreative events ranging from contraception to conception to gestation to pregnancy outcome (e.g., choosing a contraceptive method, accompanying a partner for an abortion). Those paternal roles involving some type of obligation can be assessed at various points prior to, during, and after a pregnancy has been brought to term.

A conventional definition of male procreative responsibility as it applies to either domain noted above presupposes a normative social standard.[65] This is problematic insofar as definitions of responsibility are subject to historical and subcultural interpretations as well as personal and situational vagaries. These diverse definitions will exist on a societal, community, familial, and peer group level.

Jim Levine and Ed Pitt identify several commonly held beliefs about how men can act responsibly toward their children and partner. They suggest that a responsible man does the following:

> He waits to make a baby until he is prepared emotionally and financially to support his child.
>
> He establishes his legal paternity if and when he does make a baby.
>
> He actively shares with the child's mother in the continuing emotional and physical care of their child, from pregnancy onwards.
>
> He shares with the child's mother in the continuing financial support of their child, from pregnancy onwards.[66]

These suggestions, though consistent with my own views and clearly relevant to my broader discussion about procreative responsibility, do not specifically address all aspects of men's potential involvement in the procreative realm (e.g., abortion, assisted reproductive technologies). Consequently, these suggestions do not grapple with all of the complexities of how men should express their procreative responsibility.

Discussing procreative responsibility is further complicated because men's marriage plans and their paternal conduct, such as child support payments[67] and child care practices,[68] may be influenced to some extent by external conditions beyond their control (e.g., employment schedules and opportunities) and factors that reflect personal limitations and circumstances (e.g., education, skills, knowledge, unreceptive partner). Hence, efforts should be made to determine, to the extent possible, men's desire to assume specific responsibilities in the procreative realm, irrespective of their objective ability to do so. The reference group norms being applied in any particular situation should also be taken into account. Developing strategies for identifying men who are interested in contributing to their children's well-being but restricted in their ability to do so has significant policy and programmatic implications.

From their perspective, men can try to act responsibly in different contexts within the procreative realm. Much of their behavior, though, occurs as part of an ongoing interpersonal relationship and is therefore not easily identified as one distinct action. Consequently, understanding how men's role identities affect their perceptions and behavior is difficult but vital.

Men's autonomous efforts to practice birth control and their discussions about contraception with their partners provide useful illustrations of how men can demonstrate their procreative responsibility. The two most basic types of contraceptive discussions involve method-choice and method-use decision making.[69] Both explicit discussions and more tacit decision making are relevant here.

Men's participation in the method-choice situation includes their role in discussing their present contraceptive method, if any, or simply using a method on their own without explicitly discussing it. Method-choice situations that involve explicit discussions tend to occur early on in a relationship as well as at other strategic times during the relationship's tenure (e.g., after the birth of a child, when two people agree to have a monogamous relationship). When men engage in these types of discussions as part of a sexually active couple, they tend to do so infrequently, perhaps a few times a year or even only a few times during their entire involvement with a particular partner. In many ongoing monogamous relationships, there may be no need to have repeated discussions about contraception if both partners accept their current method. However, for those men who have many partners, they may engage in a series of individual method-choice discussions with numerous women in a relatively short period of time.

Method-use decision making, the other form of contraceptive decision making, involves more short-term, recurrent types of concerns, including when to take birth control pills, use a condom, employ the withdrawal method, apply spermicides, insert a diaphragm, and so forth. If the method of choice is coitus dependent, requiring at least one of the partners to be conscientious in practicing contraception during each sexual episode (e.g., diaphragm and condom), then men will have repeated opportunities to demonstrate their attentiveness in this area. Even in those cases where the female pill is used, a man can periodically give his partner money to defer the costs of the pills and remind her on a regular basis to take them.

For those men wishing to impregnate their partner rather than prevent a pregnancy, each sexual episode may lead men to think about the prospects of inducing conception.[70] Men's involvement in this type of situation may at times be considered a form of procreative responsibility. This is especially true for those couples who go to great lengths to conceive a child. Men might, for example, help their partners chart their ovulation cycle, or take it upon themselves to learn about strategies to enhance their chances for conceiving a child.[71]

Many men also have occasion, in connection with their partner and father identities, to express their sense of procreative responsibility when they are involved in resolving an unintended pregnancy. Although some men may have clear expectations concerning their actual or potential participation in resolving a pregnancy, especially those who have had personal experience with a previous pregnancy and/or have strong religious convictions about abortion, others may be unaware of their preferences for being involved in this type of situation. Men with strong religious convictions may rely on their religious beliefs to help them interpret the responsibilities they associate with their romantic partner and father identities. Those men with conservative religious beliefs are likely to feel very strongly that they should have the right to prevent their partner from having an abortion. In some respects, they may feel as though it is their responsibility as a partner and potential father to dissuade their partner from having an abortion. Some men with more liberal religious beliefs, and even those who are not religious at all, may also feel at times that they are acting responsibly when they try to prevent their partner from aborting her pregnancy.

Similarly, men with pro-choice beliefs often find themselves in situations where they must grapple with the prospects of acting responsibly.

For these men, the most troubling situation occurs when their preference for resolving a pregnancy differs from their partner's. They recognize that their own desires are ultimately meaningless because their partner can make the final decision whether to abort or bring the pregnancy to term.[72] Thus, pro-choice men responsible for a pregnancy are likely to feel that if they are to act like a responsible partner they must not pressure their partner to resolve her pregnancy in one way or another. If their partner opts for an abortion, men can act responsibly as a partner by volunteering to participate in the abortion process to the extent their partner and the clinic policy permit.[73] In some cases, this will entail accompanying their partner during the procedure and recovery phases. If the woman chooses to bring the pregnancy to term, men may wish to demonstrate their commitment to their partner and/or father identities by participating in the childbirth procedures.[74]

When an unplanned, nonmarital conception occurs, men can adhere to traditional, mainstream social norms by formalizing their commitment to their partner and child by getting married or establishing a cohabiting arrangement.[75] Demographers have clearly documented that during the past several decades a growing proportion of men are not married to or living with the women who give birth to their children.[76] What is unclear, though, is to what extent this pattern can be attributed to an actual decline in men's perception of their procreative responsibility rather than to other factors (e.g., social structural restrictions on young men's employment opportunities and wages, women's greater economic autonomy, and greater societal acceptance of single motherhood).[77] For many men involved with teenage mothers, making a formal commitment to their partner and child depends upon whether the young woman's parents consent to such an arrangement.

A study I conducted of high school youth in 1986 provides some insight into how gender may influence teenagers' family formation intentions with respect to unplanned pregnancies.[78] Using a hypothetical scenario, I found that young men within a metropolitan high school system were actually more likely than their female peers to report that they would prefer to establish a two-parent household if their child were nonmaritally conceived within the context of an ongoing, committed relationship. One interpretation of this pattern is that, compared to young men, young women may be more realistic in assessing young men's ability to assume the provider role. This finding shows how important it is to consider external and interpersonal factors when interpreting the way men think about and express their procreative responsibility. In other words, young men may be much more willing to form committed unions with their partners than is represented by the number of men who actually live with their child and partner.[79]

Public outrage over stereotypical young fathers, specifically their apparent lack of interest in being involved in the lives of their nonmaritally conceived children, represents one slice of the larger critique of men's changing commitments to family life during the latter half of this century. Barbara Ehrenheich forcefully argued over a decade ago that men were beginning to redefine their ideas about marriage and paternity in the 1940s and 1950s prior to the women's movement of the 1960s.[80] In her opinion, men's lifestyles were being shaped by the ethics of individualism and consumerism prior to being affected by many of the other macrolevel changes that occurred during the past several decades. Growing numbers of men during the 1950s supposedly drifted away from defining themselves according to the relationships they could have with spouses and children. Given the emergence of the playboy image during this era, it is not surprising that men increasingly adopted alternative strategies for defining themselves. Few would dispute that this cultural shift has continued largely unabated into the 1990s, although some religiously based organizations, the Promise Keepers and the Nation of Islam in particular, have successfully promoted less self-centered and more family-oriented images for men.[81]

A contemporaneous and noteworthy pattern finds women becoming more economically autonomous and less willing to define themselves exclusively in terms of their relationships with men and children.[82] Thus, while many men appear to have a significantly different ethos about paternity than their counterparts who lived during the earlier half of this century, women's views about motherhood have probably changed even more. Women's changing roles, in concert with larger economic trends, will no doubt influence how men define and express themselves in the procreative realm in the future.

Modes of Procreative Consciousness

Another subtle distinction can be made when considering men's procreative consciousness as it is expressed in either the situational or global context. The two modes of consciousness described below are relevant to, but differ slightly from, the earlier distinction I made between men's temporary (situational) and more stable (global) expressions of their procreative consciousness. On the one hand, men may have personal beliefs, attitudes, and preferences about individual procreative issues that are not confined to or necessarily the result of their ongoing involvement in a particular romantic relationship. Men sometimes develop and embrace ideas about procreative issues that are completely independent of their ongoing relationship. Men cultivate this individualized orientation, sometimes with little deliberate effort, through their exposure to cultural and subcultural values (e.g., pronatalism, values associated with the pro-life and pro-choice movements), physiologically based events (e.g., puberty, sterilization), and life events (e.g., pregnancy scare, a child's birth). Men's individualized ideas and feelings about procreative issues are likely to be relatively stable for extended periods of time.

On the other hand, men sometimes develop more relationship-based perceptions and feelings about specific procreative issues. In this context, men's approach to domains of procreation is intimately tied to their involvement with a particular romantic partner at a given point in time. As a result, men's procreative consciousness and sense of responsibility can be influenced by specific facets of a romantic relationship and a female partner's views about reproductive issues. A partner's influence may be restricted to particular domains or issues associated with men's procreative consciousness (e.g., contraception but not abortion), or it may affect men's overall orientation in all domains.

Imagine for a moment the effect of a woman's repeated request that her male partner use condoms. In at least some cases, the man would probably become more attentive to his contraceptive role. Or imagine another woman who is very eager to have a baby and therefore tries to persuade her partner to have children. A man who is frequently asked to procreate will probably grow more attentive to his own procreative potential.[83] He may even agree to have fertility tests performed if he and his partner are unable to conceive a child. A partner's influence can persist after a child is born as well. For example, a female partner may be able to persuade either a resident or nonresident father to develop and/or maintain positive relationships with his children.[84]

The way men interpret and respond to particular experiences clearly depends on their level of commitment to their partner. If men are intent on securing and maintaining their partner's respect, they are more likely to accommodate their partner's expectations for how they should be involved in different aspects of the procreative realm.

While these two modes of experience can be conceptualized separately, they probably affect each other and overlap in many instances. In other words, men's individualized orientation toward procreative issues influences the way in which they deal with procreative issues with specific partners, while their relationship experiences in turn influence their more personal orientation.[85] When men pursue an exclusive, sexually based relationship for an extended period of time, the two levels of procreative experiences are likely to meld together, becoming more or less indistinguishable from one another.[86]

2

Transformations of the Procreative Man

In the early months of 1996, readers of various popular magazines, including *Esquire*, *Time*, the *New Yorker*, and *U.S. News and World Report*, were treated to stories with such titillating titles as "Downward Motility," "What's Wrong with Our Sperm," "Silent Sperm," and "Investigating the Next 'Silent Spring!'"[1] These stories chronicled biomedical scientists' most recent efforts to study and evaluate whether the quality of men's sperm, at least in some regions of the world, has significantly declined in recent decades. Those familiar with these stories were given good reason to ponder the wide ranging social and political implications of such a discovery—if, indeed, it were found to be true.[2]

Throughout the latter part of this century, the public has also been the beneficiary of a steady flow of articles describing developments in innovative male hormonal contraceptives, new reproductive technologies, the spread of DNA fingerprinting technology,[3] and the use of ultrasound technology for prenatal screening. The genre of news covering these developments appeals to individuals' curiosity about the intersection between technology and the prevention or creation of human life. On a practical level, all of these technological developments, as well as others, have helped to transform men's lives as procreative beings in recent decades.

Throughout history, cultural developments not based on technological advancements have also influenced how men experience their lives in the procreative realm. The most fundamental development can be traced back to the social processes that occurred long ago when men first learned of their role in the conception process.

No portrait of men as procreative beings would be complete without discussing how men's lives have been and will continue to be affected by technological and social innovations bearing on procreation. Assessing men's lives as procreative beings from both a historical as well as futuristic perspective is consistent with my efforts to present a comprehensive synthesis of issues associated with men in the procreative realm.

A Brief History

The discovery of biological paternity, of when and how our early ancestors acquired the basic knowledge that men contributed to the creation of babies through their ejaculation during vaginal intercourse, is a matter of considerable speculation. One reasonable explanation suggests that knowledge of paternity coincided with the domestication of animals around 9000 B.C. when people began to watch more closely the sexual and reproductive experiences of specific animals over a period of time.[4]

While our understanding of the initial discovery of paternity remains incomplete, it is quite clear that this discovery has had profound cultural, social, and political significance for diverse civilizations throughout time. One would be hard pressed to exaggerate its significance. This discovery, which has now become part of our common stock of knowledge, precipitated a revolutionary chain of significant and unforeseen consequences for men, women, and children alike. The social organization of the societies that acquired this knowledge changed forever as men sought to devise social institutions and norms that exerted legal control over their partners and children whom they believed to be their biological offspring.

Sex and Kinship Ties

Attempts to theorize about the possible links between the discovery of paternity and the establishment of kinship ties must take place in the face of an obscure record about how prehistoric modern humans organized their lives relative to one another. In the early part of this century, Freud[5] speculated that at some point at the dawn of human "societies," primary groups existed in which individual dominant males copulated with groups of females consisting of their "wives" and daughters, while secondary groups consisted of less dominant males. Males in these secondary groups may have had limited opportunities for sexual intercourse, at least during extended periods of their lives. Setting aside these speculations, it is possible to assert with confidence that at least some early men were copulating with early women.

Regardless of what types of social structures our early ancestors were accustomed to, it is safe to assume that for a considerable period of time prehistoric humans did not recognize that men played a role in reproducing children. Men had intercourse with women because it was instinctive and physiologically pleasurable. They were ignorant, though, to the fact that their sexual activity in some cases was directly related to the reproductive process and that they were at risk of impregnating their partner when they had intercourse while she was ovulating. Moreover, these males probably witnessed, or were at least aware, that the females with whom they had had sex were also undergoing physiological changes during gestation and eventually bearing children in many cases. However, for a long time they did not have a clue as to why these females were experiencing these changes.

Ira Reiss, a sociologist, has speculated that the physiologically gratifying experience of copulation, not knowledge of their paternity, first lead some males to bond with female partners and to develop feelings toward their partners' offspring.[6] Even if Freud was correct—that early human social structures resembled hordes of primates—the masculine "power" dimension to early men's and women's social organization would not by itself account for the intense, interpersonal bonds that eventually began to characterize individual male-female pairs and adult males' ties to children. With this in mind, early forms of social kinship may have evolved because of the bonding associated with copulation, even though men and women did not comprehend the technical details of the reproductive process. This thesis is consistent with at least one anthropological interpretation of the very early evolutionary history of the species.[7] In discussing the probable living patterns of the protohominids who lived some eight million years ago, Helen Fisher posits that a selection process took place where females with physiological attributes that enabled them to be more sexually active were able to gain advantages for themselves and their children. She argues that this process leads to what she refers to as the "sexual contract":

> As generations passed, selection gradually produced more and more female protohominids who copulated for a longer period of their monthly cycle; who made love during pregnancy; who had sex sooner after parturition. Protohominid females were beginning to lose their period of heat. With this daily life began to change again.[8]
>
> With the stimulus of constantly available sex, protohominids had begun the most fundamental exchange the human race would ever make. Males

and females were learning to divide their labors, to exchange meat and vegetables, to share their daily catch. Constant sex had begun to tie them to one another and economic dependence was tightening the knot.[9]

Fisher goes on to suggest that some females were supposedly more capable than others of deriving intense physical pleasures from their sexual episodes. Consequently, she argues that a selection process enhanced the chances for survival for highly sexualized females. In her words:

> These components of an extremely high sex drive are not necessary for procreation today, and they weren't necessary millions of years ago either. But they were essential to survival—because the males liked them. They were sex attractants and those who had them clinched economic ties with males. These females lived. They reproduced. Their children lived with the economic prosperity induced by male attention, and the phenomenally high sex drive of the female protohominid was passed along to the females of today.[10]

If we accept this theory of human evolution, then it is likely that men had occasion to extend their protective child care services and affection to children born to their favorite sexual partner(s). This may have occurred even though, unbeknownst to them, the children had actually been sired by other men. Thus, being involved with and taking care of children was coincidental for men in that they were available to partake in some of these activities primarily because they were interested in having sex with the children's mother. Their commitment to "their" children was therefore not based on their concern for biological relatedness, rather interpersonal ties fueled their familial commitment. Some features of this scenario are still a part of our contemporary social-sexual landscape in the sense that some women have multiple, serial sex partners during ovulation, with the consequence that their children are sometimes raised by men who assume they are the biological father when, in fact, they are not. Moreover, men often develop commitments to children that are contingent on their romantic interest in the children's mother. Unfortunately, the model I have sketched depicting reproductive activities and social kinship processes among our early ancestors does not generate hypotheses that can be easily tested with cultural or archeological artifacts. While this model stimulates fascinating cocktail conversation, it represents only a speculative reconstruction since we can only conjecture about these social kinship processes and how males came to develop an understanding of their biological paternity and paternal roles.

Discovering Biological Paternity

While knowledge of the mechanics of paternity and reproduction more generally has been a part of humans' common stock of knowledge for many, many years, it must have been a fascinating period of human history when individuals first began to incorporate this knowledge into their everyday sense of reality. From the "enlightened" vantage point of the late twentieth century, it is intriguing to speculate about the evolution and expression of the intrapsychic processes that first enabled individual men to develop a procreative consciousness. At some point in time, individual men, as well as particular cohorts of adult men, began to undergo a transformation in the way they thought about sex and reproduction. During this transformation, men (and women) developed a cursory understanding that they and/or others had contributed to the birth of infants through sexual acts.

The significance of men developing a procreative consciousness is accentuated when we consider that it coincided with the evolution of myths and religions in which the powers of creation were bestowed upon male gods. In the words of one scholar, "Once the relevance of coition to child bearing had been officially admitted[,] . . . man's religious status gradually improved, and winds or rivers were no longer given credit for impregnating women."[11] After the male deity gradually ascended to prominence over a period of about a thousand years, the final stage revealed the existence of

> a wholly new type of powerful male, the father-king who creates the world and all the living things in it, giving them names in the process. This promotion records a similar shift in the status of men in early civilizations.[12]

Mary O'Brien has argued that these early men experienced a dilemma because while they had a crude sense that babies were created through sexual intercourse, they were physiologically detached from the gestation and labor process. This, in turn, made the establishment of paternity problematic.[13] These men had no way of being absolutely certain that a child was, in fact, their child. Documenting one's paternity was consequently an act of personal faith reinforced by community cooperation. Men's tacit acceptance of other men's paternity claims provided the collusion necessary to perpetuate patriarchal social systems. In short, others in the tribe, clan, or community had to accept men's paternity claims for this system to work. O'Brien therefore asserts that men's efforts to develop an ideology of continuity that linked fathers to their offspring, solidifying the patriarchal system, necessitated that they develop social and legal institutions such as marriage in order for them to lay legal claim to their children. This practice connected the biological paternity of children and social fatherhood with men's marital relationships. Men were, in effect, indirectly appropriating their children by asserting their paternal rights vis-à-vis their legal relationship with, and ownership of, their children's mother. This perspective suggests that "fatherhood is a human social invention and patriarchy, the rule of the father, is a fundamental condition of history and of our ideas of power, authority, and of civilization itself."[14]

Procreative Mythology: Males' Search for Power

One of the central themes common to all forms of feminist ideology has been the notion that patriarchy is a system created for and perpetuated by men obsessed with power. However, social relations between men and women were not, and are not, always governed by patriarchal ideology and inequitable social structures. Some scholars have speculated, for example, that in precivilized society women may have been men's equal because of women's mysterious role in childbirth and their knowledge of plants.[15] According to this line of thinking, male domination in the form of patriarchy had to await the agricultural revolution. It supposedly was only then that men as a class of people began to subjugate women through formal and informal means.[16]

Scholars such as O'Brien point to men's sense of alienation from the reproductive process as the critical source of men's historical oppression of women. Other social philosophers, such as Engels, offer a more convincing explanation of the origins of patriarchy by focusing on the structural features of prehistoric social life, but it is still plausible that men's alienation from the reproductive process may have shaped and reinforced patriarchal institutions once they emerged. Whatever the origins of patriarchy may be, it is clear that men have attempted to develop indirect ways of exerting control over reproduction and the meaning of paternity because they have been physiologically isolated from the reproductive process.[17]

While numerous historical and cross-cultural examples illustrate how some men in various historical epochs have sought to salvage and glorify their reproductive role, one example warrants special mention here. The ancient Greeks are well known for the myths they propagated regarding reproduction and the incredible powers embodied by a man's sperm. Writing in patriarchal Greek society, Aristotle (c. 384–322 B.C.) was one of the most ardent proponents of the male's superior contribution in the reproductive process.[18] He elevated the significance of the man's sperm, suggesting that a woman played a passive role and did not produce any type of "seed." Although Aristotle did not stand alone in his views, it appears to have been a minority perspective during this period since many others adhered to a two-seed theory of reproduction. Nevertheless, even when both men and women were assigned a contributory role in reproduction, mythology sometimes conveyed the notion that a child's soul and vitality were contained in the man's sperm. The significance of a woman's egg was consequently downplayed. A woman's role in reproduction was actually likened to a vessel for the production of a man's children. As a result, Greek men could assuage their potential sense of alienation during their partner's pregnancy with their "knowledge" that their sperm contained the most important aspect of life—a person's soul or spirit.

This brief discussion of some of the sociohistorical aspects to sex and reproduction, while limited in scope, illustrates that the social organization of societies is tied to the way individuals perceive and experience the interrelationship between the sexual and reproductive areas of social life. Now we can turn our attention to more recent social developments and innovations related to men's experiences in the reproductive realm in western industrialized societies.

Recent and Contemporary Developments

Today in industrialized societies we are in the midst of another important period for the social construction of fatherhood and men's attitudes and experiences in the procreative realm. Men appear to be expressing, and in some instances avoiding, their procreative consciousness and sense of responsibility in new ways. The distinctive nature of the current period involves several interrelated developments that include recent behavioral patterns, shifts in cultural values and social policies related to fertility and fatherhood, and developments in technology as well as the health care profession. While I hesitate to identify a particular year as the starting point of this period, my evidence points to the early 1960s, with the introduction of the female contraceptive pill, as the dawn of a new era in procreative issues.

Many societies, especially western industrialized ones, have experienced significant changes in their childbearing, marriage, divorce, and remarriage patterns in recent decades. A consequence of these patterns is that growing numbers of men at some point in their life are assuming paternal roles for children who are not biologically related to them.[19] Our current era is not unique in this respect. In earlier centuries, because people's life spans were much shorter, large numbers of children interacted with males who assumed father-figure roles but were not their biological fathers.[20] However, the major difference between social life today and in previous centuries is that a significant proportion of children are currently experiencing alternative father figures, even though their biological fathers are still alive and in some cases actively involved with them.

The cultural scenarios germane to fatherhood, the stockpile of ideas related to how persons should and do express particular paternal roles, have become more varied in recent years. The basic definition of fatherhood has become more inclusive as a result of this greater diversity of paternal roles.[21] The demographic and cultural trends mentioned above have prompted a series of lively academic and public debates that explore the definition and nature of family, kinship, and fatherhood.[22] Laypersons in industrialized countries are slowly changing how they perceive the meaning of these concepts. Questions that explore whether socially constructed relationships can be as thick as or thicker than blood ties take on new meaning in this type of cultural climate.[23] Thus, the meaning of biological paternity and social fatherhood are in a state of flux.

These contemporary discourses are occurring alongside remarkable scientific and biosocial developments that affect the nature of the reproductive process. The development and increasing use of innovations in reproductive technology overlaps recent advances in contraceptive technology. The "Age of Contraception," as O'Brien refers to this development, represents the second major period in the history of reproduction—the discovery of biological paternity being the first.[24] Both earlier and ongoing advances in contraception have provided women (and men) expanded opportunities to exert control over their reproductive potential without abstaining from sexual intercourse. Contraception, especially in its most technologically advanced forms, has made it possible to separate the potential reproductive aspects of intercourse from the sexual pleasures associated with it. One of the consequences of this development is that, although women can sometimes still use sex as a form of leverage to keep men interested in them and their children, modern contraceptive technology now provides men with greater ease in having sex outside of a familial context without worrying about pregnancy—and women have the same opportunities for sex outside an ongoing relationship. In addition, the introduction of modern forms of female birth control, coupled with the legalization of abortion, has eroded many women's ability to form stable unions and secure men's long-term commitment without offering sex in return. In recent decades, men have many more options to have sexual relationships without promising marriage.

Developments in contraceptive technology and the availability of abortion have also prompted men to reevaluate the notion of paternal responsibility when children are conceived outside of marriage:

> The fact that the birth of the baby is now a *choice* of the mother has implications for the decisions of the father. The sexual revolution, by making the birth of the child the physical choice of the mother, makes marriage and child support a social *choice* of the father. (Italics in original)[25]

In short, these developments have lead to the decline in the rate of shotgun marriages, where social norms had previously portrayed men's willingness to legitimate conceptions that occurred outside of marriage as the honorable and responsible thing to do.

Advances in modern reproductive technologies have also begun to revolutionize how we think about parenthood. These technologies can now separate biological paternity from sexual intercourse, and biological paternity from social fatherhood. Reproductive technologies are currently blurring the traditional images of "father," "mother," and "family relations."[26] The increasing prevalence of sperm banks, donor insemination, and surrogate motherhood has heightened the public's awareness of images that depart from the conventional process of biological fatherhood through intercourse. Relatively speaking, these innovative options are not widely used at this time. Nevertheless, men do have options to become fathers through nontraditional means and are increasingly using them.

The public's concern in recent years about fatherhood—and parenthood more generally—is captured by two competing themes. The first theme challenges the once privileged position of paternal claims based solely on biological relations. Challenges to the genetic position come from both those interested in expanding the definitions of fatherhood and those interested in accentuating women's unique reproductive experiences. Some observers argue that genetic fathers should demonstrate a threshold level of responsibility toward their children if they are to retain their formal or informal rights. According to this view, the notion of social fatherhood—the acts associated with paternal caregiving—take precedence over genetic ties. In a related vein, some feminists voice concern about the privileging of genetic connections in reproduction in terms of the male seed. They contend that this orientation negates women's reproductive experiences and, in the process, inappropriately defines women's contribution to reproduction in terms similar to those applicable to men. Barbara Rothman laments that the *"central concept of patriarchy, the importance of the seed, was retained by extending it to women* [italics in original]." She adds that "women do not gain their rights to their children in this society as *mothers*, but as *father equivalents*, as equivalent sources of seed."[27] From this perspective, when too much emphasis is placed on the basic genetic connection, the importance of women's nurturing efforts during gestation is disregarded.

The second theme reasserts, under certain conditions, the centrality of biological connections between fathers and their children. Legal efforts to reunite biological fathers with their children are consistent with this theme, even when this means taking children away from social fathers who have fulfilled their "father" roles admirably. Similarly, those who emphasize this position support recent efforts to create registries within state governments that would provide men the opportunity to protect themselves from inadvertently relinquishing their paternal rights to biological children they may have unknowingly fathered.

One expression of men's interest in biological paternity involves their concern about their fecundity, their ability to procreate. Men today may be slightly less concerned about their fecundity than their pre-1970s counterparts because voluntary childlessness, smaller families, abortion, and nonmarital childbearing are more common and fertility norms are less rigid.[28] The direction and magnitude of this shift cannot be assessed precisely, however, because data are not available that would enable researchers to determine how cohorts of similarly aged men have felt about their potential to procreate at various times during this century. Trend data based on Gallop polls do indicate that white men have reported a lower ideal family size over the years;[29] and a relatively recent national study (1982) documented that 8.6 percent of never married males, ages 17 to 25, expected to have no children.[30] Unfortunately, these data do not adequately address the fecundity issue per se because they do not explore men's perceptions about their ability to procreate if they so desired. While two men without children may each indicate that they would like to have at least one child, one man may be much more devastated than the other if he is unable to procreate. In addition, men who have already sired a child may tend to view their fecundity differently than those men who have not yet proven their procreative prowess.

Women's increased participation in the labor force is another significant behavioral change associated with the family-related demographic patterns mentioned earlier (e.g., high rates of divorce and out-of-wedlock parenting). Men's procreative consciousness will probably continue to be affected by women's participation in the workforce, as large numbers of women continue to delay the timing of their first marriage and child, choose to be child free, and have smaller families when they do have children.[31] On the one hand, men involved with women who are interested in postponing or avoiding childbearing completely will have fewer opportunities and less incentive to think about their fecundity and associate it with their various identities. On the other hand, if nontraditional women (and presumably men) are beginning to think of children as "consumer goods,"[32] and if nontraditional women with strong career commitments are evaluating their potential maternal roles in the context of a complex image of self, one in which motherhood is but one identity, then men's procreative consciousness will be altered. In such cases, men are likely to perceive that their partner does not intend to accept full or perhaps even the majority of responsibility for child care. As a result, men and women are more likely than in the past to negotiate explicitly their concerns about the appropriate timing and number of children as well as child care arrangements. Growing numbers of men, therefore, may be forced to reevaluate the relative importance and meaning of their father and partner identities in comparison to their work identity. In other words, some men may need to convince themselves and their partners, prior to conception, that their work life will not prevent them from assuming an equitable share of the child care responsibilities, while being supportive of their partner's needs at the same time.

One factor that has probably affected the apparent decline in men's sense of financial responsibility to their children during this century is the growing public perception of women as autonomous economic beings. As women (whites in particular) became more economically self-sufficient beginning in the early 1900s, and as female gender roles grew to accommodate paid labor, men became increasingly less inclined to fulfill as a matter of duty the provider role for their partner and child. Women's increased participation in the paid labor force, coupled with the late nineteenth- and twentieth-century policy to give mothers preferential treatment in child custody decisions,[33] provided many men with the opportunity to rationalize their declining financial commitment to their children.[34] Furthermore, women's employment patterns and economic autonomy in the United States have been accompanied by a decrease in the real income of working and lower middle-class men, due primarily to the transition from a manufacturing to a service-based economy. Men's declining financial clout has restricted many men's ability to fulfill the traditional, sole-provider role.[35] The extent to which formal and informal initiatives to promote paternal responsibility will curtail or perhaps reverse the consequences associated with these trends in the economic arena remains to be seen.

In terms of paternal responsibilities, LaRossa identified one important feature of the contemporary cultural landscape that may influence men's views and behavior.[36] He posited that the cultural image of the "new father" as someone who assumes a more active role in parenting was a reaction to the growing influx of women into the workforce. The social perception that men have become more conscientious fathers to compensate for the void created by working mothers implies that men have developed a more responsible attitude toward child care. However, what exists as a cultural image may bear little resemblance to fathers' everyday life experiences in child care—or child support. The stark reality is that men on the whole have not been very active in the areas of child care and child support in recent decades,[37] although fathers' involvement in child care appears to have increased slightly[38] and may continue to do so in the future. In reality, while men may on one level feel they should be responsible for a range of supportive behaviors toward their children, their actual behavior is often inconsistent with the emerging cultural image of the new father and their own expectations.[39] If women put more pressure on men to get involved, the gap between the culture and conduct of fatherhood is likely to narrow. Whether women, in fact, will demand that men get more involved is unclear. Surveys from the 1970s and 1980s show that a majority of women in two-parent households are actually content with their partner's level of involvement in domestic activities and their children's lives.[40]

While public expectations for men to be more involved with their children have risen, the public has seemingly placed less pressure on men to procreate. Thus if current patterns of family life and work continue to alter pro-childbearing norms in the United States, those men who do become fathers, compared to fathers of previous generations, may represent a more select group of individuals because they will be making a conscious commitment to sacrifice time, energy, and money to have a child even though they have other options. As such, men who become fathers in the near future may represent a more self-selected group and be more committed than fathers from previous generations to provide financial, emotional, and practical support to their children.[41]

In recent years, social policymakers and the public at large have shown a greater willingness to reinforce the "new" image of fatherhood through a steadfast commitment to altering men's procreative consciousness. Issues involving male procreative responsibility in particular are becoming more highly politicized as conservative and progressive interest groups alike are attempting to alter men's relationship to various aspects of the procreative realm.[42] For example, policymakers[43] and social service providers[44] have accelerated efforts to impart a message to young men that it is irresponsible to beget children without having the desire and capability to make a commitment to social father roles. One message created by the National Urban League along these lines is poignantly depicted in a poster that displays in the foreground an African American baby, sitting naked and diapered in a shadowy, vacant room on a splintery, old wooden floor. The camera angle moves the viewer's eyes, first to the child's frightened expression, and then to the archway leading to a lit hallway where a tall, young black man, with his back to the infant, walks away. The young man's shadow mysteriously reaches back to the child; sadly, one is left to imagine that, to the man, this shadow represents the essence of their relationship. Above this scene, the bold caption reads: "Don't make a baby if you can't be a father."

In addition to these types of media messages, efforts are underway to explore strategies to improve young men's opportunities to play an active role financially and interpersonally in their children's lives. On a legislative front, the Reagan administration introduced a program during the 1980s to increase the establishment of paternity and enforce fathers' child support payments. Paternity can be established when a man voluntarily signs a declaration or birth certificate acknowledging that he is the father of the child or when a man is forced to undergo genetic testing. In either case, establishing paternity means that the man is expected to provide for his child financially and is likely to have legal rights in relation to his child as well. Subsequent administrations have attempted to refine this program, and various states have also introduced innovative legislation to address these issues.[45] Whether these continuing efforts, and the publicity they receive, will alter the way a significant number of men conceptualize and practice procreative responsibility remains to be seen. Evidence is starting to mount, though, that suggests that some states have been able to increase the rate of paternity establishment in recent years. In West Virginia, for instance, the rate of paternity establishment for unwed fathers rose from 15 to 60 percent in a recent three-year period.[46] One of the key factors was training maternity nurses in birthing hospitals to expect and encourage men to establish paternity while they are in the hospital. On a national level during the 1992 to 1996 period, child support collections increased by 50 percent and paternity establishments by 55 percent.[47] These new initiatives are likely to influence at least those men who are forced to pay child support payments.[48]

The final broad set of factors that has influenced, and will continue to influence, men's procreative consciousness and sense of responsibility are recent changes in technology and health care services. Biological paternity, due to recent developments in the DNA fingerprinting technique, is now being cast in a new light because it is possible to document the shared genetic heritage of fathers and their children.[49] The DNA fingerprinting innovation has been particularly useful for documenting paternity in cases where attempts are made to hold biological fathers accountable for the financial support of their children. This technology, used under less punitive circumstances, provides curious individuals the chance to determine for one reason or another whether they are biologically related.[50] The revolutionary and practical implication of this innovation is that individuals' beliefs about the possible genetic relationship between particular men and children need no longer be based solely on faith.

Other advances in modern technology that are designed to monitor the pregnancy and labor process, such as amniocentesis and sonography, currently allow fathers to experience the reproductive process and the fetus in a more intimate manner than their counterparts who became fathers a few decades ago. Some of the major moments in the pregnancy process, such as hearing heartbeats and seeing fetal movements, are now more readily accessible to expectant fathers, particularly those who are in committed relationships and are not economically disadvantaged.[51]

Anecdotal accounts indicate that prospective fathers are fascinated with the opportunity to view their offspring during the gestation process and monitor their partner's labor.

While these developments may enable some men to feel more connected to their father-in-waiting roles, not everyone feels comfortable with them. Some feminists worry that modern technologies and recent medical policies will usurp women of some of their reproductive power and that the male-dominated medical community and prospective fathers will now have additional opportunities to assert control over women's reproductive process. Rothman's apprehension about prenatal diagnostic technology can be gleaned from her discussion of what she labels the "tentative pregnancy."[52] She underscores the notion that women who receive modern prenatal care have access to data that can be used to evaluate the status of their fetus. Pregnant women, and all those privy to the diagnostic information, can learn of the fetus's physical well-being and sex. As a result, they find themselves in a position to pass judgment as to whether or not the pregnancy should be brought to term. Rothman fears that women have been, and will continue to be, subjected to various forms of undue pressure to abort pregnancies that they might otherwise, with or without access to prenatal screening information, choose to bring to term.

Modern contraceptive technology has, of course, also affected men's experiences in the procreative realm by allowing them to have sex with greater certainty that they will not impregnate their partner. These developments have altered men's interpersonal relationships with women since they now have more opportunities to engage in casual sex.[53] While I discuss men's attitudes toward and involvement in contraception in chapter 4, I comment briefly here on some of the implications the contraceptive revolution has had for men in the United States and other industrialized countries. Women in these countries experienced more autonomy once they were able to use highly effective female-oriented birth control methods such as the female contraceptive pill and IUD. At the same time, the shift in contraceptive technology to more effective female-oriented methods has had the effect of minimizing men's opportunities for participating as actively as they had previously in selecting a contraceptive.[54]

However, incremental advances are being made in developing male contraceptive technology. These technologies could alter once again the nature of the contraceptive decision-making process. The development of male-oriented, chemical contraceptives, although still a number of years away from being mass-marketed in the United States,[55] eventually could provide an impetus for some men to alter their views about contraceptive responsibility.

Individuals can use either tacit or explicit decision-making strategies when they negotiate the adoption of a contraceptive method. Some partners may have one or more direct conversations about what type of contraception they wish to use. In other situations, partners may make decisions about contraception based on unspoken assumptions regarding their sense of contraceptive responsibility. The marketing of a reliable male pill, hormonal injection, or reversible vasectomy for men could change the dynamics of these processes and increase the extent to which couples engage in explicit discussions. Some men on their own initiative might give more serious thought to their procreative potential and role in assuming responsibility for contraception. Men's greater involvement might also be due to their partner's insistence that they consider taking direct responsibility for contraception for a period of time.

In terms of health care services, the increased availability (although geographically uneven) and use of abortion services since the early 1970s represents an important development with ambiguous consequences for how men experience the procreative realm.[56] For some men, increased abortion access has probably reduced their attentiveness to procreative issues, their vigilance about procreative responsibilities in particular, because they reason that their partner can have an abortion if she becomes pregnant. At the same time, greater access to abortion produces strong negative responses from men with firm conservative religious beliefs.[57] Legalized abortion has probably provided a significant number of men who possess conservative views on abortion with more opportunities to think about their involvement, or lack of involvement, in this aspect of the procreative realm. Those men with the strongest political convictions about abortion, whether they be conservative or liberal, have devoted much time and effort to shaping the cultural scenarios that deal with pregnancy-resolution issues. I discuss these matters more extensively in chapter 5 when I focus on men's involvement in abortion issues.

For those who are willing to support their partner during the abortion process, their opportunities to be supportive—in a sense, to demonstrate a kind of procreative responsibility, are influenced by abortion clinic policies regarding men's participation in the abortion procedure and recovery phases. While reliable data are not available to document how many clinics allow men to be present with their partner during the abortion procedure or the recovery phase, one study of clinics surveyed in the early 1980s found that only 12 percent allowed men to be present during the procedure and a similar percent permitted men to be with their partner in the clinic's recovery room.[58] My informal discussions with several health care professionals working in clinics that perform abortions has lead me to conclude that clinics have not changed their policies dramatically in the past decade.

Research indicates that men's willingness to play a more active role in supporting their partner during the abortion process is much greater than their opportunities for doing so. Findings from several studies conducted in 1983, including my own needs assessment of an abortion clinic in Columbus, Ohio, reveal that among men who accompany their partner to an abortion clinic, between 56 and 80 percent are willing to be with her during the procedure and over 90 percent would like to be with her during the recovery phase.[59] Thus some men's options for expressing themselves in this domain of the procreative realm are restricted by clinic policies. Other men may be hindered because their female partners simply do not want them to participate. If some men are able to gain more firsthand experience with abortion procedures, and the gender politics associated with abortion in the United States continue to escalate, increasing numbers of men will probably experience their procreative consciousness and sense of responsibility in new ways as they contemplate their options for resolving an unplanned pregnancy.

Meanwhile, beginning in the mid 1940s, men's opportunities in the pregnancy and childbirth processes have improved because of the natural childbirth movement and related initiatives such as prepared childbirth classes. These classes educate prospective parents on the pregnancy and childbirthing processes while providing fathers with a chance to experience a "rite of passage." When an obstetrician named Grantly Dick Read began to publish material in the 1960s about his practice of allowing fathers to be with their partner throughout labor and delivery, it prompted fathers' greater involvement in childbirth.[60] Read introduced the idea of the "husband-coached delivery" to the United States, which, in turn, eventually lead to an institutionalized role for fathers during the birthing process.[61] Remarkably, whereas only about 27 percent of fathers were present at their child's birth in 1972[62] and 35 percent of physicians refused fathers access to the delivery room in 1975,[63] these patterns have shifted dramatically so that now the vast majority of fathers (between 80 and 90 percent), especially economically advantaged fathers, are in attendance when their child is born, and they are highly motivated to be there.[64]

A final noteworthy development affecting men's involvement in the procreative realm, the HIV/AIDS epidemic, has prompted a number of researchers in recent years to study men's experiences with condoms. This epidemic has apparently indirectly altered the way some men experience the procreative realm. In general, condom use seems to have increased during the late 1980s and early 1990s, a pattern attributable in part to some men's concerns about STD prevention.[65] However, it is not clear to what extent, if any, men's increased use of condoms has prompted them to become more aware of their procreative potential. Using a condom, irrespective of the reason for doing so, may encourage at least some men to pause and think about the prospects of fathering a child.

As the preceding discussion indicates, the transformation of men's lives as procreative beings is being aided by an array of technological and social innovations. Men's relatively new experiences, and those that lie ahead, are also tied to the gendered nature of the reproductive realm. I develop this theme more fully in the next chapter, where I juxtapose the sexual and reproductive domains, while exploring how they each are structured by gender themes that contribute to men's and women's unique experiences.

3

Gender, Sex,
and Reproduction

That men and women think about and experience aspects of their sexual and reproductive lives quite differently seems obvious, and it is borne out by both recent scientific evidence and common everyday experience.[1] Most scholars and laypersons recognize that individuals' biological sex and the social aspects of their gender profoundly shape their experiences with sex and reproduction, both directly and indirectly. This commonsensical notion has persisted throughout the past several decades despite concerted efforts by many to discount, disregard, or eliminate gender-related patterns.

The 1960s ushered in a political climate, particularly within academia, where it was fashionable to challenge the scientific evidence and folk wisdom supporting gender differences in some areas. While this type of critique has considerable merit in many instances (e.g., child care abilities), it often came at the expense of the notion that biological factors could affect people's sexual and reproductive lives in a significant way.[2] These attempts to challenge orthodox views were often motivated by efforts to eliminate sexual double standards and promote gender equality. This stance was consistent with the larger intellectual movement that decisively favored the "nurture" side of the "nature-nurture" debate, or what has at times been referred to as the "blank slate" image of human beings.

In recent years, however, the pendulum has shifted to acknowledge more balanced approaches to these issues. These perspectives acknowledge that the biological and psychosocial factors associated with sexuality and reproduction affect men and women differently and are interrelated in complex ways.[3] Sharing this view, I highlight how gender differences in reproductive anatomy help to create distinctive contexts within which men and women experience sexual and reproductive phenomena. Psychiatrist Willard Gaylin has recently outlined the personal, social, and cultural implications related to men's and women's anatomical differences.⁴ My analysis draws extensively from his work.

Since reproduction is typically associated with vaginal intercourse and coitus has been portrayed as being the most valued form of sexuality within a patriarchal society, I discuss sexuality issues, most notably sexual intercourse, as they pertain to procreation. My primary objective in this chapter, though, is to examine how the reproductive realm is organized according to gender themes. This domain of life is structured and experienced in ways that are fundamentally shaped by physiological and social dimensions related to biological sex and gender. I therefore focus on both of these dimensions when considering the origins of men's and women's diverse experiences in the reproductive realm. Moreover, I show how men's perceptions about masculinity shape their views and experiences with regard to procreative issues. Juxtaposing men's and women's lives in this way accentuates the unique aspects of men as procreative beings.

Aspects of Reproduction

Men are anatomically and hormonally different from women, although some differences may not be well understood. Physiological differences between men and women are significant in their own right and in combination with individuals' perceptions about what is appropriate gender role behavior.⁵

Though vital in conceptions that result from sexual intercourse, men's participation in the reproductive process is, in effect, limited to their contribution of sperm. Their physical body is not even directly connected to the moment of conception, which occurs long after the sexual act is complete. Their role in the biological aspects of sexually based reproduction is restricted to the few brief seconds during intercourse in which they experience an ejaculation. Men often experience these fleeting seconds primarily, or exclusively, in conjunction with the erotic moments they share with their partner. In other words, as they reach their sexual climax they are unlikely to be thinking about their possible contribution to the conception of a fetus, or the potential long-term father roles that might result from this sexual encounter. Instead, they focus on their erotic experience and fantasies. Granted, women may seldom have thoughts about reproduction while they are having sex, but they have subsequent chances to experience aspects of the reproductive realm directly if they do become pregnant. If men and women do have different types of thoughts during a sexual episode, women are probably more likely to worry about the possibility of unplanned pregnancy since they are more directly affected by it.

The actual moment of conception occurs sometime after a man and woman have discontinued their sexual episode, although technically they might be engaged in a subsequent sexual episode when the egg is actually fertilized by sperm from the successful initial encounter. In cases of conceptions resulting from coitus, conception takes place inside the woman's body (although the woman is initially oblivious to this process, at least in the immediate sense), and only the woman directly experiences the pregnancy. She alone has the firsthand physiological sensations associated with the gestation process.

Presumably only a small percentage of men are envious of women's direct role in the reproductive process.[6] Notwithstanding men's indifference, the biological realities of sexually induced reproduction have limited men's experiential opportunities during pregnancy and childbirth. The biological processes associated with sex and reproduction therefore represent the foundation for men's emotional and psychological alienation from the reproductive process.

While men's and women's prenatal experiences in the reproductive realm are based on fundamentally different physiological and social realities, men and women, especially those who are in a serious relationship, may have similar experiences prior to the onset of a pregnancy. For couples who are attempting to conceive a child, an episode of sexual intercourse may focus each partner's attention on the couple's shared reproductive potential. The interpersonal bond partners experience during sex may be quite powerful, and their feelings may extend well beyond the sexual realm. Partners may infuse their lovemaking with private or shared fantasies about the prospects of forming a coparental bond. They may at times candidly talk about their feelings, or they may simply share an implicit understanding. During these sexual episodes, and perhaps in their everyday discussions about their desire to share the pregnancy and parental experience, the similarities in how they think about having a child, especially when it would be the woman's first pregnancy, may be more striking than any dissimilarities they experience. Gender differences are probably least prominent in situations where neither the man nor the woman have had previous firsthand experience with childbirth. Those who have already experienced a pregnancy may be more immersed in the traditional, gendered aspects of reproduction.

Most of the time when individuals have intercourse, they do not want a pregnancy to occur. Consequently, just as men who are attempting to impregnate their partner may sometimes be aware of their procreative self during their sexual episodes, those men who want to avoid becoming a father during a specific act of intercourse are also likely to be conscious of their ability to impregnate their partner. Men who use a male-oriented approach to pregnancy prevention (i.e., a condom or the withdrawal method) can be viewed as taking their procreative potential directly into account. As such, men are more likely to have a heightened sense of procreative consciousness when they play an active, ongoing role in preventing a pregnancy, as compared to situations where they are not directly involved in birth control or only involved in a passive way. When men rely on condoms or the withdrawal method, they place themselves in a situation where they may reflect on their ability to procreate, even if it is for a fleeting moment. However, many men who use these techniques for pregnancy prevention may not spend much time thinking about their ability to procreate. Men's awareness is likely to be heightened in those situations where their attempt to use one of these techniques is disrupted (a condom breaks or slips off during intercourse or the man does not successfully withdraw prior to ejaculation). These predicaments typically shift the man away from the erotic realm[7] and into the procreative realm and the everyday world.

Men who have chosen to have a vasectomy or one of the new reversible sterilization alternatives described in chapter 4 (e.g., vas deferens plug) may be less likely than men who use condoms or the withdrawal method to have a heightened sense of procreative consciousness or sense of responsibility during any given sexual episode. Those who have been sterilized probably do not think about their condition every time they have sex, and this pattern is likely to be more pervasive as time lapses after their operation.

The type of contraception women use also affects whether they, and in some instances whether men, are constantly reminded of their fecundity. If women need to attend to their method on a regular basis (e.g., female pill, diaphragm), they may be more conscious of their reproductive self than if they do not need to attend to it very often (e.g., Norplant, Depo-Provera).

In industrialized countries today, many men play at best a passive contraceptive role because their partner has taken the initiative to use a modern form of contraception. Consequently, men are probably less likely than women to express their procreative self in connection with contraception.[8] In many instances, men's procreative consciousness may only be activated if their partner becomes pregnant and tells them about their impending paternity.

Men's and women's prenatal experiences tend to be quite different for physiological and social reasons, though there are still opportunities for at least some men and women to have similar intrapsychic experiences. The possible similarities in men's and women's experiences in the reproductive realm should not obscure the fact that men, unlike women, are unable to participate directly in the reproductive process.[9] Because men's biological endowment reduces them to experiencing procreation from a distance, their emotional and psychological reactions to the procreative process are often experienced vicariously through their partner. At best, they must frame their prenatal experiences in the context of being potentially involved in the creation of a fetus, or if they are aware that a conception has occurred, they must await the delivery of their child before their interpersonal connection with their child can approach that of the mother-child bond. Even though men may not know for certain that they are responsible for their partner's pregnancy during gestation, most simply assume that this is the case. Some men, however, find themselves confronting the uncertainty of their paternity status when they suspect, or know, that their partner has recently had sex with another man.

Modern ultrasound technology has at least provided some men with an alternative means to visualize a fetus and an opportunity to develop a more practical understanding of their future identity as a father. However, since women have this opportunity, too, this technology does not really close the gap between men's and women's experiences. Men are still unable to experience the physiological sensations associated with pregnancy, labor, and delivery. Men's prenatal perspective, then, evolves around their assumed and pending paternity and their secondhand understanding of their partner's experiences. Meanwhile, women's prenatal experiences are grounded in their ongoing and concrete physiological gestation of a fetus.

It is one of the basic ironies of human life that, despite men's disproportionate social, political, and economic power, they have remained alienated in some ways from the reproductive process. Men's power in the key nonreproductive areas, if we accept O'Brien's thesis about the origins of patriarchy, may actually be a function of their alienation from the reproductive process. What is clear is that men's direct physiological contribution and experience in procreation, particularly in western societies, is restricted to their sperm. Women's reproductive physiology, on the other hand, affords them the opportunity to experience the gestation process directly and intimately. It is quite common for women to speak fondly of the unique bond they develop with the fetus that grows inside them, a bond that to most outweighs the physical hardships and risks associated with pregnancy and childbirth. Women are also more likely than men to be emotionally distraught by a couple's infertility, irrespective of the reason, because maternal roles, on average, tend to assume a more central position in women's overall identity.[10] Interestingly, as growing numbers of women develop career ambitions and stronger ties to the workforce and as more men take a greater interest in the nurturing aspects of parenthood, the gap between women's and men's experiences of infertility may converge.

Gender and physiology also combine to shape individuals' reproductive experiences because the relationship between sexual and reproductive functioning differ for men and women. A case can be made that the relationship between sexuality and reproduction is, from one perspective, unique and much stronger for men than women because men's ability to procreate is essentially contingent upon their ability to be sexually aroused and ejaculate.[11] Simply put, men typically cannot impregnate a woman without first being sexually aroused. Men's biological functioning therefore links sexual performance with procreative virility; the erotic and procreative realms are closely intertwined. Women, on the other hand, can ovulate, have sex, and then conceive a child without reaching any type of sexual climax or even being sexually aroused. Moreover, whereas sperm is typically associated with men's procreative efforts as well as their sexuality, ova are only directly associated with women's reproductive capacity.

Cultural scenarios and individual perceptions about how images of masculinity are associated with both sexual ability and procreative potency help to solidify the connection people make between these two aspects of men's lives. One of the most noteworthy and ubiquitous public images or cultural icons found in many societies, including the United States, is the erect phallic symbol. This symbol, in all of its varied forms, implicitly links sexual prowess with a masculine expression of power. Indirectly, it often stands for procreative potency. These cultural patterns persist because many persons associate masculinity with both sexual prowess and procreative virility, and, as mentioned earlier, procreation typically depends upon a man being able to have an erection and ejaculate. The connection between sexual vigor and procreative potency is likely to be reinforced by most men's perception that their sexuality depends upon the quality of their erectile functioning—including ejaculation.

While the extent to which individuals associate sexual and procreative potency will vary due to cultural norms as well as the age of the men in question, this connection appears to be an important facet of many men's experiences. Impotency is stigmatized in all societies, and involuntary sterility elicits negative reactions in varying degrees worldwide. Men who have been unable to father a child, for whatever reason, are often seen as less than "real men" by at least some segment of the population. Some men internalize these social perceptions and begin to question their masculinity. Furthermore, while men in the United States who undergo a vasectomy are largely immune from stigmas associated with infertility, particularly if they have already proven themselves by fathering children, many men are reluctant to have a vasectomy for psychological reasons. Even fathers who do not want any more children are sometimes opposed to it. Since these men often associate their masculinity with their ability to have erections and sometimes to sire children,[12] they see a vasectomy as a potentially emasculating experience. The fact that their sexual abilities will be unaffected by this procedure from a physiological standpoint may be of little consequence to them. The erroneous perceptions that many men, and some women, have about the relationship between procreative potential and sexual functioning are quite powerful.

This situation contrasts sharply with women's lives. There is no sexual image comparable to the phallic symbol that would depict "power" derived from femininity or the power women have whether or not they present themselves as feminine. Women's physical attributes in U.S. society continue to be objectified with great regularity, but the cultural images associated with this process (e.g., models with large breasts, slender legs, and high cheek bones or commercial products with seductive curves that resemble an idealized feminine form) do not reference women's power. Some of the imagery indirectly suggests that heterosexual women have the means (or power) to seduce men into being a part of a predatory, captive audience, but the nature of this process is quite different from the sense of proactive power conveyed by the phallic symbol. Furthermore, women's sexuality is seldom portrayed as being associated with their reproductive capacity. Cultural representations of pregnant women, especially in the United States, often desexualize them. There are, of course, plenty of cultural artifacts from around the world that glorify women's role as childbearers, in the past and present, but they seem to focus on women's reproductive role while conveying few if any impressions about their sexuality.[13]

One fairly recent and controversial exception to this pattern in contemporary U.S. society involved the well-known actress Demi Moore, who posed seminude on the August 1991 cover of *Vanity Fair* magazine during the eighth month of her pregnancy. Her notoriety as a Hollywood sex symbol, coupled with her alluring presence, represented a unique departure from the cultural pattern that reinforces the separation of images of female sexuality and reproduction. The magazine cover created quite a public uproar for challenging this pattern, although some thought it was long overdue. While similar attempts to bridge the gap between women's reproductive and sexual identities may be on the horizon, they are unlikely to alter one of the fundamental gender differences in cultural imagery: people tend to perceive visual representations of men's procreative and sexual prowess as being linked in a fundamental way, whereas the connections they might make for women are optional and less powerful.

On a more practical level, and as noted above, women can be impregnated whether or not they are sexually aroused. Consequently, women may be more likely in their own minds to separate their sexual and reproductive self-images in a manner that is somewhat different than is the case for men. Unfortunately, these observations are largely speculative at this point since empirical work has not systematically addressed these issues in detail.

Gendered Bonding Patterns

Sex and reproduction overlap in many ways and, in a sense, are inseparable. However, the essence of these two realms can be examined separately. Much can be gained by clarifying, for example, how gender role norms shape the way men and women experience each of these domains.[14] Some norms are referred to as "feeling rules" because they provide men and women with guidelines for how they should express their emotions in specific types of situations.[15]

Boys and men often engage in interpersonal bonding that takes place in a homosocial setting where an erotic reality is accentuated through the combined effect of sexually imbued activity, visual imagery, and conversation. For example, many young boys explore aspects of their sexuality within same-gender groups. The imagery of boy culture is replete with examples of groups of boys gazing at one of *Sports Illustrated's* annual swimsuit issues, hording around a *Playboy* magazine, or watching an X-rated movie on the VCR. Young boys sometimes fashion these situations in a way that enables them to experience a shared sense of adventure and solidarity among their friends. Thus, these sexualized episodes afford boys an opportunity to develop and strengthen their interpersonal ties within a homosocial environment. The same thing occurs when young men—and some older men, too—foster their "male bonding" by organizing group experiences, which include trips to strip joints and live sex shows as well as bachelor parties complete with erotic female dancers. The feeling rules associated with these types of rituals encourage men to remain emotionally detached from the women they are objectifying while at the same time acknowledging their sense of comradery with their male companions. These rituals serve much the same purpose as those situations where males brag among themselves about their sexual exploits with females, although these latter occasions are not typically ones where males are immersed in erotic reality.[16] Unfortunately, researchers have not yet documented the extent to which boys and men experience the erotic realm in conjunction with homosocial bonding episodes. The degree to which these types of homosocial experiences affect how males view and experience their sexuality is also unclear.

Although many men engage in interpersonal, platonic bonding as they experience aspects of the sexual realm, they tend not to have the same type of group-oriented experiences in the procreative realm, particularly in industrialized countries. While there are a few innovative social programs that bring men together to talk about their experiences about becoming a father, being a partner to a woman who is undergoing an abortion, or dealing with the frustrations associated with assisted reproductive technologies, these programs are rare.[17] Likewise, few men ever throw a baby shower for a prospective father, and once a child is born, men seldom rally around a new father to assist him with his infant care responsibilities. As with most social patterns, there are exceptions. For example, in one guide to organizing baby showers, the author encourages organizers to get men and women involved by planning "couples showers" and having guests buy gifts for the father as well as the child and mother.[18] There may even be a trend toward more men participating in these types of situations. Nevertheless, anecdotal reports suggest that a distinct gender difference still exists in who participates in baby showers.[19]

Turning an eye to young girls' activities in the United States, it may be the case that some girls spend time occasionally in same-gender groups looking at adult magazines, watching X-rated movies, or talking about sex. Young women may also hire male strippers for bachelorette parties or arrange for a group of women to go and watch Chippendale dancers. My impression is that even though groups of females may be immersing themselves into the subworld of erotic reality more frequently than in the past, they are still less likely to do so than their male counterparts.[20]

The significance of this gender difference may be offset partially because, compared to their male counterparts, young girls and women engage in more subtle activities with other females. While not as deeply embedded in the erotic realm as men's group experiences, females' experiences probably still have implications for their sexual self-concept. These activities are not typically viewed as erotic experiences; however, they enable females to experience aspects of their sexual identity while they interact with other females. For instance, it is not uncommon for female friends to embark on shopping excursions that result in conversations about how specific clothes either enhance or diminish their sex appeal. Likewise, females are probably more apt than men to incorporate same-gender friends into their preparation rituals for dates, especially those that precede first dates.[21] To my knowledge, researchers have not explored the significance of these types of ritualistic experiences for females' sexual self-concept. I suspect, though, that these experiences may affect individuals differently than encounters where persons are engrossed more intensely in an erotic reality where they are sexualizing others. Females probably share the subtle interpersonal rituals mentioned above more often throughout their lives than men spend experiencing their more explicit forms of group bonding that accentuate the erotic realm. Consequently, women may be affected to a greater extent by their experiences than men are influenced by their own.

Women are much more likely than men, however, to participate in bonding rituals that evolve around reproductive and parenting experiences. For example, baby showers have historically been a female-dominated ritual that enable a pregnant woman to celebrate her status as a "mother-to-be" with her female friends and relatives. Other postnatal gatherings that facilitate bonding include occasions when females assist a recent mother's recovery shortly after the birth of a child or situations where a lactating mother allows her female friends to observe her breast-feeding her infant. Women's interpersonal ties can also be strengthened when women support other women during and after an abortion procedure.

To what extent do these types of experiences actually contribute to gender differences in individuals' sexual and reproductive identities and experiences? How often and in what types of situations do men engage in homosocial activities where they sexualize females? Does extensive participation in these activities reinforce their sexual consciousness while downplaying their procreative roles? Does women's participation in group encounters focused on aspects of the reproductive realm influence their sense of self? These questions have yet to be studied systematically.

Data are available that offer clues about how men and women differ in the way they experience a particular aspect of reproduction. An intriguing comparison can be made between men who donate sperm and those women who, as surrogates, arrange to carry a pregnancy to term and then give the newborn to someone else, usually a married couple. While I discuss at length various alternative strategies for reproducing children in chapter 6, I briefly review here the gendered nature of the reproductive realm by examining various aspects of sperm donation and surrogacy. Ragoné's unique study of surrogate motherhood reveals the gendered nature of the reproductive realm and provides the foundation for this discussion.[22]

Surrogacy and donor insemination both violate conventional taboos about conceiving children independent of sexual intercourse and outside the marital bond. Gestational surrogacy, where one of several techniques is used to transfer both the male and female partners' genetic contribution for their child to the surrogate who then gestates the fetus, seems to be perceived by the general public as being less deviant than traditional surrogacy, which incorporates the social father's sperm and the surrogate's ovum. Because surrogacy and donor insemination are viewed with suspicion, even the individuals who use these alternative reproductive techniques may be ambivalent about them. Their confusion often stems from the fact that they, as well as others, have a difficult time separating sexuality from procreation. A man's relationship with a traditional surrogate who supplies her own egg may be seen by some as a kind of adulterous relationship since the product of their association, a child, is typically the byproduct of a sexual union (women who use sperm donors may also experience this ambivalence). Ragoné astutely observes the irony that underlies individuals' efforts to manipulate how the surrogacy arrangement is socially constructed:

> Although biogenetic relatedness is the initial motivation for, and the ultimate goal of, surrogacy and the facet of surrogacy that makes it consistent with the biogenetic basis of American kinship ideology, such relatedness must be deemphasized, even devalued, by all the participants in order to make surrogacy consistent with American cultural values about appropriate relations between wives and husbands.[23]

The major differences in the way donor insemination and surrogacy are perceived can be traced back to the distinctive features of men's and women's reproductive physiologies. Commercial sperm donors are excluded from the reproductive process and, in most cases, remain anonymous and have no direct contact with the individuals who use their sperm or the children who may be born from it. Surrogates, on the other hand, often form relatively close attachments with the adoptive or social mother. They often accompany one another to the doctor's office or birthing classes. Furthermore, unlike sperm donors, most surrogates are married—85 percent.[24] Thus, surrogacy provides another example of how women use an aspect of the reproductive realm as an opportunity to bond with one another. Ragoné notes that both surrogates and adoptive mothers view the reproductive process as "woman's business." Their bonding efforts are partially motivated by their desire to make the situation seem socially acceptable. Toward this end, surrogates usually de-emphasize their biological link to the child and emphasize the adoptive mother's roles.

This type of female bonding frequently occurs at the expense of the biological father's relationship with the surrogate. It serves the important function of minimizing the appearance of an adulterous relationship between the man and the surrogate that is symbolically represented by their joint contribution to the surrogate's pregnancy. Despite the participants' efforts to downplay the relationship between the man and the surrogate, some men do recognize a special type of connection with the surrogate. In the words of one thirty-eight-year-old man,

> I would be prepared to pay her [surrogate] another fee so that she would not have a child for someone else. It's something so special to do it for one

couple, and if she did it for another couple, she would be too much of a baby machine. You [interviewer] didn't ask me, but I wouldn't do it with another surrogate.[25]

The sperm donor's role in the reproductive process contrasts sharply with the surrogate's role because his contribution is typically far less personal and emotional. This difference is, at its most fundamental level, produced by men's and women's distinctive reproductive physiologies. Men can donate sperm, but they cannot gestate a fetus. The social conventions that have arisen in response to these procedures have also reinforced commercial sperm donors' anonymity. While the same can be said of women who donate their ova, women in general have the option of becoming more intimately involved through surrogacy if they wish. While it is only possible to speculate, I imagine that men would not be very eager to donate sperm if they had to incur the types of "inconveniences" that pregnant women experience. I also expect that it would be quite rare for sperm donors and social fathers to make a concerted effort to associate with one another if sperm donorship were not an anonymous process.

I close with another specific illustration of how men's experiences in the reproductive realm differ from those of women. Prospective fathers in the United States have essentially no legal rights concerning whether a pregnancy is carried through or terminated.[26] This means that prospective fathers, unlike pregnant women, cannot unilaterally opt to have a pregnancy terminated nor can they ensure that a pregnancy be brought to term. Although the landmark 1973 *Roe v. Wade* abortion decision allowed states to place legal restrictions on women's options for having abortions after the first trimester of pregnancy, women have complete autonomy over abortion decisions during the first trimester. The effect of these stipulations is that men's voices, at least in a legal sense, have been silenced on the abortion question. This does not mean that men cannot and do not frequently play an active role in attempting to persuade or force their pregnant partner to resolve her pregnancy in accord with their wishes. In some cases, men have actually attempted to petition courts to file injunctions against women in order to prevent them from having an abortion, though the women had abortions anyway.[27]

The previous examples illustrate that whether it be asexual forms of reproduction, pregnancy, abortion, or birth control, men and women experience the diverse aspects of the reproductive realm in unique ways, largely because of physiological differences and gendered social patterns. Creating a detailed portrait of men's experiences in these areas rests on showing how men's procreative lives differ from those of women. Furthermore, it requires an understanding that men's sexual and procreative experiences are in some ways uniquely intertwined. Because men's experiences with birth control represents a primary area in which men can express themselves as procreative beings, these issues warrant a more extensive discussion.

4

Birth Control

Among their varied roles as procreative beings, men are often involved, actively or passively, in trying to prevent conceptions from occurring. Men's experiences with birth control are best understood in the context of their interpersonal exchanges and negotiations with their partners. These interactions are, in turn, imbedded within a larger cultural milieu where social forces and technologies shape individuals' birth control practices.

Birth control, when viewed in its broadest sense, includes efforts to plan as well as avoid pregnancies. However, the term is typically used to refer to practices involving the latter.[1] Most of the research on men's birth control activities focuses on men's approach to contraception—those strategies that lower men's risk of impregnating women. This is the issue I attend to here.

As noted earlier, our male ancestors experienced a revolutionary shift in their procreative consciousness when they developed a better sense of the physiological processes associated with conception, pregnancy, and childbirth while also discovering the "secrets" of their specific role in procreation. Further, while it's not clear when men first showed an interest in controlling their fertility, individuals have been concerned with these issues for at least the last twenty-five hundred years.[2]

One of the most significant recent scientific developments affecting birth control practices occurred in the 1950s when Gregory Pincus began to study synthetic hormones, research that eventually lead to the development of an oral contraceptive pill in 1960. The pill, which quickly won wide medical acceptance, altered the nature of birth control for millions of men and women. Since its introduction, the contraceptive industry has continued to supply highly effective chemical forms of birth control to women. Some of the more recent developments include Norplant and Depo-Provera.

These recent technological advances in contraceptive technology have been viewed positively or negatively, depending upon one's point of view:

Women, it was realized, had gained more effective methods of birth control only at the price of assuming full responsibility for the inconveniences and risks involved. No one wanted to have to rely again on coitus interruptus, but the argument could be made that, as unsatisfactory as it might have been, it at least required a high level of male involvement.[3]

In today's world of high-tech contraceptives, the selection of a birth control approach, a contraceptive method in particular, is fundamentally related to the types of contraceptives commercially available. The implications of this are that the current selection process explicitly or implicitly involves the selection of either a female-oriented or a male-oriented method. The relatively recent development of modern forms of female-oriented contraception has created an uneven array of contraceptives designed for women's use. This pattern, in turn, has shifted contraceptive responsibility much more fully to women.[4] Thus the new options of the late 1900s, which are highly effective and enhance spontaneity, have qualitatively and quantitatively altered the set of alternatives from which couples can make their selection.

Men have few choices in contraception. The condom and vasectomy represent the most reliable contraceptive methods available for men in the United States. While men can also play a role in contraception by choosing withdrawal—which is often thought of as a male technique—few adult men in the United States use this technique on a regular basis, in part, because it is not as reliable as other methods and because many people still believe that pregnancy can result from a man's pre-ejaculatory fluid.[5]

One unintentional consequence of women having the most effective contraceptive options targeted at them is that the decision-making process for selecting a method is simplified. Even though 78 percent of adult men in a recent national survey report that men and women should share equal responsibility for decisions about contraception,[6] partners are less apt to negotiate the possible adoption of gender-specific methods because the options for men and women aren't comparable. Women continue to assume the dominant role in decisions about contraceptive use although many men do play a role.[7]

Future developments in male-oriented contraceptives, specifically a reliable male birth control pill, hormonal injection, or reversible sterilization will undoubtedly alter the nature of contraceptive decision making. Men would no longer have the convenient excuse of stating that male methods are inferior. Today, they can argue that vasectomies are often irreversible and condoms inhibit spontaneity, detract from sexual gratification, and are "somewhat" unreliable.[8] A more balanced set of modern contraceptives should produce more lively negotiations between partners over the selection of a female- or male-oriented method. Consequently, if a male pill, hormonal injection, or reliable form of reversible vasectomy were commercially marketed, contraceptive decision making would likely become more complex and potentially confrontational for many couples.[9]

The uneven supply of effective and reversible contraceptive methods available to men and women is unlikely to change dramatically in the near future, though there is some hope that significant developments in male methods will be developed eventually. Several organizations around the world are currently attempting to refine vasectomy procedures so that they can be reversed by choice more easily. In addition, a small group of scientists are experimenting with new nonhormonal and hormonal strategies to regulate men's fertility.[10] Social scientists have also contributed to our understanding of individuals' willingness to try different types of male-oriented fertility control methods once they have been marketed.[11]

Condom Use

Before I describe some of the current and future developments in male methods, and the implications they may have for how men experience aspects of the procreative realm, it is instructive to discuss heterosexual men's recent patterns of condom use. The public's interest in condom use has grown considerably since the HIV/AIDS epidemic captured the public's attention in the early 1980s. The public's and policymakers' concern over this epidemic provided researchers with a unique opportunity to secure funding to study men's views about and use of condoms. Much has been learned in particular from two nationally representative samples of men, the three waves of the National Survey of Adolescent Males (NSAM-1, NSAM-2, NSAM-3) first fielded in 1988 and the 1991 National Survey of Men (NSM). The funding for these types of studies, linked as it is to the whims of the political process, indicates that many policymakers welcome, or at least are willing to tolerate, research that explores men's sexual and reproductive experiences. In many instances, policymakers support this type of research because they are concerned not only with the implications of HIV/AIDS, but also welfare reform and single-parenthood issues.

National surveys reveal that most adult American men have at some point in their lives used a condom as a form of birth control, STD prevention, or both. Results from the NSM show that about 89 percent of men between the ages of 20 and 39 have used a condom on at least one occasion. Younger men aged 20 to 24 were actually the most likely to have used a condom in their lifetime (91 percent), whereas 35- to 39-year-olds were the least likely (86 percent).[12]

Has heterosexual men's use of condoms increased since the early 1980s as a result of the HIV/AIDS epidemic? While there may be some disagreement about the magnitude of the change, several data sources suggest that condom use at an aggregate level has increased during the past decade, especially among particular subgroups of men. Data from the 1988 NSAM-1, for instance, showed that young men 15 to 19 years of age living in metropolitan areas were significantly more likely to report condom use than their counterparts of a decade earlier. When asked about the use of condoms at last intercourse, 57 percent of sexually active respondents in the 1988 survey reported that they had used a condom, whereas only 21 percent of respondents in a comparable 1979 survey offered a similar reply.[13] In addition, data from the National Survey of Family Growth showed that 13 percent of never-married women 15 to 44 years of age in 1990 reported condoms as their current method compared to 8.2 and 4.1 percent of similar aged cohorts in 1988 and 1982, respectively.[14] Finally, condom manufacturers experienced double-digit annual sales increases in the late 1980s and have continued to report more modest annual growth in the 1990s of about 3 percent.[15] While purchasing condoms does not necessarily indicate their use, we can assume that a significant proportion of the increase in condom sales has translated into higher levels of use.[16]

Though the health care community has made a concerted effort to promote the use of condoms as a means to prevent STD and HIV transmission, most young men continue to cite pregnancy prevention as the major reason they use condoms.[17] In fact, a recent study reported that 83 percent of the young men in the 1990–91 NSAM-2 who used a condom in the previous two years told interviewers that they had used a condom to prevent a pregnancy.[18] Meanwhile, among all respondents in the NSM, 49 percent reported using a condom during the four weeks prior to the interview for birth control reasons only, while another 43 percent said they had used condoms for both birth control and STD prevention.[19] Significant differences appeared between married and single men. Whereas 83 percent of married men said that they had used condoms for birth control only and another 16 percent said they used it for both birth control and STD prevention, the comparable figures for single men were 24 and 63 percent, respectively. Men's racial background was also related to their reasons for using condoms. White men were much more likely than black men to say they used condoms only for birth control reasons (55 percent to 18 percent). Likewise, men 30 years of age and older were significantly more likely than their younger counterparts to report that they used condoms only for birth control purposes (59 percent to 41 percent), a finding that is confounded, though, by older men's greater likelihood of being married.

This NSAM-2 study revealed significant differences in African American and white men's reported condom use over the four-week period preceding their interviews. Among 20- to 24-year-olds, almost 57 percent of black men reported using a condom during the preceding four-week period, while only 36 percent of whites said they did. A similar, though less pronounced, pattern was found among each of the five-year age categories used in this study. This condom use pattern was partly due to black men's greater likelihood of using a condom when they were single and without a regular sexual partner. Faced with this type of relationship situation, 69 percent of blacks reported using a condom in the four weeks prior to their interview, whereas only 42 percent of whites used a condom. The difference in condom use was much smaller, though, between married black and white men (24 to 18 percent).[20]

African American and white men have also been found to differ in how they assess psychological and interpersonal dimensions of using condoms. Black men are more likely to report that men can demonstrate that they are concerned and caring persons by using condoms. At the same time, however, black men are also more likely than white men to say that when a man uses condoms or suggests that they should be used, he conveys an implicit message about his and his partner's HIV/AIDS status. In other words, black men are more likely to believe that if a man shows an interest in using condoms, the man will imply that he is wondering about his partner's infectious status or will induce his partner to believe that he is infected. Either way, the positive message associating condom use with caring for one's partner is more likely to be offset for blacks than whites by concerns about the stigma of possible HIV/AIDS infection raised by condom use.[21]

We can usefully consider several key themes that highlight the different ways condom use patterns can be assessed using cross-sectional and longitudinal data. When taken together, they provide the basis for what has been referred to as the "sawtooth hypothesis."[22] This hypothesis might be better described as a theoretical explanation for condom use that includes several interrelated hypotheses. Simply put, this explanation suggests that condom use is more likely to occur during the early phases of a relationship and that it declines as a function of men's age, for several possible reasons.

The first theme underscores men's lack of consistency in using condoms during each successive act of intercourse. While some men use condoms faithfully without exception for an extended period of time, the more common scenario is for men to use them irregularly during the tenure of their involvement with particular partners. One study with the NSAM-1 found that 35 percent of sexually active teenage men aged 15 to 19 reported using a condom all of the time during the previous year, another 43 percent used them intermittently, and 22 percent had not used them at all.[23] Another study with the same data found that black adolescent males were, contrary to popular stereotype, more consistent condom users than whites.[24]

A second theme suggests that consistency of condom use declines with age. Cross-sectional data from the NSAM-1 and the NSM documents that older men use condoms less frequently than younger men. NSAM-1 cross-sectional data reveal that 59 percent of young men 17 to 18 years of age reported using a condom the first time they had sex with their most recent partner, whereas 56 percent of 19- to 20-year-olds and 46 percent of 21- to 22-year-olds reported condom use in similar situations. Consistent with these findings, cross-sectional data from the NSM indicated that each successive five-year age cohort of the sample of men aged 20 to 39 were less likely to report having used a condom during the four weeks prior to their interview.[25] In addition to these cross-sectional data, longitudinal analyses using the NSAM showed that young men are less likely to use condoms as they get older.[26] This pattern is largely due to the increased likelihood that young men's female partners become regular users of some type of modern contraception (e.g., pill, Norplant).

The third theme relevant to men and condoms highlights how men's condom use is affected by the nature of their relationship with their partner. Some research has found that men are more likely to use condoms with casual or secondary partners than with more serious partners,[27] although other research has failed to document this pattern.[28] One set of analyses actually revealed that young men were less likely to use a condom with women they thought were at high risk for HIV/AIDS and more likely to use a condom when they had sex with a woman they suspected had never had intercourse.[29] Young men may be more likely to use condoms with young women they suspect are less experienced because these partners are probably less likely to be using birth control.

Although men continue to cite pregnancy prevention as the primary or exclusive reason why they used condoms, especially older men, some researchers have speculated that this reporting pattern may be a function of the way survey questions are posed. Men may be reluctant to indicate that they used a condom for STD or HIV prevention because they might want to avoid conveying the negative impression that they or their partner might have been infected. Research has shown, though, that young men's consistent condom use is correlated with their personal concerns about AIDS. Likewise, condom use is positively associated with young men's perceptions about their partner's desire for them to use a condom and negatively related to men's reported concerns about embarrassment and reduced sexual pleasure.[30]

Researchers have used several types of theoretical models to interpret survey data on men's condom use patterns. One of the more popular general models has been the cognitive or rational choice model. This model basically holds that there is an important rational component to the way individuals think and act when they engage in sexual intercourse. The research team responsible for fielding the NSAM, for example, has used a variant of the basic rational choice model, the subjective expected utility theory.[31] A basic assumption of this theory is that individuals' behavior is a product of two considerations. First, individuals evaluate what they perceive to be the positive and negative outcomes associated with a behavior. Second, they assess the probability that each of these outcomes is likely to occur. When these considerations are combined, they represent a measure of a person's perception of the utility or disutility of a particular course of action (e.g., using a condom).

One of the strengths of this model is that it enables researchers to assess individuals' perceptions about the different costs and benefits they associate with using condoms as well as their overall orientation toward the use of condoms. In one analysis with the NSAM-1 comparing sexually inexperienced and sexually experienced young men, researchers found that the latter group were less likely to anticipate that future condom use would be embarrassing but they were more likely to believe that condom use would inhibit their physical pleasure. Having a favorable attitude toward contraceptive responsibility was a significant predictor of young men's intention to use a condom during their next sexual episode. This variable was a more powerful predictor of young men's intention than were the specific consequences they associated with condom use.[32]

Unfortunately, rational choice theory does not adequately address many of the emotional and dynamic features of men's interpersonal sexual episodes in which decisions about condom use are made. This theory is limited because it does not take into account the way men actually define their partners and particular situations. It also does not consider how information is processed during these sexual episodes. When do men feel that it is "safe" or "reasonable" from a health standpoint to be sexually active with their partner without using a condom? What about from a pregnancy-prevention standpoint? How do their feelings toward their partner interact with these types of concerns? If men feel they are in love with their partner, do they typically perceive their risk as lower or are they simply more willing to take the risk of contracting a disease or impregnating their partner? How often do men who are in love use condoms because they are concerned about protecting their partners from contracting an STD or HIV? Addressing these questions is difficult because the standard survey methodology used to operationalize the rational choice theory does not adequately capture how individuals come to form impressions of their partners and particular situations. Survey-based research should therefore be supplemented with more qualitatively oriented research that examines how men (and women) develop their perceptions of whether their partner is safe and free of infectious diseases. It should also consider how men's feelings toward their partners might lead them to risk contracting a disease or being responsible for an unplanned pregnancy. Likewise, research should explore how men's feelings might prompt them to take steps to protect their partner from possible health and pregnancy risks.

Men's choices to use or not use a condom may be affected by how they characterize their relationship. More specifically, men may on occasion use stereotypes to define their partner or may draw upon some type of schema to categorize the type of relationship (e.g., serious versus casual) they feel they have with their sexual partner. Men's perceptions of whether a situation is one in which a condom should or should not be used may depend, in part, on their interaction with their partner, their perception of her reputation, and their feelings for her. When men define relationships or situations in a particular way, they may feel more or less confident that their partner is free of contagious diseases and perhaps be willing to assume paternal responsibilities if a pregnancy and birth should result. It should not be overlooked, though, that a woman can also play an important role in allowing, perhaps even encouraging, sex to occur without a condom—whether or not she is using contraception herself. These types of considerations are influenced by the cultural and subcultural scenarios that individuals use to guide their intrapsychic and interpersonal scripting.

Current research has yet to answer a number of significant questions concerning the relationship between condom use and procreative issues. Has condom use affected men's procreative consciousness or their attentiveness to their procreative abilities to any discernable degree? Do specific reproductive events influence men's contraceptive behavior? For example, do men who have had unplanned pregnancies subsequently become more attentive to their procreative potential and engage in more responsible contraceptive behavior? Contrary to what I expected, I found in one of my analyses with the NSAM-1 data that those young men who had had previous experience with impregnating someone were actually not as diligent about their contraceptive behavior as those who had no prior knowledge of being an expectant father.[33] On the other hand, Mercer Sullivan, in his ethnographic study of young New York City men, found that personal experiences and knowledge of others' experiences did encourage some young men to reduce their risky sexual behavior: "The experiences of suspected pregnancy, actual pregnancy, and childbearing by their partners were key turning points in the contraceptive behaviors of many of these young males."[34]

Vasectomy Use

In addition to the condom, vasectomy represents the other effective method readily available to men—and one disproportionately used by married men. During much of this century, men in the United States and numerous other countries have been able to limit their fertility by undergoing a vasectomy. While more women than men choose sterilization, a growing proportion of men have chosen to have vasectomies in recent years in the United States and Britain, although men in other European countries, Latin America, and Asia—not including China and India—are much less likely to pursue this option.[35] Data from the 1990 National Survey of Family Growth (NSFG) showed that among a sample of U.S. women 15 to 44 years of age, 17.5 percent reported being surgically sterile and 7.5 percent relied on their male partner being surgically sterilized.[36] Comparable figures for 1982 were 13 and 6 percent, respectively. Among currently married women 15 to 44 years of age, roughly 37 percent relied on some form of surgical sterilization as their method of birth control (24 percent female method, 14 percent male method). The relative likelihood of couples choosing male sterilization is significantly higher in Britain than the United States. Data from the 10,000 British respondents in the annual General Household Survey, where the female partner was aged 18 to 44, revealed that vasectomy has become more prevalent and is actually chosen slightly more frequently than female sterilizations (12 percent to 11 percent).[37]

Another way to assess the relative prevalence of male sterilization is to focus only on the subsample of women in 1990 who reported using any method of contraception. When this approach is used, about 30 percent of women reported relying on female sterilization and 13 percent used male sterilization. It has been estimated that about 500,000 men are sterilized each year.[38]

Analyses using the 1988 NSFG found that after couples made a decision to use some form of contraceptive sterilization, they were more likely to opt for a vasectomy when they had fewer children, higher education, higher-status jobs, and a higher household income.[39] A study based on the 1991 NSM also found that white husbands are significantly more likely than black husbands to elect male over female sterilization.[40] Though it is difficult to say for sure, Bruce Stokes's observation made nearly twenty years ago may still ring true:

> The deeply felt fear among some black Americans that government-funded sterilization programs are really attempts at black genocide has apparently kept some men from turning to this method of contraception and may inhibit the government from actively promoting vasectomies in minority communities.[41]

Why do some men decide to have a vasectomy while others do not? A variety of factors can affect men's vasectomy decision. Some of these factors may relate to men's personal attitudes while others are associated with the dynamics of their relationship with their partner. Men's anxieties about sterilization are possibly related to their more general procreative consciousness. For those men who associate their presumed procreative ability with their masculine gender-role identity, the idea of voluntarily submitting to sterilization could be devastating. Such concerns are probably reinforced by fears of being stigmatized by others if they were to have a vasectomy. While some men may feel this way even though they have absolutely no desire to have children, others may be more worried about being sterilized and then wanting to have additional children. Some men may, therefore, have practical concerns as they contemplate having a vasectomy. They may worry about feeling helpless if a future partner wants to have a child who would jointly share their genetic makeup. Or, they may simply be afraid of the actual surgical procedure. Men's perceptions about vasectomy and advancements in microsurgical techniques are especially relevant to the present discussion. Thus, "males desire to keep their reproductive options open for much longer than is operatively and culturally feasible for women, but many also fear the real or imagined sequelae of vasectomy."[42] Finally, those men who are involved with assertive women may be more likely to agree to have a vasectomy than men whose partners tacitly assume that it is their own responsibility to be sterilized or use some other form of birth control.

One of the consequences of recent patterns of divorce and delayed childbearing has been that a growing proportion of middle-aged men are finding themselves in the unenviable position of being sterilized and unable to satisfy their new partner's (and perhaps their own) desire for children. Two therapists have reported on their sessions with British couples who found themselves in this situation and were referred to counseling because they were considering donor insemination.[43] Data from these couples provide preliminary evidence that the proportion of couples whose predicament was caused by an irreversible vasectomy increased during the 1980s. One of the possible implications of this pattern, as speculated by these therapists, is that more men may consider banking their sperm prior to having a vasectomy. Currently only a very small percentage of individuals make arrangements to have their sperm frozen. If cryopreservation of a man's sperm were to become more commonplace, a prospect that seems unlikely at least in the foreseeable future, the link between the sexual and reproductive spheres could be lessened for a subset of men and women. The number of unplanned pregnancies, especially among the more affluent segment of society, would also probably decrease. I discuss the potential significance of cryopreservation more fully when I explore the alternative pathways to fatherhood in chapter 6.

A related trend of some import involves recent improvements in the surgical techniques used to perform vasectomies. These new technologies are quite significant because the method's potential irreversibility continues to be one of the key obstacles to its adoption. The two key technical improvements in the surgical procedures for vasectomy are "the isolation and ligation of the vas through a puncture (non-scalpel) opening in the skin; and the development of a technique for the percutaneous injection into the vas lumen of sclerosing or occluding agents through a hypodermic needle."[44] These new procedures have helped to increase surgically sterilized men's chances of having their vasectomy reversed. The no-scalpel vasectomy operation has been performed on between four and eight million men in China, though relatively few men outside of China.[45] In time, more and more men in the United States and elsewhere will be able to have a no-scalpel vasectomy as experience with this innovation becomes more widespread.[46]

If the reversibility of vasectomy can be improved, peoples' perception of vasectomy could change dramatically. Vasectomy would no longer automatically be considered the final event in a man's procreative life. In certain instances, a vasectomy might be perceived as a way to address a man's (and sometimes his partner's) immediate birth control needs without negating the man's future ability to procreate. Thus, sometime in the future, men may have the option of using vasectomy as a temporary birth control strategy, which would in effect allow them to have sex more freely without the fear of impregnating their partner, while feeling confident that they could regain their procreative ability if they decided to have additional children. Another impediment to widespread acceptance of vasectomy today is that some men are quite nervous about having surgery performed on what they have come to define as the most vulnerable region of their body because this region, comprised of their penis and testicles, also happens to be linked inextricably to their masculine identity and sexuality. It should come as no surprise then that some men fear being emasculated by having their procreative ability eliminated.

An additional concern for some men in recent years has been the perceived safety of surgical vasectomy owing to its association with both preexisting testicular tumors and an increased risk of cardiovascular ill-health, as well as its *perceived* role in predisposing patients to prostate cancer.[47] Researchers have produced mixed results in their attempt to determine the safety of vasectomy, but recent and extensive reviews of the available evidence appear to have allayed safety concerns to some extent.[48]

Withdrawal

The third method of birth control, often labeled as a male method, is withdrawal. Very little effort has been devoted to understanding this widely used method.[49] Family planning professionals typically neglect discussing this method in favor of the much more reliable modern female methods. Rates of withdrawal use are relatively low in developed countries such as the United States and Japan, although teenagers in the United States do exhibit higher usage rates.[50] In addition, its use is much greater in selective countries such as Belgium, France, Hungary, Spain, and Turkey.[51]

While the withdrawal method is clearly less reliable than the other male methods, disinterest in this method in the United Stated is based on the misperception that pre-ejaculate fluid is a significant factor in conceptions. Of the handful of studies relevant to the debate about the viability of pre-ejaculatory fluid, the most detailed studies have found no viable sperm in pre-ejaculatory fluid.[52] Research indicates that the number of sperm needed for fertilization do not appear in pre-ejaculatory fluid.[53] While it is difficult to identify the actual use-effectiveness of the withdrawal method—and estimates from available studies range from 7 to 37 percent[54]—it is suspected that contraceptive failures are due to inadequate withdrawal, not sperm in the pre-ejaculatory fluid.[55]

New Nonhormonal Techniques

While the condom, vasectomy, and withdrawal are currently the available male-oriented methods, a variety of other innovative nonhormonal techniques are being experimented with throughout the world.[56] I highlight the key features of several of the more promising methods.

One strategy is to develop a permanent form of contraception that closes off the vas deferens through the injection of chemicals rather than use of a surgical procedure. For those interested in a potentially reversible form of contraception, research is being conducted on an injectable vas deferens plug. As with many other experimental contraceptive methods for men, China is at the forefront of clinical human trials with this technique. Over 512,000 men have used this technique. It has had a 98 percent effectiveness rate, and all of the men who have had their plugs removed for at least a year have regained their fertility. Clearly optimistic about this approach, the World Health Organization is interested in pursuing trials with it in various parts of the world.

Another method employs a kind of soft silicone vas deferens plug ("shug") that is surgically implanted in an operation that is similar to a vasectomy. A major advantage of this approach, its use of two plugs with a small space in between, makes it more leak-free and therefore more effective than the injectable vas deferens plug. Sperm that might leak past the first plug should be trapped in the space between the two plugs. The development and testing of this method is proceeding slowly with small clinic trials being conducted in the Chicago area.

Animal studies have been conducted on a third type of experimental method that involves application of a sperm-killing solution to the interior of the vas deferens through injection. At present, the effects of this injection are for up to five years and can be reversed at any time with another simple injection. Studies over the past ten years have shown this method to be safe and effective in animals. While human trials are being conducted in India, similar trials have yet to occur in the United States.

These research efforts on male fertility regulation are the latest in a series of studies that began during the 1970s and early 1980s. Much of this early research was conducted at two institutes in the People's Republic of China beginning in the early 1970s. Large-scale clinical trials based on more than 8,000 Chinese men were run to study how effective gossypol (a derivative of cottonseed oil) was on lowering sperm counts.[57] While the findings from the Chinese research were fragmentary at best, this early research program generated a considerable amount of enthusiasm. More recently, however, the scientific community has concluded that gossypol should not be used in connection with contraception because of the problems of irreversibility and side effects.[58]

Male Hormonal Contraception

In addition to these nonhormonal strategies for male fertility regulation, research on various chemically based contraceptive methods have been conducted for several decades.[59] Because male contraceptive innovations could have such a profound impact on how men experience aspects of the procreative realm, I review the status of the biomedical research in this area in some detail.

The basic objective of male hormonal contraception is to bring about temporary infertility by reducing the production of viable spermatozoa on a consistent basis.[60] Research on this type of contraception has been and continues to be conducted on several fronts. A brief review, published in 1978, summarized the major efforts to discover viable forms of male contraceptive agents other than gossypol.[61] It focused on the work of three of the most active organizations in this type of research: the Population Council's International Committee for Contraceptive Research (ICCR), the Contraceptive Development Branch of the U.S. National Institute of Child Health and Human Development (NICHD), and the World Health Organization's (WHO) Special Programme of Research, Development and Research Training in Human Reproduction. At the time of this review, these organizations were still struggling to discover a suitable agent and regimen to reduce sperm counts.[62]

Research conducted by WHO during the 1970s involved combined regimes of androgens and progestins in a series of clinical trials in eight countries. As was the case with the earlier studies mentioned above, no regimen was found to be fully effective. Side effects experienced in this study were similar to those found in other research; among those experienced with one or more of the different agents and regimens studied by these organizations were acne, weight gain, libido loss, and delayed orgasm. An important finding consistent across all three organizations was that, generally speaking, a minimum of six to eight weeks were required after the initiation of treatment for sperm counts to reach their lowest levels. Furthermore, twelve to eighteen months usually constituted the recovery period for sperm counts to regain their pretreatment levels after cessation of treatment.

During the 1986 to 1990 year period, the first-ever multicenter contraceptive efficacy study was conducted with 271 men from Australia, China, Finland, France, Sweden, the United Kingdom, and the United States who had no known fertility problems and were in stable relationships. These men received weekly injections of 200 milligrams of testosterone enanthate. Initial reports from this research suggest that progress is being made toward developing a male hormonal antifertility agent.[63] Sixty-five percent of these men became azoospermic (the absence of sperm). Meanwhile, another study conducted clinical trials with men in nine countries (Australia, China, France, Hungary, Singapore, Sweden, Thailand, the United Kingdom, and the United States) between 1990 and 1994. The men in this second set of trials also received weekly injections of 200 milligrams of testosterone enanthate, but the assessment phase of the study began after men reached the state of oligozoospermia (less than 3 million sperm/ml.). Of the 289 men who stayed in the study, 97 percent reached this state of subfertility.[64] Finally, two recent clinical studies of Indonesian men explored the effectiveness of different progestogen-androgen combinations in bringing about azoospermia. One advantage of this type of regimen is that it would require a smaller dose of androgen than those regimens that use only androgens. In one Indonesian study, three injections at monthly intervals resulted in the suppression of spermatogenesis to azoospermia in 19 out of 20 men.[65]

As the scientific community makes incremental advances toward the eventual marketing of effective male hormonal methods, social science research that explores the acceptability of experimental hormonal methods will take on greater importance. These studies will focus more directly on men's perceptions about, and possible use of, more realistic male birth control options.[66] They will be essential for determining men's (and women's) willingness to accept particular male methods that may be highly effective in reducing sperm counts but fall short of producing azoospermia.

An important question, and one highly relevant to those marketing a male pill or hormonal injection, involves the acceptability of specific types of product characteristics. As one study cautions: "It is imperative that before any male pill [or hormonal injection] is marketed all necessary information about its biomedical properties be obtained."[67] What are the side effects and health risks associated with these modern forms of male birth control? How long does it take for sperm counts to reach acceptable levels? How long does it take for sperm counts to revert back to their normal level after discontinuance of the technique? How reliable is it and how often must it be administered? Some combination of these and other product features will influence the acceptability of a hormonal strategy for male birth control. Men's responses to these product features will vary considerably, and this variation is likely to be associated with, among other factors, individual's age, educational background, gender role attitudes, and phase in the family life course. Social science research designed to explore the relationship between social factors and product features should contribute to our understanding of individuals' willingness to use these innovative male-oriented contraceptives.

Focus group discussions with men from some of the countries participating in the two multisite studies mentioned above provide researchers with some clues as to what factors might influence men's (couples') use of a hormonal injection. All but 2 of the 154 focus group participants in the 1990 to 1994 study reported that "doing a good thing for my partner" was at least a "somewhat important" motivational factor for their involvement in the trials. As one respondent said, "My wife had been taking the pill for nine years. I felt that she was helpless, so why shouldn't it be my turn?"[68] Clinical trial participants were most often deterred by the frequency of the weekly injections. Eight-two percent reported that they would prefer a three-month injectable, hormonal form of male birth control. Interestingly, most focus group participants noted a slight increase in their libido during the trial of about 10 to 20 percent.

After reviewing the status of the biomedical research on male-oriented contraception, it should be apparent that a panacea is not yet on the immediate horizon (within the next several years). Developing a qualitatively new contraceptive is clearly not without its scientific and political impediments. For some time now, observers within the scientific community have speculated about the prospects that a viable antifertility regimen for men would be developed and marketed in the near future. In the early 1980s, Bruce Shearer of the Population Council conservatively estimated that a male pill was feasible and could be developed and marketed by 1990,[69] while Carl Djerassi, a chemistry professor, projected in 1981 that it could occur within the next 12 to 20 years.[70] Others offered even more optimistic time frames,[71] although such assertions have tended to sensationalize the development of a male pill. More recently, Djerassi and Leibo offered one of the bleaker prognostications by stating in 1994,

> The prognosis for a new male contraceptive by the year 2000 is nil, because the development, testing and regulatory approval of a truly novel, systemic male contraceptive requires 15–20 years. Given the absence of serious research and development in male contraception by major pharmaceutical companies—and only they can bring such a product to the general public—the expectation for a "male Pill" even after 2010 is dismal.[72]

Other observers are more cautiously optimistic that it is simply a matter of time before chemical contraceptives for men are produced. The director of male contraceptive research at Vanderbilt University Medical Center, Dr. Spyros Pavloy, boldly asserted in the early 1990s that "if we had all the money we need, we could have a male contraceptive in the next five or six years."[73] A researcher at WHO offered a more measured response in 1993 by suggesting,

> The research to develop male antifertility methods is lively and progressive. There is reasonable hope that, by the year 2000, there may be methods for men based on infrequent steroid injections, reversible vas occlusive systems and possibly other affordable options. However, unless serendipity turns up a post-testicular drug already in clinical use for another application, it seems unlikely that any newly discovered drug could be developed through the long and expensive route of toxicological and regulatory requirements by the end of the century.[74]

The quest for male methods could be accelerated by several events. One of these developments would be the renewed interest of the pharmaceutical industry, which may not be as completely disinterested as it is sometimes portrayed. The "identification of simple biochemical tests of sperm function, together with their transformation into home-use, 'dipstick', methods by which a man could check his own fertility status, would be one significant achievement."[75] Finally, it seems safe to conclude that since clinic studies are able to enroll men in contraceptive efficacy studies with relative ease today, large numbers of men throughout the world would be willing to assume greater responsibility in contraception if the technology were available to them. Since all of the projections offered during the 1980s have not or will not come to pass, it is difficult to assess the more recent predictions about when modern, effective contraceptives will be available for men.

Research and Politics

While observers of the biomedical research on male methods may not share similar views on the prospects for developing these methods, they do share a consensus that the scientific development of highly effective hormonal (and nonhormonal) contraceptive methods for men takes place within a larger sociopolitical context. During the past several decades, women's rights activists have voiced their concern about the orientation of contraceptive research by arguing that contraceptive research has focused primarily on developing and refining female-oriented techniques because of women's disadvantaged position within society. One of the more vocal proponents of this position, Barbara Seaman, argued twenty-five years ago,

> If you doubt that there has been sex discrimination in the development of the pill, try to answer this question: Why isn't there a pill for men? Studies of the male reproductive system are well advanced and a man's organs, being handily placed outside the body, are easier to work with than a woman's.[76]

Assertions that contraceptive research has been fueled by a pervasive sexist ideology have not gone unchallenged. Some have conceded that most contraceptive research has been geared toward female methods, but they do not believe that this has been due to a male chauvinist plot to exploit women. Instead, they suggest that compared to the male reproductive system, female physiology offers more opportunities to inhibit conception.[77] Consequently, many observers assume that contraceptive research has been guided largely by the scientific community's recognition of the differences in reproductive physiology between males and females.

Ironically, it could be argued that if a patriarchal conspiracy were responsible for the direction of contraceptive research, more, not fewer, resources would have been allocated to develop male birth control methods. If only male methods had been developed initially, men alone would ultimately have had the capacity to regulate fertility, to the extent that technology and their motivation to use it dictated. Women would have been unable to regulate their own fertility unless they abstained from sexual intercourse (an unrealistic proposition for most married women) or sought abortions. Under these circumstances, men's coercive control of women could have flourished. Women would have sensed that having vaginal intercourse outside of committed relationships was fraught with unwarranted risks because of the fear of pregnancy, a realistic fear if some of their male partners chose not to use contraception. Hence, men's subjugation of women could have been strengthened if only male-oriented methods had been developed.

This line of reasoning should not be permitted, however, to mask the fundamental and legitimate issues raised about women's health. The highly effective female-oriented contraceptives on the market today have potential side effects and are associated with serious health risks. If modern hormonal birth control methods are to be used, women, not men, must deal with these problematic features, given the types of highly effective contraceptives currently available. Contraceptive research is, therefore, often viewed as sexist because women have been expected to tolerate many of the potential consequences associated with modern contraception, and this technology is rooted in a male-dominated research community and commercial industry. Some feminists point to the controversy surrounding the development and marketing of the defective Dalkon Shield (an IUD popular in the 1970s), where company officials apparently continued to manufacture and sell this IUD even after reviews within their company revealed that it had design flaws that were hazardous to women's health. These feminists have argued that women's health frequently takes a back seat to such male-dominated companies' interest in monetary gain.[78]

Although the underlying motivation that guides contraceptive research may be questionable, the disproportionate amount of funding that goes to support research on female methods cannot be disputed. A 1980 report found that 71 percent of the $34 million dollars spent in 1979 on developing new birth control techniques was targeted at female methods.[79] The remainder went to methods suitable only for men or both men and women.

Relatively speaking, the funding pipeline of research and development funds continues to be geared toward female methods today. Recent congressional testimony reporting on new National Institute of Health (NIH) contraceptive products indicated that six of the nine products under study were intended for female use. Female methods accounted for 63 percent of the total $10.5 million dollars NIH spent on contraceptive research during the fiscal years 1990 and 1991.[80] This pattern in contraceptive funding is also documented by reviewing results from my computer search of articles using the Medline database (January 1991 to November 1995), which identified studies on male and female contraceptives and the type of funding that supported them. Of the 8,593 published reports in this area during the specified time frame, only 10 percent dealt with male contraceptives. Moreover, only 6 percent of the 1,234 reports funded by the U.S. Public Health Service and only 5 percent of the 264 articles funded by U.S. government agencies outside the Public Health Service were based on male contraceptives. Finally, 11 percent of the published articles funded by sources other than the U.S. government dealt with male contraceptives. These figures reveal that the amount of funding and effort being devoted to male contraceptive research pales in comparison to what is being done in connection with female strategies.

The decision to undertake male contraceptive research, or any contraceptive research for that matter, necessitates a serious commitment from a sponsor organization because of the considerable expenditure of monies and other resources.[81] Pharmaceutical companies prior to the early 1970s were responsible in large part for assuming the costs of contraceptive research. More recently, these companies have been reluctant to invest large sums of money into developing new methods.[82] This is especially true with regard to male contraceptives since an element of doubt prevails as to whether or not a market exists for such a product and, if so, whether or not it would be cost effective to pursue. Pharmaceutical companies' willingness to invest resources into the development of male-oriented contraceptive methods will therefore hinge to some extent on findings from social science and consumer behavior research that explores men's willingness to use these types of methods.[83]

As pharmaceutical companies began to curtail their contraceptive research expenditures in the early 1970s, nonprofit organizations such as WHO, the Population Council, the Ford Foundation, and the National Institute of Child Health and Human Development (NICHD) were able to fill the void to an extent.[84] The funding for these organizations, however, has been trimmed over the years, and consequently, research projects have been either curtailed, eliminated, or not initiated. Given this funding scenario, the development of new male methods has not been a major priority.

The operating funds for the nonprofit organizations are connected to the whims of a political process. Thus, the allocation of resources for contraceptive research is politicized in many cases. As such, "it is the politics of contraception, rather than science, that now plays the dominant role in shaping the [contraception] future."[85]

Although sophisticated male birth control methods are not currently available (and there is considerable ambiguity about when, if ever, modern male methods will be introduced), there can be no doubt that the development and effective marketing of a male oral contraceptive, a reversible and inexpensive vasectomy procedure, or some form of hormonal injection could prompt a revolutionary change in how contraception is conceptualized and practiced in general. A revolutionary change does not mean, though, that all contracepting men and women would seriously consider any or all of these innovative male-oriented technologies.

Male hormonal contraceptives, for example, would not be appealing to those who are opposed categorically to hormonal contraceptives. While many men may believe in sharing contraceptive responsibility, some of these men may also be opposed to medicalized forms of birth control that would alter their body chemistry. These men may, therefore, be opposed to using a male pill or hormonal injection, but it may be on the grounds that its use could have negative health consequences for them, rather than their dissatisfaction with assuming contraceptive responsibility in principle.

In addition, many women involved in casual sexual encounters would probably be reluctant to trust that their male partners were using a method that they could not observe. Since women ultimately experience the physiological consequences related to a pregnancy and delivery, they are unlikely to rely on men to assume contraceptive responsibility unless they feel their partners can be trusted.

For one of the innovations noted above to be adopted on a widespread basis, numerous men would need to experience a major shift in the way they perceive their contraceptive role. Some men, however, would already possess attitudes amenable to the use of a male-oriented technique and would adopt it with little, if any, hesitation, especially if their partner(s) were supportive. Men in committed relationships would probably be the most likely to adopt one of these innovative methods. The discussions men would probably have with their partners about the use of these methods would serve to heighten men's procreative consciousness and sense of responsibility.

In all likelihood, men in the United States will be able to choose from among several new types of modern male contraceptives sometime early in the next century. This development will represent another revolutionary moment in men's experiences in the procreative realm. The implications associated with technological breakthroughs in male-oriented contraception, though less profound than those associated with the introduction of modern female methods, should be comparable to those produced by the introduction of the condom and vasectomy. Although it is only possible to speculate on the implications these innovations will have for men and women, as men's options for playing a more active role in contraception increase, many of them are likely to experience aspects of the procreative realm quite differently.

The sociopolitical controversy over the orientation of contraceptive research draws attention to an important feature of this research that bears on the development of a male-oriented birth control pill or other types of hormonal contraceptives for men. Just as men are unlikely to use these types of contraceptives if they hold strong traditional gender role views, so, too, is it unlikely that sufficient interest and/or the necessary funding to carry out research on male contraceptive methods will exist if persons in critical positions cling to a gender-biased view about contraception. However, a political and scientific environment characterized by a liberal or modern gender role orientation is not sufficient to stimulate aggressive research in male methods. Scientific and business-related considerations are just as important, if not more so.

5

Abortion and
Gender Politics

Abortion, the most controversial resolution of pregnancy, exposes men's gender-related limits in the procreative realm and, more generally, provides an excellent example of how gender issues organize and politicize reproduction. Women are now empowered by the U.S. legal system to make abortion decisions unilaterally during the first trimester, and at no time during a pregnancy do male partners have a legal voice in the matter. Individuals' decisions about whether to bring a pregnancy to term, and if so, what to do with the child once he or she is born are shaped by many factors, including gender differences in reproductive physiology and gender role norms, as well as political ideologies and legal rulings that deal with gender issues.

The abortion issue, more than any other aspect of the procreative realm, accentuates how different facets of men's lives as procreative beings overlap. Men's beliefs and actions involving sex, contraception, paternity, and responsibilities toward children are all implicated when abortion issues are examined from a male perspective.[1] Given this set of circumstances, and the fact that abortion has wide-ranging social, psychological, ethical, and political implications, it's worth focusing on men's roles. In particular, examining men's thoughts about and experiences with a partner's abortion allows a closer look at ways in which abortion can shape their views about procreation.

Men's and women's reproductive physiology obviously places men at a disadvantage when it comes to controlling abortion decisions. While men may attempt to persuade or coerce their partners to either terminate or bring a pregnancy to term, they ultimately are at the mercy of their partners, who are gestating the fetus. Aside from possibly trying to assault their partner to induce a miscarriage, men have no direct or legal means to intervene in the reproductive process.

While the most volatile and highly visible debates about abortion in the United States (and other industrialized countries where abortion is legal) are sustained by interest groups associated with pro-life and pro-choice social movements, the debate is further complicated because it is politicized along gender lines. Thus, a key dimension to the public abortion debate involves the gendered nature of the interest group politics that surround them,[2] as well as the moral and legal dilemmas they create.[3] Though the general conflict among men and women is played out at the interest group level, it can also be expressed on a micro or personal level when sexual partners disagree about how a pregnancy should be resolved.

Confrontations over abortion, both at the interest group and the personal levels, may be just one of many hotbeds of conflict between men and women in the immediate future because of the growing gender distrust that appears to be permeating U.S. culture, most vividly demonstrated by the high rates of divorce. At times, these additional sources of tension may exacerbate men's and women's difficulties as they try to make decisions about abortion and related issues involving child custody and support. As such, my purpose here is to discuss the gender-related and political dimensions to the abortion controversy, while highlighting how men's procreative consciousness and sense of responsibility are expressed within this larger sociopolitical context.

In recent years, this gender distrust may be particularly pervasive among African Americans.[4] The apparent increase in tension among black men and women may be due to the economic restructuring of inner-city areas and the resulting decline in the "eligible" pool of black males, those men residing in the civilian population who are perceived as desirable mates for black women.[5] As a growing proportion of African American adult males are either killed or commit suicide, imprisoned or placed on probation, committed to mental hospitals, or unemployed/underemployed, the rising imbalance in the ratio of adult women to men creates an alarming situation that strains relations between black men and women.[6] How this imbalance in the sex ratio—or other race-related factors—affects men's and women's interpersonal conflicts over abortion is unclear.

Earlier research suggested that the difference between men's and women's views of legalized abortion was larger among African Americans than among whites,[7] with black men being less approving of abortion than black women. We also know that over time African American and white men's attitudes about legalized abortion have been converging.

Recent national data from the General Social Survey shows that beginning in the late 1980s there were no longer statistically significant race differences in men's views about legalized abortion. From this period onward, black men have become more supportive, while support among white men has declined slightly.[8] Similarly, among women forty-four years of age and younger, black and white women do not differ significantly from one another, although there appear to be significant shifts over time in the factors shaping black women's views.[9]

One conclusion consistent with these recent studies is that the changing economic and social conditions of inner cities have affected how black women think about abortion. That is, black women may have increasingly come to perceive abortion as a practical consideration rather than a moral issue. Since the consequences of childbearing and parenthood tend to be more pronounced for poor African American women than men, the meaning of abortion is in some ways tied more directly to women's everyday life experiences of living in poverty. As such, the potential gender conflict between black men and women may be conditioned by social class standing. Moreover, given their relatively poor economic circumstances, black men are in a relatively less desirable bargaining position than white men to persuade their partners to bring an unplanned pregnancy to term.

Other data can be used to supplement our understanding of black and white men's views about abortion. I found in my collaborative study with Constance Shehan, using national data for young men aged 15 to 19 in 1988, that when confronted with a vignette involving a young man who impregnates a partner whom he likes but does not love, teenage black men were somewhat less likely to prefer abortion than their white counterparts (13 to 20 percent).[10] However, this race difference in selecting the abortion option disappeared when background factors were statistically controlled. Meanwhile, young males living in very good neighborhoods were twice as likely (22 to 11 percent) as their peers living in poor neighborhoods to choose the abortion option in this study. Other data using a metropolitan high school sample from 1985 revealed that while 22 percent of whites reported that they would prefer to terminate a pregnancy if they impregnated their girlfriend of one year, only 10 percent of blacks felt this way.[11] While none of the black male respondents who had at least one parent with a college education chose abortion, 40 percent of white men with a college-educated parent selected the abortion option.

Clearly, we know very little about men's and women's actual decision-making processes that result in decisions about abortion. However, it is quite likely that factors associated with race and social class influence the way partners confront and resolve unplanned conceptions.

One of the major reasons the decision to either abort a pregnancy or carry it to term is highly politicized is that it has implications for the establishment of fathers' child support obligations. Obviously, abortion renders moot the need for child support. However, if a decision is made to bring a pregnancy to term and rear a child, concerns about child support become highly relevant, as does men's role in the decision-making process.

Although reliable statistics are not available to document the number of partners who disagree about how a pregnancy should be resolved, disputes are probably not uncommon. A 1982 survey of 521 males who accompanied their partner to the Midwest Health Center for Women in Minneapolis, Minnesota, revealed that 93 percent had discussed the decision with their partner.[12] Overall, 88 percent of all of the respondents agreed with the abortion decision, 2 percent disagreed, and 10 percent did not provide an answer. The restricted nature of the sample for this survey precluded any type of analysis of those who did not accompany their partner to the health center. We can assume that a higher percentage of men who did not accompany their partners to the clinic, compared to those who did go, disagreed with their partners' decision to have an abortion. One crude estimate based on clinic staffers' impressions from a study of twenty-six different abortion clinics suggests that at least 6 percent of the men who do not attend a clinic with their partner are absent because they are opposed to their partners' abortion decision, another 4 percent are too upset to join their partner, and 14 percent are unaware that their partner is having an abortion. The rest of the men stay away because they are either aware that their partners are having abortions but have been told not to join them (14 percent), the women prefer to have female companions (16 percent), they are working (27 percent), or they are absent for other reasons (19 percent).[13] In another survey of women who attended a full-service family planning center in Granite City, Illinois, none of the married women in this sample reported that their husband disapproved of the abortion decision.[14]

In the Granite City survey, almost 90 percent of the women reported that they told the coconceiver of their pregnancy, and about 83 percent indicated that their coconceiver was aware of their decision to have an abortion. Single women were no more likely than married women to inform the coconceiver. However, women who were married and not involved in extramarital affairs, those who were engaged, those living with the coconceiver, and those who described their relationships as "going steady" were all quite likely to inform their partner of their pregnancy. Over 95 percent of these women notified their coconceiver. In those instances where women told their husbands of their pregnancy, 12 percent reported that their husbands expressed anger, 6 percent were described as upset, 9 percent indicated that their husband blamed them for the pregnancy, and in one instance a woman was verbally abused. The other women apparently had more civil discussions with their spouses. While 6 percent of these couples discussed the possibility of adoption and 43 percent discussed the idea of having the baby, more than half never discussed the idea of whether to terminate the pregnancy. According to these wives, about half of the husbands expressed their feelings to them and 47 percent asked them about their feelings. The authors concluded that they found no evidence to suggest that couples' relationships improved as a result of these disclosures and discussions, contrary to what many proponents of spousal notification laws tend to expect. Moreover, they concluded, after examining wives who had mixed feelings about telling their husbands and those who did not, that women in intimate relationships were capable of making a fairly reliable guess about how their relationship's harmony would be affected by notification.

Although it appears that a large proportion of partners agree with whether a pregnancy should be aborted, it is still important to consider those couples where partners disagree. It should also not be overlooked that some men who disagree with their partner about how a pregnancy should be resolved prefer that a pregnancy be terminated. Thus, a significant number of men become fathers even though they would have preferred to have resolved a pregnancy by having their partner undergo an abortion. Most of these men are expected to make child support payments toward their unplanned children, although many do not fulfill their financial obligations.[15]

The potential struggles between men and women over the abortion issue are shaped by many factors, including competing ideologies about family life and gender roles. These ideologies are expressed most forcefully in versions of Christian religious doctrine, feminist principles, and the philosophy of men's rights groups. These ideologies need to be taken into account because they help shape social policy, law, and the programmatic guidelines that deal with men and reproductive issues. In this context, it is essential to note how social institutions—the legal system in particular—help to structure men's experiences in specific areas of reproduction. These institutions affect men's involvement or exclusion from the processes leading to the resolution of a pregnancy, in addition to affecting child support policies.

Men's Personal Experiences with Abortion

Little is known about how men express their procreative consciousness in connection with the general process of resolving a pregnancy or with respect to abortion in particular. Research has seldom explored men's emotional reactions and coping styles in this area.[16] This is unfortunate because even though men do not directly experience the pregnancy or abortion process as do women, many have feelings about those pregnancies their partners bring to term or terminate. Men have a range of emotions, some of which are related to their disagreement with their partners about how the pregnancy should be handled. Understanding men's involvement in the abortion decision-making process is important because some research suggests that male partners' coping expectations affect women's adjustment to having an abortion, especially among women who have low coping expectations themselves.[17]

As one might expect, men vary considerably in how they emotionally react to the abortion process. In the early 1980s, a seminal study was conducted with 1,000 men who accompanied their partner to one of thirty abortion clinics located throughout the United States; it remains the most extensive study of men's personal responses to abortion.[18] One of the major conclusions of this study is that the prevailing public image of men as largely uninvolved and uninterested bystanders in the abortion process misrepresents many men's experiences. This research reveals that around the time of the abortion, 29 percent of the men surveyed reported having frequent thoughts about the fetus and some continued to ruminate about the fetus after the abortion. Experiencing an abortion with their partner left some men with a deep sense of loss.[19] Several respondents' comments illustrate this point:

> Sometimes I regret it. I have friends who have young or infant children, and when I go there, I kind of regret it. Maybe you love kids when they're someone else's.

I personally really love kids, so it was kind of rough for me. . . . So, I kind of always wonder what kind of kid would this have been.

Now, often, I wonder what the baby might have been like. And for a while after I thought about asking her if she wanted to try it all over again. We broke up about six months after it.[20]

Although many men are upset by their partner's abortion, at least for a brief period of time, many others are indifferent to their partner's abortion. Some men are simply relieved that they do not have to assume any social or financial responsibilities. Irrespective of their response, it is significant that men are often confronted with the knowledge that their partner plans to abort (or already has aborted) a fetus that they helped conceive.

A number of interrelated factors affect men's reactions to learning that they might become, or could have been, a biological father. Their attitudes toward becoming a father at this point in their life, their views about the morality of abortion, and their feelings toward their partner are some of the more important factors that are likely to influence how they deal with the process of resolving a pregnancy and making decisions about abortion in particular. When contemplating abortion, men with pro-choice views are unlikely to experience a great deal of emotional trauma if they feel as though having a child right now would disrupt their daily routine and life plans too dramatically. However, the same cannot be said of men who embrace a pro-life stance. An abortion is much more likely to upset men with pro-life views, especially if these men feel they could be a responsible parent at this point in their life.

In some respects, men's moral concerns about abortion and the type and quality of the relationship they have with their partner may be linked. Men involved in committed relationships, especially men who are either married or cohabiting, are probably more likely to be confused about the morality or soundness of their choice. Men's sentiments about how their feelings toward abortion are related to the way they feel about their partner are poignantly captured by one respondent:

It's hard for me to talk, but I've got to do it. I'm an emotional guy. There are friends that don't give a shit. It's programmed in them to think like that, but I don't think they love the women they've gotten pregnant.

If I were to get a woman pregnant on a one-night stand, abortion would be right. With my girlfriend, I loved her, I loved what was inside her. It still bugs me; it's always going to bug me. I had plans to someday marry this girl and have a family. I'm just trying to cope with it. It's hard, really hard. I'll never forget about it, never. Sometimes I feel like a killer, a killer . . . and I could have changed it.[21]

These remarks reveal this man's unresolved feelings about his involvement with an abortion that he apparently was either opposed to or ambivalent about at the time. There is little doubt that his abortion attitudes and feelings are interwoven with his loving feelings toward his partner. While it is unclear how many other men share feelings as intense as these, this man surely does not stand alone in his grief.

Not all men, whether they love their partner or not, are as troubled by their partner having an abortion. Men who do not wish to become a father in a particular situation (or ever) and who tend to have pro-choice views may be largely indifferent toward their partner's abortion. In these situations, an abortion is unlikely to have a significant effect on men's procreative consciousness, although their concern for their partner's well-being may encourage them to contemplate their potential fatherhood status and attempt to fulfill their partner role in a loving, supportive fashion.

To abort or bring a pregnancy to term is clearly the most fundamental decision relevant to the process of resolving a pregnancy, but it represents only one of several possible decisions that can produce conflict between partners. Even if both partners agree that a pregnancy should be brought to term, they may disagree about whether they should place the child for adoption, live together and raise the child, or raise the child either separately or jointly but live apart. It therefore seems prudent to consider men's responses to abortion in light of the larger set of options that are relevant to decisions about how a pregnancy should be resolved.

Whether partners agree on which option to choose can affect men considerably because they have less control than their female partner over this decision. Men are likely to feel uneasy and perhaps angry if they perceive that an important decision with personal consequences has been made despite their objections. For example, in those situations where women opt for an abortion against men's wishes, men are likely to feel very powerless. Some men's ill feelings may be due only partially though to their remorse over not being able to play a role in their biological offspring's life. In some cases, men's feelings are exaggerated because they were, in the end, left out of the decision-making loop—without a sense of control, their emotional well-being is likely to suffer.

The abortion decision can also be a relevant issue for men who prefer to terminate a pregnancy but whose partner chooses to bring it to term. Men are likely to be disgruntled about their paternity status when their preference for abortion goes unheeded, but they are still expected to fulfill child support obligations. This may be especially troubling to men who are denied the opportunity to live with their child.

Some men may have no desire to assume fatherhood responsibilities at this point in their life, although they may be reluctant to assert their preference if they are in love with a partner who forcefully asserts her desire to give birth to their child. In this type of situation, it is often the case that men's procreative consciousness is interwoven with their feelings toward their partner identity. Because some men may not wish to disappoint their beloved, they may cope with an unplanned pregnancy by fantasizing about how their paternal and partner identities may be connected. In other words, they may attempt to become more enthusiastic about becoming a father because they realize that their father roles will provide them an opportunity to affirm their relationship with their partner. If this is the case, fathers may for a period of time develop an appreciation for their child vicariously through their partner if the pregnancy is brought to term. Over time, men's socioemotional relationship with their child may or may not become more direct. They may begin to develop a bond with their child that is independent of their ongoing or previous romantic relationship with their child's mother. However, in some cases they may continue to allow their connection to their child to be mediated by their relationship with the child's mother or, perhaps, a new romantic companion. These types of situations underscore the dynamic nature to men's procreative consciousness, in addition to showing how its expression is fostered by men's interrelated role identities.

Men can in numerous ways display their sense of procreative responsibility by their actions in relation to the pregnancy, abortion, and the child (if the pregnancy is brought to term). When both partners prefer to terminate a pregnancy, men can demonstrate responsible behavior by offering to accompany their partner during the procedure and recovery phases of an abortion. Men can also offer to cover the expenses associated with this procedure. Men's responsible behavior in this area of the procreative realm, as alluded to above, is closely linked to their partner identity. Those men who wish to demonstrate their sense of responsibility are likely to feel that being a good partner requires them to "be there" for their partner and face the consequences of impregnating her.

Defining responsible behavior for those men who object to their partner aborting her pregnancy is a much more difficult task. While men may be unwilling to assist their partner through the abortion process, they may be very committed to assuming the responsibilities associated with their potential paternal identity. These men will face a type of role conflict involving their partner and paternal identities. This unpleasant dilemma will arise because they want to be compassionate toward their partner, but at the same time, they oppose abortion either for ideological or emotional reasons—they may even want to be a father. Their definition of responsible behavior will be based fundamentally on their religious or ethical beliefs as well as the views on appropriate family and gender role behavior.

In terms of child support, nonresident fathers who feel a strong commitment to their social father roles, and perhaps their partner and male roles as well, are likely to act in a responsible fashion and provide their child with some type of financial support, assuming employment opportunities exist for them. Because men's sense of responsibility to their children is often linked to their feelings toward the child's mother rather than to the child per se,[22] fathers' commitment to providing for their child financially may be moderated by their feelings toward their child's mother. Nonresident fathers' investment in their child may therefore represent some men's attempt to maintain their role identity as, say, a traditional family man who fulfills his financial obligations to his offspring or even, in some cases, a particular type of loyal partner (or former partner) who sticks by his partner's side through difficult times.

Political Ideologies and Procreative Issues

Political ideologies relevant to family and gender role issues directly and indirectly affect the way in which men perceive and experience aspects of the procreative realm, including abortion and child support. The two most basic philosophies that shape the general public's approach to fertility and family-related matters, as well as that of policymakers, have been labeled "conservative" and "progressive."[23] Those who embrace these competing ideologies have very different perceptions about men's and women's roles, as well as about fertility issues. Consequently, they tend to support divergent social policies for the procreative realm and family life more generally.

Conservative and progressive ideologies have implications for how key social institutions are used to structure men's specific procreative experiences, including those related to abortion. These ideologies, as represented within the various institutions, help shape the context within which men experience aspects of their procreative consciousness and sense of responsibility.[24] The institutional context is often influenced, too, by the fact that men, unlike women, cannot directly experience some of the physiological dimensions associated with the reproductive realm.

Proponents of the conservative perspective,[25] with its religious underpinnings and patriarchal ideals, support social policies and programs that advance a pro-life stance and men's breadwinner role with respect to their partner and children. They typically view abortion as morally repugnant, with the possible exception of those instances where extreme mitigating circumstances are present (e.g., if a pregnancy or childbirth would endanger the mother's life, in rape, in incest). In short, abortion should be banned and, at the very least, women should be denied unilateral power in this regard so long as it is legal. According to this perspective, men should be able to prevent their partners from having an abortion. When men do become fathers, they are expected to support their children financially whether they live with them or not.

The pro-life movement's orientation toward men's role in the abortion process clearly emphasizes a position that advocates a gender equality theme under certain circumstances. For example, one pamphlet specifically directed at men states,

> When men promote abortion for their partners it is typified as coercion, lack of caring, insensitivity and selfishness. When women choose abortion it is the exclamation of women's rights, an affirmation of the right to health and freedom from male oppression, and a confirmation of sovereign territoriality over the female body and reproductive functions. . . . Many men are victims of abortion along with women and unborn children. For now, they are often silent sufferers, bewildered and frustrated by their responses to abortion. With time, perhaps a true equality of the sexes will provide for more democratic decisions, more love and less pain and the realization that abortion is no solution at all.[26]

The basic progressive viewpoint, on the other hand, draws heavily on versions of liberal feminism while advocating the economic autonomy of women.[27] Most progressives, and presumably the vast majority of persons who call themselves feminists,[28] endorse in principle a woman's autonomy over her body. They also recognize that, given comparable incomes, men and women should be equally responsible for the financial support of their children, although there may be some disagreement when specific circumstances are considered. For example, some feminists[29] are reluctant, as are members of men's rights groups,[30] to assert that men should always be held financially accountable for their children if only women have the power to make abortion decisions. Over a decade ago, a former president of the National Organization of Women argued,

> Justice . . . dictates that if a woman makes a unilateral decision to bring [a] pregnancy to term, and the biological father does not, and cannot share in this decision, he should not be liable for 21 years of support. Or, put another way, autonomous women making independent decisions about their lives should not expect men to finance their choice.[31]

Similarly, another spokesperson for this position observed,

> To saddle a man with at least eighteen years of expensive, exhausting child support liability on the basis of a haphazard vicissitude of life seems to shock the conscience and be arbitrary, capricious, and unreasonable, where childbirth results from the mother's free choice.[32]

However, many who espouse basic feminist principles would not agree with these statements. Some would argue that while men are free to choose whether or not they wish to have sex with a woman, assuming that she consents, they do not have the right to ignore their financial commitment to children they beget from these encounters. According to this view, we can assume that by having intercourse, men are implicitly acknowledging their willingness to provide financial support to any potential children they may sire.[33] Overall, then, the progressive ideology is consistent with social policy and legislation that enables women to retain the ultimate power to make decisions about abortion in consultation with their physician. However, there is disagreement as to whether men should automatically be obligated to pay child support if the mother decides, contrary to the prospective father's wishes, to bring the pregnancy to term and raise the child, especially when the child is born to unmarried parents.

In recent years, men's rights organizations (e.g., the National Center for Men) have lobbied aggressively for new abortion policies and legal provisions that would balance men's and women's rights in this area. These groups have a unique position that does not neatly parallel either a conventional or progressive perspective. In a sense, these groups incorporate aspects of both the conventional and progressive positions. While men's rights activists generally support women's access to abortion, they have recently increased their efforts to promote policies and draft legal initiatives that would balance men's and women's rights with respect to abortion and child support. Their orientation is guided by two key considerations.

The first issue is related to single men who do not wish to accept fatherhood responsibilities after accidental pregnancies. Some men who are involved with unplanned pregnancies would prefer that their sexual partners have abortions. In other instances, men may not care whether their partners bring their pregnancies to term or not. They may not even mind if their partner places the child for adoption or raises the child by herself. They do insist, however, that they should not be shouldered with fatherhood obligations, irrespective of the mother's choice, if they had never indicated prior to conception or during the early phase of the prenatal period that they had wanted their partner to have their child. In 1992, the National Center for Men (NCM) proposed a specific strategy to address these issues. This organization developed a controversial consent form called the "Consensual Sex Contract" that outlines the terms under which heterosexual partners might agree to have sexual relations. This document currently has no legal bearing in court, although the NCM believes it should. The intent of the document is to ensure that partners are aware of each others' sexual and reproductive expectations. While most of this document deals with sexuality concerns, one item affords partners the opportunity to agree to the following condition: "We're not ready to be parents now. If an unplanned pregnancy occurs, neither one of us will try to force the other into parenthood." A man can therefore indicate that although he is having sexual relations by choice, he is not consenting to fatherhood responsibilities should his partner get pregnant.

In January 1996, the NCM officially unveiled a second controversial document called the Reproductive Rights Affidavit in conjunction with its Reproductive Rights Project, which is designed to balance men's and women's reproductive rights. A portion of this document reads,

I hereby relinquish all legal rights and responsibilities for the child referred to in this affidavit. I have made no commitment to, and will accept no obligation for this child. I will not recognize the authority of a court to strip me of my constitutional right to reproductive choice and I will challenge any court order that seeks to impose a parental obligation upon me against my will. By filing the affidavit with a court of law I am joining with others in an act of peaceful resistance to unfair and unjust laws.

The NCM's innovative proposals have provoked heated discussions among the limited number of individuals familiar with them. One of the major criticisms of these approaches, even from those who are somewhat sympathetic to them, is that the proposals do not address the best interests of children who are conceived from the sexual liaisons in question. For this reason, it is unlikely that this document will receive government or court support anytime soon. In the final chapter, I highlight some of the key issues relevant to this debate by proposing my own formal strategy that would enable heterosexual partners to define their reproductive expectations and obligations explicitly, though in a very restricted set of circumstances.

The second issue relevant to the men's rights orientation is pertinent to men when they want their sexual partner to bring a pregnancy to term even though she prefers to have an abortion. Many of these men are interested in sharing the responsibility of raising their children with their sexual partner. Some are even willing to assume primary care as single fathers. To date, men's legal efforts to prevent their wife or their unrelated sexual partner from having an abortion have failed.[34] While some prospective fathers have been successful in having lower courts issue restraining orders on their partner, the women have had abortions anyway. The notion that men should have a legal right to determine how a pregnancy is resolved is consistent with the major tenets of conventional family ideology that espouse both a patriarchal view of gender relations and a pro-life stance toward abortion. Some scholars argue that men who are interested in expanding their abortion rights in this regard tend to be concerned with reaffirming a traditional ideal of manhood; consequently, they differ considerably from those men who align themselves with the pro-feminist men's movement.[35] Nevertheless, most activists in the men's rights organizations probably share pro-feminists' views that women should have the discretion to have a legal abortion. They are primarily interested in enhancing men's legal option of being able to relinquish, prior to conception, any potential paternity rights or responsibilities.

Men's Legal Standing and Attitudes

During the past fifteen years or so, there has been extensive discussion about the extent to which conservative ideologies might influence judicial decisions and state legislation in a manner that would curtail women's abortion rights and, in turn, expand the rights of male partners in this area, sometimes indirectly through the protection of the fetus's rights.[36] In addition, men's rights groups have played an increasingly active role in championing social policies and legal reforms that would provide men with more leverage in the areas of abortion and child support. Conservative ideologies have also played a major role in shaping child support policies. The conservative Reagan and Bush administrations each advocated more aggressive methods for establishing the paternity of nonresident fathers and collecting child support payments.[37] The Clinton administration, which has typically supported a more progressive ideology, has likewise continued to support these earlier policies. Thus, unlike the ideological debates over abortion, progressive and feminist groups have often allied themselves with conventional groups in order to increase fathers' financial accountability to their children. We should not forget, though, that these competing interest groups, despite their single-issue alliance, have very different views of men's procreative roles.

Today, neither unmarried male partners or husbands have any legal recourse in terminating or bringing their partner's pregnancy to term, although ten states have laws that stipulate (but are not enforced) that a woman must gain consent from or notify her husband before she aborts a pregnancy.[38] The U.S. Supreme Court ruled in 1992, in *Planned Parenthood of Southeastern Pennsylvania v. Casey*, that the provision in a Pennsylvania law requiring spousal notification prior to abortion was unconstitutional. In a prior ruling, the Court held in *Planned Parenthood of Central Missouri v. Danforth* (1976) that when a married couple disagrees about whether to abort a pregnancy, the decision should go in the wife's favor since she is the one who bears the child and is more directly and immediately affected by the pregnancy. The justices argued that states could not require women to obtain their husbands' consent in order to terminate a pregnancy because the court could not delegate to husbands veto power that the government itself is prohibited from exercising during the first trimester of pregnancy.

Notwithstanding the U.S. Supreme Court rulings, recent research suggests that there is substantial public support among North American males for greater male authority in making decisions about abortion. I found that 60 percent of young males aged 15 to 19 in a national survey conducted in 1988 disagreed at least a little that it was all right for an unmarried woman to have an abortion when her partner objected.[39] Unfortunately, the phrasing of the survey item in this instance does not explicitly tap men's views on what a woman's legal right should be, rather it appears to capture men's moral sentiments about abortion in different circumstances. In another study, only slightly more than one-third of Canadian male respondents reported that they would support a law that allowed a woman to have an abortion without her husband's consent.[40] These findings are consistent with the results from an anonymous survey I conducted in 1992 of 400 first-year college students enrolled in an honors course. Thirty percent of the young men in the sample strongly agreed that an unmarried, twenty-year-old prospective father "should have the legal right to prevent his partner from having an abortion" if he is "prepared to pay for all of her medical expenses and he intends to raise the child by himself with the help of his family." Only 10 percent of the female respondents gave a similar response.

In the area of child support, biological fathers can be held financially responsible for their children irrespective of their preconception or prebirth preference for how the pregnancy should have been resolved or their willingness to pay for an abortion.[41] Men's dilemma in this area is sometimes acknowledged, but it is often concluded that pro-feminist men must recognize women's autonomy over their bodies; men's power is restricted to their ability to control their own sexuality.[42] Put differently, men are free to refrain from having sexual intercourse with a woman if they perceive that their position on abortion is inconsistent with their partner's or if they are unwilling to accept the consequences of fathering a child. Although this position is not without merit, it does not go far enough in proposing a strategy that would balance the potential gender struggles over sexuality, pregnancy, abortion, and child support issues.[43]

6

Pathways to Paternity
and Social Fatherhood

We have thus far explored two significant aspects of men's procreative lives, contraception and abortion. Let's now turn to what is certainly the central aspect to men's lives as procreative beings, their experiences with becoming a father. The public, which helps to construct the meanings associated with these experiences, is most likely to view men as procreative beings in their fullest sense when they demonstrate their physical ability to create life. However, comprehensively studying men as procreative beings requires consideration of a variety of issues related to biological and social fatherhood. To do this, it is best to focus on different types of men, including biological fathers with legal rights toward their children, sperm donors who have no connection to their genetic offspring, stepfathers, adoptive fathers, and biological and nonbiological fathers who achieve their father status through assisted reproductive technologies (ART).[1]

Defining men as procreative beings in this broader fashion is consistent with the important historical transition underway in the social construction of fatherhood. In recent years, the process and implications of becoming a biological and/or social father have become much more complex. Part of this growing complexity is due to parents' and children's shifting experiences over the life course and to the growing recognition of men's expanding paternal roles.[2] Moreover, the cultural scenarios and definitions associated with fatherhood have become increasingly varied due to changing demographic patterns related to childbearing, marriage, divorce, and remarriage.[3] An important consequence of these patterns is that men are more often playing fatherlike roles to children who are not biologically related to them.[4] In some instances, these men may even see themselves as fathers, and the children may view them similarly. These types of changes in the nonmaterial aspects of the culture of fatherhood are occurring while developments closely linked to the material culture of reproductive technologies (e.g., in-vitro fertilization) and biosocial innovations (e.g., sperm banks, surrogacy) are unfolding. The overriding question is: How do each of these changes affect men's experiences of siring children and/or assuming paternal responsibilities for children?

The demographic trends just mentioned have prompted a series of lively academic and public debates that explore the definition of family, kinship, and fatherhood.[5] A consequence of this ongoing debate is that people in industrialized societies are slowly changing the way they define "family." More and more people emphasize the interpersonal aspects of committed, primary relationships between persons rather than the more formal connections based on either blood, marriage, or legal ties.[6] These traditional bonds still count, but people seem more willing to think of their closest friends and their romantic partner's children as family, too.[7] This raises important questions about the significance and meaning of such socially constructed familial ties. When, if ever, can these socially constructed types of relationships (including those produced through reproductive technologies using donor sperm and/or ova) be considered to be comparable in strength to those based on a shared biological connection?

Despite this trend toward accentuating socially constructed bonds, individuals continue to place a great deal of importance on biological relationships. This tendency is evidenced by couples' willingness to use donor sperm or a surrogate so that at least one partner will have a biogenetic relationship to their offspring. Some individuals submit themselves to extraordinary hardships as they experiment with these alternative reproductive strategies. A disgruntled infertile couple, responding in writing to a state legislature's pending bill to criminalize commercial surrogacy in 1989, capture this sentiment about biological relations:

> Dear Legislature:
> Please don't deny us our biological lineage. Surrogate parenting is our only hope to preserve it. We are law-abiding citizens and all we want is the opportunity to have a baby. If we are unable to conceive a biological child, thousands of years of family evolution and lineage will end. It's not fair to deny us this most fundamental and essential need.
> Also please don't deny surrogate mothers the opportunity to give the ultimate gift. Life.
> Yes, the alternative is adoption. And yes, we will take advantage

of this wonderful possibility. It's just that the core of our existence is tied up in having a biological child. Please don't deny us this chance.[8]

This heartfelt letter highlights the significance that many men and women still place on the biological dimension to family in its conventional sense.

The public and private discourses that address questions dealing with the definition and meaning of family are complicated by the recent developments in how the reproductive process is sometimes experienced. The medicalization of artificial insemination procedures and the introduction of the more sophisticated ARTs have helped to underscore the notion that biological paternity can be separated from sexual intercourse. These patterns also add another dimension to the mix of shifting cultural images and legal rulings that interpret the theoretical and practical significance of differentiating biological paternity from social fatherhood. The contemporary use of reproductive technologies is thus blurring the traditional images of father, mother, and family relations, in some cases.[9]

Modern technology informs these debates in yet another way because biological paternity is reaching new levels of certainty due to recent developments in the DNA fingerprinting technique I described in chapter 2. Medical professionals' ability to establish with near certainty the shared genetic heritage of fathers and their children reinforces the uniqueness and, for some, the significance of biological paternity. Now that the guesswork has been eliminated from the process of establishing paternity,[10] men can more easily be held accountable for their children's financial welfare, or in some cases assert their paternal rights.

Although many still believe that biological relations should be the basis for paternal rights and that these relations should assume a privileged position relative to nonbiological connections, a significant number of people are willing to challenge this position. A growing number of people feel that genetic fathers must demonstrate a minimal level of responsibility toward their children to retain their formal or informal rights. Responsibility, they argue, is much more important than biology in this age of parental instability. A father's biological tie with his children is not a sufficient basis for conferring paternal rights. It is not surprising, then, that the practical value of social fatherhood is being accentuated by many in a historical period marked by relatively high rates of divorce, single parenthood, and cohabitation.

One example of this emphasis on social fatherhood can be found in discussions about revamping paternity law. A legal scholar, Jill Anderson, proposes that states move away from a strictly biological or marital basis for determining paternity. Instead, she advances the provocative idea that the paternity standard should be based on her notion of the "functioning father," who she defines as "a man who initiates positive, consensual interactions with a child on a regular basis and provides for the child's care and support in proportion to his ability to do so."[11] If adopted, this approach would require the court system to weigh more heavily the man's involvement with the child, rather than either the man's biological relationship to the child or his marital relationship to the child's mother. It would not apply to stepfathers, who could formalize their relationship to a child through adoption. Anderson goes on to support the adoption of her functioning father standard by arguing that its adoption would be cost-effective. She cites three major reasons why the functioning father strategy would be cost-effective:

> First, it would protect men who act as fathers, thus encouraging, rather than discouraging, an emotional and material commitment to a child who otherwise would have no father. Second, voluntary monetary support is cheaper for society than court enforced support. Third, protecting a functioning relationship would decrease the number of psychological impairments due to father absence, thus reducing mental health costs.[12]

Ironically, at the same time our society is witnessing an increase in the number of proponents of social fatherhood, the modern assisted reproductive technologies and DNA-testing techniques have arrived on the scene to highlight biological paternity. Describing the competing array of developments that are affecting the way paternity and social fatherhood are perceived and experienced is relatively easy; trying to predict their long-term implications for men and others is not.

Paths to Procreation

The paths to paternity and social fatherhood are numerous, as are situations where the genetic and social dimensions of fatherhood are not con-

nected in a tidy, conventional manner. Men who impregnate their partner in the typical fashion through sexual intercourse represent one class
of fathers. A second category includes those men who are involved with
a partner who conceives a child through artificial means using their
sperm. Men in the second category are similar to those who experience
sexually based procreation in the sense that they both have a genetic tie
to their child. Included in a third and smaller category are those men who
are involved with a partner who attempts to become pregnant using
donor sperm. While men in this third category will be in a position to assume the social responsibilities associated with fatherhood, they obviously don't have a direct biological connection with their child.

Formal adoption and informal stepfathering arrangements represent
additional paths by which men can become fathers. These paths to fatherhood are largely beyond the scope of my discussion since they do not
deal specifically with procreative issues. I would be remiss, though, not
to comment on these paths to fatherhood because they involve key issues
pertaining to men's needs for siring biological progeny, as well as their
generativity needs to nurture future generations of children.[13]

The final and most unconventional way for men to experience a form
of biological paternity is by donating sperm. Because many births resulting from ARTs involve donated sperm, this form of detached, asexual paternity warrants attention. Fertility clinics, if they are to assist couples
with male-based infertility problems, must depend on men to donate
sperm in sufficient quantities and, in the process, sire genetic offspring
they will never know. In the United States, this type of anonymity currently means that they will have no legal rights or obligations in connection with the children conceived through the use of their sperm.[14] Examining men's motivation for, and reservations about donating sperm under
these circumstances offers an intriguing opportunity to view men as procreative beings.

Men's Perceptions

In one sense, men's paternity experiences originate with the views they
have about procreation that are separate from and occur prior to their
impregnating a woman. Men generally have some idea of whether they
want to have children eventually, whether they want more children than
they already have, or whether they desire to have a child at this particu-

lar point in their life.[15] The extent to which men have consciously and rationally formed opinions about these issues is likely to vary depending upon their age, previous fertility experiences, and their current relationship status. Teenage boys who have never, to their knowledge, impregnated a girl and are not in a serious relationship probably spend little time thinking about their paternity expectations, whereas young married men in their late twenties or early thirties, some of whom have already impregnated a partner, probably spend more time thinking about paternity issues, a consequence perhaps of being involved with women who are interested in having children in the near future. These older men also probably have more well-defined views about procreative issues. In either case, teenage boys and young adult men should be able to generate ideas about these issues if they are asked to articulate them.

Men's perceptions about procreation and social fatherhood can be explored in a systematic fashion by applying the conceptual framework I described in chapter 1. Procreative consciousness, one of the key concepts of this framework, captures both the cognitive and emotional aspects to men's lives as procreative beings. Men's motivations and wishes to have children represent important cognitive elements in this regard. While theorists tend to focus on the cognitive aspects of procreative consciousness, we must recognize that men's views are intimately related to their emotional needs—of which some they may not be completely aware.

Men's motivation to sire children, or become a social father to children not genetically related to them, can be thought of as a kind of enduring disposition or personality characteristic.[16] This disposition includes both "energizing" as well as "directional" qualities, providing men with a "readiness to act" and a direction or agenda for their actions. Many times men do not experience this type of motivation in an active fashion because it is neither influencing their behavior or being expressed as part of their "wide-awake" consciousness. It may still reside, though, within what I have referred to as men's latent procreative consciousness. In certain situations, often those involving a specific romantic relationship, men's paternal motivation becomes a part of their active consciousness and influences their behavior. Thus, for some men their motivation to become a father can be viewed as untapped potential that must be activated in order for their desires to be manifested.

A related way of thinking about men's procreative consciousness, particularly their perceptions about having a child, is to talk about how men may "wish" for children.[17] This notion suggests that there is both a "change" and "timing" element to men's experience. The first element reveals that men experience some type of uncomfortable mental incongruity between what the present situation is like and possible alternatives. Men consequently possess a wish or desire to bring about a change. Meanwhile, the timing component refers to men's sense of when the change would be desired. Do men want it to occur now, soon, or simply at some unspecified time in the future? A "latent wish" is thought to exist in those situations where an incongruity exists but men do nothing to remove or diminish it. A "manifest wish" is operative when men engage in actions that are designed to bring about a change or merely make a conscious choice to do so.

While theorists have offered intriguing ways of thinking about men's ideas and feelings about paternity, the data are rather limited. Several surveys conducted during the past two decades provide some clues about men's expectations for begetting children, but these data sources provide only a crude profile of men's fertility attitudes and beliefs. They also do not clarify how important the ability to father a biological child is to men's self-image. Further, little is known about the social-psychological mechanisms or processes that influence men's views on paternity.[18]

National surveys do indicate that most teenage and adult men express an interest in having children at some point in their life.[19] About 92 percent of the never married male respondents aged 17 to 25 in 1982 from the National Longitudinal Survey of Labor Market Experience and 89 percent of never married men aged 15 to 19 in 1988 who were respondents for the National Survey of Adolescent Males (NSAM-1) expected to father a child. Data from the first wave of the National Survey of Families and Households (NSFH) conducted in 1987 to 1988 indicated that among a sample of married men who had not fathered a child (mean age 30), 87 percent responded "yes" to the question "Do you intend to have a child sometime?"[20] while 81 percent of unmarried male respondents in the NSFH intended to have a child.[21]

In addition to documenting the proportion of men who report that they expect to have a child, some research has explored men's (women's) views about the possible types of positive and negative factors associated with fathering a child. This research is relevant to the literature that explores how the symbolic meaning of children and parenthood has changed over time[22] and how the benefits and costs associated with having children may differ among men and women.[23] There has been considerable discussion in recent decades that adults are now assessing in a much more rational fashion whether or not they want to have children. The decline in many men's earning power, some parents' misperceptions that the average financial costs of raising children are increasing,[24] and women's increased participation in the labor market have apparently lead many adults to view childbearing in a manner similar to the purchase of expensive consumer goods. Individuals appear to be increasingly willing to take into account the ways in which childbearing may hinder their ability to fulfill their individual and family goals. Despite this movement toward a more rational decision-making style about fertility, some couples are still unsure about the large set of both positive and negative consequences associated with having and raising children. As a result, their decision making in this area is haphazard; they tend to "experience their pregnancies as happenings, unplanned events, occurrences, or the will of God."[25]

One study found that when husbands and wives were asked to assess consequences they associate with parenting, husbands rated positive consequences significantly lower and negative consequences significantly higher than did wives.[26] This study also considered the overall and relative importance of three clusters of factors thought to be associated with men's perceptions about the positive and negative consequences of fathering a child. The sets of factors included experiences during childhood and adolescence (e.g., family religion, father's care pattern, positive mothering, mother's employment patterns, frequency of teen child care), adult experiences (e.g., education, occupation, religiosity, marital discord), and personality traits (e.g., nurturance, affiliation, autonomy, and achievement). A number of these factors were significantly correlated with husbands' childbearing motivations, especially those measuring positive consequences in a bivariate context. When a variety of factors were examined in a multivariate context, men were found to be more likely to have a positive childbearing motivation when they married their current wife at a younger age, had completed fewer years of school, were Roman Catholic, expressed a nurturing and affiliative personality, and had mothers who were employed more regularly when they were children and adolescents. Furthermore, events during the young adult years were much more important predictors of positive motivation than negative motivation. The latter may be already established at an early age and change little over the course of a person's life.

Two additional studies using national data[27] shed light on men's fertility attitudes and childbearing motivations. Surprisingly, in the first study, comparing the fertility views of married men and women who had not yet had a child, men were significantly more likely to indicate that it is better to have a child than to remain childless.[28] Another unexpected finding was that men and women did not differ in how important they felt the overall benefits and costs associated with having a child were. However, when individuals assessed specific concerns, several gender differences were present. Men had different views than women on four of sixteen separate issues. They were more concerned than women that having a child would limit their ability to make major purchases, but they were less likely than women to report that their fertility preferences would be affected by their age, being stressed and worried, or wanting to have someone to care for them in their later years of life.

The second study compared married and single men's attitudes toward parenthood who had not yet fathered a child.[29] More specifically, it focused on the relationship between men's intention to have a child and six different considerations related to parenthood. These concerns were "the stress and worry of raising children," "having time and energy for my career," "being able to make major purchases," "having time for leisure or social activities," "having someone to care for me when I am old," and "having someone to love." Both married and single men indicated that their most important consideration for having a child was to have someone to love. Overall, 65 percent of this sample reported that having someone to love was an important reason for having a child. These findings are consistent with a small-scale study in which ninety men attending a community college in Texas were asked to indicate the relative importance of ten different assigned reasons why men in general have children.[30] The number one reason chosen was to "bring love and emotional satisfaction to the family," while the responses to "carry on the name or bloodline" and children "are fun to be with" were ranked a distant second and third.

Compared to single men, married men tended to be significantly less concerned about the first five outcomes listed above. The largest gap between married and single men's attitudes occurred with respect to the first three concerns. Whereas only about 43, 39, and 40 percent of married men reported that the first three concerns were important, the comparable replies for single men were much higher—61 percent, 59 percent, and 56 percent, respectively. The difference between married and single men remained when multivariate analyses were conducted using these six concerns as separate dependent variables. These analyses also showed that younger men were more likely than older men to allow these concerns to affect their fertility attitudes. Likewise, men who attained higher levels of education were more likely to emphasize their concerns about having enough time for their career and for their leisure and social activities. Meanwhile, more educated men's fertility attitudes were less likely to be related to their concerns about having someone to love.

These studies provide some insight into men's (and women's) perceptions about childbearing and parenting. Some of the findings illustrate the notion that the reproductive realm is gendered, although the results also suggest that men and women may possess relatively similar views in some respects. Although there is some evidence that demographic factors such as age, education, and marital status may affect how different categories of men think about having a child, much more needs to be done to understand the way men think about children, both in general, and in relation to the specific paths men can use to experience paternity and social fatherhood.

Paternity through Sex

The most common path by which a man becomes a biological and social father is through sexual intercourse. Unfortunately, the quantity and quality of information we have collected over the years on men's fertility patterns has been inferior to what has been gathered on women.[31] The quantity issue was recently addressed by the Census Bureau's 1992 Survey of Income and Program Participation (SIPP), which included a national household sample of 16,777 men who were at least 18 years of age, as well as 19,204 women aged 15 and over.[32] Sixty-six percent of those men who responded to a question on this survey about whether they had ever sired a child reported having at least one child. More specifically, 15 percent said they had one child, 24 percent indicated having two children, 14 percent reported three children, and 13 percent had fathered at least four children.[33] Men who had not completed high school were clearly more likely to report having fathered more children than men who had completed higher levels of formal schooling. On average, those men who were not high school graduates reported 2.2 children, whereas those who had completed one or more years of college had fathered 1.5 children. The figures for white, black, and Hispanic men were 1.7, 1.8, and 1.9 respectively.

Among men involved in a heterosexual relationship, the ideal fertility situation includes a man and woman who agree prior to engaging in intercourse that they want to conceive a child through their sexual union. In addition, each may confirm his or her commitment to care for the resulting child, or in a very small percentage of cases, they may informally agree that only one of them (usually the woman) will assume the formal parental responsibilities. Women on rare occasions, in other words, solicit men's participation in sex in order to conceive children with the expressed intention of assuming sole parental responsibility as single mothers. Irrespective of the specific details, the sexual partners involved in these ideal types of situations have a clear sense of their expectations and obligations prior to conception.

While many conceptions and births are indeed planned, a large percentage are not. It has been estimated that in 1988 roughly 56 percent of the 36 million pregnancies were unintended with roughly 44 percent of these unintended pregnancies being resolved through abortion.[34] These estimates are probably on the conservative side because some respondents may be reluctant to admit that their pregnancy was unplanned. Thus, while many unintended pregnancies never result in a live birth, more than half are brought to term. On numerous occasions, these men and/or their partners did attempt to use contraception, but for one reason or another were unsuccessful in their attempt to avoid a conception.

Men's willingness to make a commitment to their social father roles may be influenced by whether or not the pregnancy is planned, but the more important factor is probably the nature of their relationship with their partner. Those who are seriously involved with their partner are likely to be more interested in assuming these prenatal and postnatal father roles. In some situations, even though men may be uninvolved throughout the pregnancy, they may become more committed to their social father roles over time.

All things being equal, men who actively plan a pregnancy are probably more likely to be involved throughout the pregnancy and at least in the early stages of their child's life. Perhaps the most extreme example of this would be those men who are associated with pregnancies and births brought about by some form of ART. Men who are involved with ART should be quite pleased with their prenatal and social fatherhood roles given the amount of time, effort, and money they have spent to bring about a conception.

Men and Pregnancy

Although men have a very restricted physiological role in the fertility process because their contribution begins and ends with their ejaculation, they are still able to play an indirect role in the gestation process through their involvement with their partner. Opportunities for men living in industrialized societies to experience their anticipated paternity during their partner's pregnancy have grown in recent years due to innovative technologies and health care practices.

While research on men's physiological and psychological experiences during gestation is somewhat limited, a number of scholars from several disciplines, especially the health care professions, have focused on men's lives during this period.[35] Insight into the physiological and psychological aspects of fathers' lives during this transitional period can be gleaned from a variety of small-scale qualitative studies of expectant fathers. These studies also highlight how men's paternal, partner, and gender role identities are related to aspects of their involvement in the pregnancy process.

Perhaps one of the most intriguing physiological processes related to men during the gestational period is commonly referred to as the couvade syndrome.[36] The condition, as I mentioned briefly in chapter 1, represents the involuntary and unconscious bodily symptoms some men report experiencing in conjunction with their partner's pregnancy. These symptoms occur without a recognizable physiological basis and are found in diverse types of societies.[37] In preindustrialized societies, there are also a wide range of conscious and voluntary ritual couvade behaviors.[38]

The most typical couvade symptoms include gastrointestinal disorders (nausea and vomiting, abdominal bloating/pain, heartburn), aches and pains (toothaches, leg cramps, backaches, urogenital irritations), and behavioral manifestations (change in appetite, change in sleep habits, anxiety, restlessness).[39] Researchers' current sense of the incidence of these paternal bodily symptoms and their understanding of why they occur remains sketchy. It appears as though a significant number of men in diverse cultures report having pregnancylike symptoms when their partner is pregnant. Estimates based on research in the United States and Great

Britain range from 11 to 79 percent owing to different inclusion criteria and methodologies.[40]

One prospective study of eighty-one Swedish men and their partners found that older men and men whose partners reported worrying about their pregnancy and delivery were more likely to suffer from the couvade syndrome.[41] Some research suggests that the extent to which men experience these symptoms varies throughout their partner's pregnancy, with symptoms occurring most frequently during the first trimester and then again in the third trimester immediately before birth.[42] Meanwhile, another study showed elevated symptoms for prospective fathers during the second trimester, although symptoms occurred most frequently during the third trimester.[43] Men who had fathered children previously were no more likely than first-time fathers to experience symptoms, although they were more likely to experience a greater number of symptoms than their inexperienced counterparts. Likewise, those men who indicated that the pregnancy was unplanned reported more symptoms than those men responsible for planned pregnancies.

The search for a better understanding of how some expectant fathers respond physiologically to pregnancy led one research team to compare the health-care-seeking behavior of a group of 212 married expectant fathers working in Rochester, New York, with a group of married nonexpectant fathers matched for age, number of prior children, and home maintenance organization membership.[44] These researchers found, contrary to expectations, that prospective fathers were significantly less likely to initiate health care visits during the pregnancy than they were to do so prior to conception or after delivery. Moreover, the control group exhibited a steady visit rate during the three data collection intervals and there were no between-group differences in the visit rate over the designated intervals. The researchers qualify their findings by noting that since they used health-seeking behavior as their outcome variable, their study does not rule out the possibility that expectant fathers experienced more symptoms than their nonexpectant counterparts but chose not to seek medical attention.

In addition to studying prospective fathers' physiological changes, researchers have considered men's psychological state of mind as well as the way they interact with their partner during this transitional period. One retrospective study focused on the feelings and fantasies of 103 first-time fathers of children who were born prematurely.[45] Common themes were identified and the psychological processes the fathers reported experiencing during pregnancy were divided into six different time periods. A sizeable number of prospective fathers reported having more and different types of fantasies while making love during the end of the first trimester period. These fantasies were noteworthy because they emphasized themes related to men's imminent father status. Commenting on those fathers who appeared to be most attuned to their procreative consciousness, the author of this study observed that "fathers reported feelings and images of themselves as nurturing or fertilizing their fetuses, their wives and the pregnancy. It is interesting that feelings of 'having to give' and 'feeding' the fetus during intercourse were prevalent."[46]

These reports illustrate how the sexual and reproductive realms are interrelated for many men. In this instance, sexual episodes provide men an opportunity to experience their paternal identity intrapsychically. While the overall impact of these episodes may be rather limited given their brevity, they may still reinforce men's attachment to the fetus and men's awareness of their paternal identity.

In addition to the intrapsychic, symbolic processes men use to express their paternal identity, prospective fathers sometimes experience unconscious manifestations of their paternal concerns. Analyzing expectant fathers' dreams represents one strategy for exploring prospective fathers' latent feelings and thoughts.[47] Luis Zayas, a clinician, analyzed and compared the dreams of ten well-educated, middle-class white men who were first-time expectant fathers and ten married men who were not fathers. These fathers-in-waiting recorded their dreams during three specific periods while their partners were pregnant. Based on his analysis of these prospective fathers' dreams, Zayas concluded that there appears to be a developmental process underlying how these men psychically adapt to different phases of their partner's pregnancy. While Zayas's comments must be viewed quite cautiously, given his small and narrowly defined sample, I find his summary observations provocative enough to quote at length:

> In the early stages of the pregnancy, the dreams of the expectant father largely involve a sense of awe and curiosity about the pregnancy. He is curious about the uterus, its inner space, and its contents. Positioned at the beginning of the pregnancy, when there are few visible indicators of pregnancy, the expectant father appears apprehensive about the long journey he and his wife will undergo. His dreams are filled with images that suggest this mystery and incomplete understanding about the pregnancy, birth, and child. The dreams also suggest that the expectant father must

continue to deal with reality demands in waking life. This is most evident in early pregnancy dreams. . . .

Although, in the final stages of pregnancy, the expectant father comes to view himself as a member of a family and network of friends, initially he is beset by a sense of isolation from others. This sense of exclusion finds its expression in the manifest dream as his wife receives the attention of others and he feels spurned by her as she turns her attention inward to the physiological changes taking place in the "inner space" from which a life will come. The expectant father's dependency needs are disrupted by virtue of this exclusion and his dreams depict this in images of exclusion and loneliness.[48]

Perhaps one of the most important lessons to be learned from Zayas's work is that dynamic developmental processes shape the lives of many expectant fathers. Consequently, prospective fathers' intrapsychic processes need to be assessed while taking into account the phase of their partners' pregnancy. Prospective fathers are therefore likely to experience numerous changes in their procreative consciousness throughout the pregnancy, and they are influenced by their partner's efforts to incorporate or exclude them from the pregnancy process.

Men's experiences during pregnancy can also be discussed on a more interpersonal level by using May's typology of how expectant fathers are involved in a pregnancy. This typology, based on a study of twenty expectant fathers, identifies three different behavioral styles prospective fathers display during their partner's pregnancy.[49] It categorizes men's pregnancy experience as either "observer," "expressive," or "instrumental." The prospective father who acts as an observer exhibits a degree of emotional detachment from the pregnancy. Men who display this style are largely uninvolved in decision making related to the pregnancy. Expressive fathers-in-waiting view themselves as having a full role to play during the pregnancy and anticipate playing an active role in parenting their child. Finally, the instrumental style is characterized by men who take a task-oriented approach to their partner's pregnancy. They are interested in being a caretaker for their partner and a kind of manager of the pregnancy. They are less emotional than expressive fathers; consequently, they attend to the practical details of directing the pregnancy. For instance, instrumental fathers often take it upon themselves to plan their partner's doctor's visits, supervise their partner's diet, and make major purchases and decisions for their infant.

Expectant fathers who exhibit an expressive or instrumental style are probably most likely to accompany their partner to prepared childbirth classes. Men's increased participation in these classes provides them with a chance to confirm their commitment to their paternal and partner identities. Although men focus primarily on their partner during these sessions, they can also receive social support from other men who acknowledge their efforts. In some settings, leaders of these prepared childbirth classes separate men into all-male groups during the initial meeting to provide them with a kind of male-bonding ritual. This ritual enables men to share with one another their feelings about their participation in the prepared childbirth class and their partner's pregnancy more generally.[50]

Men's involvement in labor and delivery, as well as their initial interaction with their newborn baby, symbolize additional defining moments in many fathers' lives as procreative beings. As noted in chapter 2, fathers' opportunities to be included in the childbirth scene have increased dramatically in recent decades. Some earlier research found that fathers' involvement during this period is related to their heightened attachment to their baby[51] and greater participation in early child care activities.[52] One more recent study of 114 couples also found that fathers who were assigned to a conventional birth setting compared to a modern birth room were more involved in helping and encouraging their partners at midlabor.[53] The researchers speculate that this might be attributed to fathers' perception of how their laboring partners were being affected by "environmental deficiencies." Meanwhile, fathers' parenting behavior when their children were three and twelve months old respectively was not related to the type of birth setting they experienced.

Paternity without Sex

While many men are involved in relationships in which they have the ability (planned or unplanned) to father a child through sexual intercourse, a sizeable proportion of men do not have this option. It has been estimated that among U.S. couples where the woman is of childbearing age, at least 8 percent are infertile (when infertility is defined as the failure to conceive after one year of regular sexual intercourse without the use of contraceptives).[54] Some estimates for couple infertility are closer to 15 or 20 percent.[55] Among those couples who are defined as being infertile, it is further estimated that about 35 percent are unable to procreate because of a sperm-related problem, another 35 percent are unable to reproduce through sexual relations with their current partner because the woman is infertile, about 25 percent of subfertility problems may be due to a combination of male and female factors, and in 3.5 percent of infertile couples the source of infertility is ambiguous.[56] Whatever the etiology of the infertility, asexual reproductive methods represent the only chance for men involved in this type of relationship to become a father of a newly conceived child (one who is not adopted or a stepchild). These methods at the same time create opportunities for men to express their procreative consciousness and sense of procreative responsibility as they relate to their father-in-waiting, partner, and gender role identities.

The medicalization and increased use of technological developments such as artificial insemination (AI),[57] in-vitro fertilization (IVF), and embryo transfer (ET),[58] in combination with biosocial innovations, most notably sperm banks and the practice of surrogacy,[59] have provided men with numerous ways to become a father other than through sexual intercourse. With an estimated 300 IVF clinics in the United States and hundreds of other clinics around the world, the number of children born through this technique is thought to be doubling each year.[60] As of 1994, the Society for Assisted Reproduction estimated that roughly 28,000 babies had been born in the United States using one of the assisted reproductive technologies. In 1993 alone, 8,741 of the 41,209 assisted reproductive procedures reported to the American Society for Reproductive Medicine resulted in live births.[61] Even more impressive is the number of women who make use of AI technology. During a twelve-month period in 1986 to 1987, it was estimated that 172,000 women in the United States were artificially inseminated resulting in 65,000 births (35,000 by AIH and 30,000 by AID), and the practice is common in other industrialized countries as well.[62] The interest in this technique is likely to continue to grow around the world.[63] It provides a viable option to persons with various needs, including those who have become subfecund due to exposure to hazardous environmental materials or medications, as well as those persons who want to have input in the genetic makeup of their child. Furthermore, these technologies may serve a growing segment of the female population (and their partners) who for one reason or another delay their efforts to have children until their late thirties or early forties, at which point the women have generally experienced a decline in their fecundity.

Interest in ARTs is fueled by recent fears about the possible rising rate of male infertility. Researchers have reported that there has been a significant reduction in the quantity and quality of sperm produced by men in many countries.[64] These researchers believe that chemicals in the environment are largely responsible for this pattern, although there is an ongoing debate within the scientific community about the validity and implications of these claims. Some researchers challenge the conclusion that sperm counts are declining, and some have even argued that they can document increases in sperm counts in places such as New York City, Los Angeles, and Roseville, Minnesota.[65] What is clear is that the debate about a possible decline in sperm counts has intensified in recent years. Even if the scientific community were to conclude eventually that sperm counts have indeed declined, scientists may still not be able to conclude whether this decline is permanent and irreparable. If lower sperm counts do reduce men's fecundity, the demand for ARTs is likely to grow.

In some cases where reproductive technologies are used, the father is the genetic and social father, whereas in others he will assume only the latter role. The circumstances defining a couple's infertility determine the possibility of men using their own sperm. Men's experiences with these reproductive strategies include how they deal with the infertility treatment process, and for a subsample of men whose partner becomes pregnant, prospective fathers have the opportunity to experience aspects of the pregnancy process as well.

Aspects of men's procreative consciousness and sense of procreative responsibility, as well as their partner and gender role identities, affect their willingness to use reproductive technologies and how they experience the social processes associated with their use. Research shows that women are much more likely to initiate fertility testing than are men and that a number of male partners do not even appear at the first scheduled visit with a fertility expert.[66] These patterns are reinforced by gender differences that show that men are less likely than women to seek medical attention.[67] In particular, because women are more likely to have previous experience with visiting a gynecologist on a regular basis, they will probably feel more at ease visiting a reproductive specialist.

Men's involvement with one of the ART techniques, and the accompanying fertility experiences they encounter, may also affect their procreative consciousness and sense of procreative responsibility during the prenatal and postnatal periods. At the heart of this discussion are questions related to men's beliefs and attitudes about biological procreation and social fatherhood. It has typically been the case that the phrase "to father" has meant to procreate, whereas "to mother" has been associated with a longer-term, nurturing image.[68] To the extent this image resonates with particular men, they probably feel significantly different about their paternal identity when they are able to contribute their own sperm rather than using donor sperm.

Not all men will respond to fertility testing in the same manner. Unfortunately, little is known about why men respond differently to the social processes associated with using reproductive technologies. One important factor motivating some men to get involved is likely to be their concern for their partner and the quality of their relationship with her. Researchers who studied participants in a Canadian in-vitro fertilization clinic found that men who sought IVF treatment placed "marital completion" as the number one reason they tried these procedures, whereas women were more likely to emphasize their own gender role fulfillment.[69] Gender role fulfillment was of only secondary importance to men.

The way men view their procreative self is also likely to affect the way they deal with reproductive technologies. For example, men who tend to see biological paternity as an opportunity to demonstrate their masculinity may be reluctant to become a social father by using donor sperm. They may reason that using donor sperm would constitute a direct assault on their virility. Unfortunately, this hypothesis has not been tested in any reliable fashion.[70] On the other hand, those men who want to become a social father in order to experience the developmental phase of generativity—the need to care for younger generations or to share in the childrearing experience with their partner—may be more willing to become a social father using whatever means necessary.[71]

Men who are willing to experiment with reproductive technologies are often put off by the diagnostic and treatment demands associated with them. These demands sometimes lead men to feel anxious about their sexuality. This is especially true in terms of IVF technologies that use the sperm of the man rather than donor sperm. Men involved in these procedures are asked to produce fresh sperm during the time the woman's eggs are being retrieved. This feature of the treatment process highlights my earlier discussion in chapter 3 about how the sexual and reproductive realms are interrelated for men. More specifically, men who wish to participate in infertility testing and certain variations of the IVF treatment process are asked to perform sexually under pressure. A comical depiction of this dilemma recently found its way into popular culture in the 1995 movie *Forget Paris*, in which Billy Crystal portrayed a husband's futile efforts to produce a sperm sample in a "timely fashion" while under pressure at the fertility clinic. A real life example is found in a man's narrative of his concern about the diagnostic procedures.

> My wife was scheduled to have a postcoital test late one afternoon. Because of our work schedules, we met at a motel close to the doctor's office to have intercourse. At first, I could not maintain an erection, and when I finally achieved that, I could not ejaculate. We tried everything we knew, and after no success, we dressed, checked out, and went home . . . where we tried unsuccessfully again. This whole charade was so humiliating and painful for me that I could not imagine attempting such a thing again.[72]

Men's problems during these fertility-testing procedures are exacerbated by the fact that the medical community has not aggressively attempted to understand male infertility.[73] Little has been done to develop treatment strategies that would improve the physiological processes by which men are able to produce viable sperm. Instead, the medical approach has typically focused on the man's physiological product—sperm. Fertility specialists in many cases treat male impairments by using treatments directed at women, such as ovarian hyperstimulation followed by intrauterine insemination, in-vitro fertilization, or gamete/zygote intrafallopian transfer.[74] Incentives for conducting research on male sperm production and the need to treat men's fertility problems directly are also lessened by the increasing availability of sperm banks. This biosocial innovation has in a sense made it possible for men to be substituted for one another.

Furthering men's embarrassment, the evaluation of a man's sperm sample by a clinic's staff is often cast in judgmental terms based on its quantity, concentration, mobility, and viability, with undesirable results cast as personal failures. This relates to the central place the achievement theme has in traditional masculinity ideology.[75] Men often form impressions of their value as individuals by evaluating their accomplishments—sperm production being no exception. With this in mind, Carmeli and Birenbaum-Carmeli's interpretation of how men were treated during the fertility-testing procedures they observed as part of their field observations in Canada and Israel is revealing:

> Because the medical practice does not treat the male's body in most cases, the "successes" or "failures" were applied directly to his very nature, potency, and virility. This situation eliminated a possibility of distancing, and presented difficulties in finding social support.[76]

Put differently, men who undergo infertility testing are likely to form impressions of themselves based on their perception of others' opinions of them. They are not in a position to disassociate themselves easily from the stereotypically negative images that low sperm production engenders from others. Moreover, the stress associated with failed attempts to father a child, and perhaps the IVF treatments themselves, may negatively affect sperm parameters such as volume, concentration, motility, and morphology.[77]

For those couples who undergo AI and IVF procedures with the male partner's sperm, there are those additional pressures that are placed on the man to perform sexually according to a designated time schedule. In IVF procedures it is typical that the male is expected to produce a sperm sample during a time that coincides with the retrieval of his partner's (or surrogate donor's) eggs.[78] Men usually report feeling distressed about the process of producing sperm samples on this type of demand schedule in a clinical setting. Men are requested to produce a sperm sample in rooms that are often integrated into the clinics in a manner that minimizes a man's sense of comfort and privacy. Carmeli and Birenbaum-Carmeli offer a shrewd synopsis of men's IVF treatment experiences:

> The man knows that his partner, who has undergone a lengthy medical preparation, is being operated on for egg retrieval. He is aware of the importance of timing, and the inevitable cancellation of the cycle if the sperm is not provided on time. He also knows that the staff is expecting it. A culturally charged complex of virility-manhood (mainly in Israel), his commitment to his wife and to the treatment, and his face vis-à-vis the professionals, are all on trial at this particular moment.[79]

Is it any wonder, in the face of these awkward circumstances, that some men voice their uneasiness about using an assisted reproductive method? These experiences can be quite unnerving to many men.

My comments about diagnostic and treatment issues highlights researchers' interest in the way men deal with the stigma associated with being a member of an infertile couple. Much of the research on this topic has attempted to compare distress levels between women and men in these couples. This research has produced mixed results. While some research has found that women tend to experience more emotional and psychological problems when they are members of an infertile couple,[80] other research has found no differences.[81] Interpreting this research is complicated by the fact that much of it does not control for whether instances of infertility were due to male or female factors. Some of the samples used in this research have also been skewed because they had a disproportionate number of couples who were infertile because of a female factor.[82] Men seem only to experience significant amounts of distress if they are personally responsible for a couple's infertility.[83] Nachtigall and his colleagues concluded, based on their study of thirty-six infertile couples, that "men's response to infertility will closely approximate that of women if the infertility has been attributed to a male factor but will be significantly less if a male factor is not found."[84] This study found that the inability to have a child, for whatever reason, affected women's gender role identity more than it affected men's. Men and women may, in fact, think quite differently about their potential parental roles as they relate to their larger self-image. Nachtigall and his colleagues observe,

> Women are affected from the time they decide to seek infertility treatment because they define the problem as a failure to fulfill the motherhood role, which is not dependent on the identification of an actual fertility factor. Men will not share the intensity of women's emotional response, however, unless and until a male factor is identified in the infertility evaluation. Thus, men's response to infertility will be delayed relative to their partners, and if no male factor is found, their lack of identification may inhibit their recognition of infertility as a problem.[85]

Men appear to be less concerned than women about the possibility of not having the opportunity to assume a parental role. But some men may still feel uneasy about their personal inability to procreate because they see this problem as an affront to their virility and sense of masculinity. Men therefore appear to link the fertility problem more closely with their gender role identity than their identity as a father. Because the empirical evidence in this area is quite thin, researchers can only speculate on how the use of donor sperm affects social fathers.

If men's probable responses to the processes involving asexual assisted reproduction are to be assessed systematically, it is important to distinguish between the different methods available.[86] I illustrate in figure 1 how a social or nurturing father involved in ART can establish a paternal relationship to a child through AI (AIH or AID) or IVF in at least eight different ways. While some of these eight combinations are much more prevalent than others, and the absolute and relative frequency of some of these permutations may increase in the future (e.g., those involving surrogacy), I will discuss each of them in turn. Note that case sce-

FIGURE 1
Eight Permutations of Assisted Reproduction among Heterosexual Couples

	Sperm[+]		Ovum[++]		Gestation Body	
Case Scenario	Own	Donor	Partner	Donor	Partner	Surrogate
1	*		*		*	
2	*		*			*
3	*			*	*	
4	*			*		*
5		*	*		*	
6		*	*			*
7		*		*	*	
8		*		*		*

[+] In some cases a semen specimen includes both the social father's sperm and sperm from a donor. I have excluded this variable from the table because it rarely occurs and its inclusion would make the conceptualization less manageable.

[++] In many cases of IVF, more than one ovum will be used during any given treatment.

Case Scenarios:

Male's Own Sperm
 1. Own sperm, partner's ovum, partner's gestation body
 2. Own sperm, partner's ovum, surrogate mother's gestation body
 3. Own sperm, donor's ovum, partner's gestation body
 4. Own sperm, donor's ovum, surrogate mother's gestation body

Donor's Sperm
 5. Donor's sperm, partner's ovum, partner's gestation body
 6. Donor's sperm, partner's ovum, surrogate mother's gestation body
 7. Donor's sperm, donor's ovum, partner's gestation body
 8. Donor's sperm, donor's ovum, surrogate mother's gestation body

narios 1 and 2 preserve the genetic relations of both social parents to the child, 3 and 4 preserve only the social father's genetic ties, 5 and 6 preserve only the mother's genetic relations, and 7 and 8 preserve neither social parent's genetic ties (however, the mother's direct contribution during gestation is preserved in 7).

Given my focus on heterosexual men in this book, I will simplify my discussion by assuming that the partners using an assisted reproductive strategy comprise a heterosexual couple. I also assume that the social father knows that his partner is experimenting with an alternative form of reproduction even though in rare cases a woman might attempt to deceive her male partner and covertly use one of these technologies. According to the Uniform Parentage Act of the United States, which I discuss later in this chapter, a husband's written consent is required for a wife to be artificially inseminated.

How are men's procreative consciousness and sense of procreative responsibility likely to differ due to the unique combination of fertility circumstances they encounter when using one of the reproductive innovations? Their experiences will probably affect, as well as be affected by, their tendency to develop a commitment to a paternal identity. The first four scenarios depicted in figure 1 refer to social fathers who use their own sperm to procreate. As discussed, biological paternity may be a critical factor shaping their perception of their role as a prospective father during gestation and as a social father after their child's birth.[87] A qualitative study of fifty-seven couples who received AID between 1940 and 1980 at one clinic in the United Kingdom revealed that many fathers were concerned about whether they would be related to their child genetically.[88] Many equated their fertility potential with their level of masculinity, a position reinforced by others' tendencies to stigmatize infertile men. As one husband in this study expressed, "I know a chap at work— he and his wife they've been trying for two or three years, and the amount of stick that chap takes—virtually everyone that knows him has offered to go and do the job for him."[89]

Men probably feel the fullest psychological and emotional intensity of being a genetic father in the first case scenario. This set of fertility circumstances most closely resembles the natural reproductive process because men use their own sperm to impregnate their partner who also uses her own ovum and carries the pregnancy to term.

Those social fathers using their own sperm who are represented by the second and third scenarios are probably very similar to each other and may have experiences comparable to men in the first category. In the second scenario a man becomes a social father by using his partner's ovum and a surrogate mother's body, whereas in the third scenario he uses a donor's ovum and his partner carries the pregnancy to term herself. If men experience the second and third scenarios differently, it probably hinges on men feeling as though the use of their partner's ovum is either more or less important than the opportunity to experience the gestation process with her. The symbolic significance of these options may be quite different.[90] In either case, the man's partner would be making some type of physiological contribution to the eventual birth of the man's genetically related child.

If men do experience these two scenarios differently, it is possible that the difference may subside over time or even dissipate entirely. The way a man develops and experiences his procreative consciousness and sense of procreative responsibility during a pregnancy initiated by AI or IVF may differ from his experiences measured at some point after the child is born. The degree of similarity in the child's and mother's appearance may be one meaningful factor that comes into play in this respect. While it may not be of great consequence to prospective fathers during the prenatal period whether their partner contributes her ovum, it may be more meaningful after the child is born if the father's daughter or son does not physically resemble his partner at all. If the child does resemble the mother, then men's possible prenatal concerns about using donor ovum may be minimized.

Concerns about the partner's genetic or gestational contribution are likely to affect a father's procreative consciousness or sense of procreative responsibility only if his paternity experiences are influenced vicariously, at least in part, through his association with a partner. Prospective fathers who feel emotionally and psychologically connected to their partner may be in the best position to experience the pregnancy indirectly through her. These men, compared to those who are emotionally detached from their partners, are probably more likely to experience aspects of the couvade syndrome. The circumstances of the fourth case scenario identify a traditional surrogate situation where the man uses his own sperm but his partner plays no biological role in the child's conception or birth. Under these circumstances, men are likely to have different feelings and perceptions than men who experience one of the first three permutations. These distinctions should be accentuated during the gestation period if a man's procreative consciousness is affected by his relationship with a partner who assumes the gestational mother role. As with the first three cases, this distinction may dissipate once the child is born. On the other hand, some fathers may have a very active procreative consciousness and a strong sense of responsibility for their child under these circumstances because they share a direct tie to their child, whereas their partner does not. Much probably still depends though on how the father and social mother develop and express their parental roles once their child is born.

The remaining case scenarios 5 through 8 represent examples of AI and IVF that involve donor's sperm. Social fathers who use donor sperm are likely to experience their prenatal procreative consciousness differently than those men who contribute their own sperm. Users of donor sperm are likely to worry more about whether their child will physically resemble them and have similar personality characteristics.[91] While differences between prospective social fathers who use their own sperm and those who rely on donor sperm may be most pronounced during the prenatal period, differences between these two categories of social fathers may persist sometimes even after a child's birth.

Presumably, men who experience the combination of fertility circumstances listed in the fifth scenario are most likely, among those men using donor sperm, to have a strong sense of their paternal identity. In this instance female partners use their own ovum and also carry the pregnancy to term. Thus, men are able to draw upon their bond with their partner and her contribution to the conception, gestation, and actual birth process to reinforce their own prenatal and postnatal paternal identity and actual involvement with their child once the child is born.[92] Their partner's expectations for them to be a supportive partner during gestation may help remind them of their emerging father roles. Thus, in those situations where a man's partner can participate fully in a child's prenatal development, the prospective social father is likely to benefit if his partner is capable of making him feel that he is included in the process, too—even if his involvement is indirect.

However, some men who use donor sperm may feel alienated from the reproductive process; they may envy their partner for being able to participate fully in this important process. If this occurs, men may have difficulties embracing their paternal identity.

Those men included among the sixth scenario of cases may be particularly susceptible to feeling alienated during the time of pregnancy. They may be concerned because they have not contributed their own sperm and have probably been unable to play an active part in the pregnancy process because a surrogate mother has gestated the fetus (rare exceptions to this pattern probably occur when family or friends serve as surrogate mothers). From the social fathers' perspective, the symbolic and relative significance of having their partner serve as the gestation mother (using a donor ovum), versus having her contribute the ovum, may depend on whether men use donor sperm or their own. Men may place greater weight on their partner's genetic contribution when they are unable to make a similar contribution themselves.[93] Some men facing these fertility circumstances are likely to have some difficulty developing a paternal identity during the prenatal period.

Social fathers categorized according to the criteria for the seventh scenario may tend to have a stronger sense of their paternal identity, especially during the prenatal period, than men depicted by the sixth scenario. Although men in the seventh scenario depend upon a donor's sperm and a donor's ovum, their partner is responsible for carrying the fertilized egg to term. Consequently, the man is able to be a daily witness to the pregnancy process and may even have the opportunity to visualize the fetus using ultrasonography. Aspects of the man's procreative consciousness are likely to be reinforced repeatedly as he and his partner experience the daily interaction rituals (including prepared childbirth classes) that usually attend the pregnancy process when shared by two people who have actively gone through a pregnancy and have access to modern prenatal care. Many of these men also have an opportunity to be with their partner throughout the labor and delivery process.

Of the eight permutations, the final one most closely resembles the dynamics of parenthood through adoption. Those extremely rare cases where men depend on donated sperm, a donated ovum, and a surrogate carrier for the pregnancy typically include men with the least well-developed paternal identity. This should be especially true during the pregnancy. Men who become social fathers under these circumstances may still be quite committed to their father roles. However, they have a greater chance to feel unsettled about their paternal identity than those who are genetically related to their child or were at least indirectly involved in their child's birth due to their association with a partner who made a genetic and/or gestational contribution.

Sperm Donors

While social fathers' reactions to using reproductive techniques that rely on donor sperm are important, a basic feature of these methods is that a sperm donor can potentially become a progenitor to a child if the assisted reproductive technique is successful in a given instance. The systematic study of sperm banks and donors is essential then because donors are indispensable to the success of many forms of asexual assisted reproduction, and techniques that rely on donated sperm are widely used. Though it is beyond the scope of my discussion to address sperm donors' possible motivations and concerns about their genetic contribution at length,[94] several issues associated with sperm donation, particularly how donating sperm may influence men's procreative consciousness in unique ways, deserve comment.

A major innovation that increased the use of donor sperm for reproductive purposes occurred in the 1950s when scientists developed techniques to freeze sperm intact. The first human pregnancies resulting from frozen sperm took place at the University of Arkansas in 1953.[95] Less than twenty years later, in 1970, the first commercial sperm bank appeared in the United States.[96] In 1990, it was estimated that 400 commercial sperm banks existed in the United States with the world's largest being located in New York City.[97] This New York sperm bank, with over 30,000 specimens, has been responsible for more than 11,000 babies since 1971.[98]

The general population tends to know very little about sperm banks. One intriguing facet of these businesses is the room where sperm is actually collected. A journalist, Doug Hill, presents a behind-the-scenes snapshot of what the staff at BioGenetics, a national sperm bank located in Mountainside, New Jersey, call the "cupping room."

> It's a brightly lit, windowless chamber, about twelve feet square with a high ceiling, decorated in muted grays. Its central object is a turquoise lounge chair, which faces a TV set and video machine. On top of the TV are two x-rated videotapes; the selection is changed monthly. A magazine rack stocked with *Playboy* magazines is within arm's reach; on the walls are framed posters of naked women, including a nude shot of Marilyn Monroe. Against the far wall is a sink and, beside it, a hamper filled with shrink-wrapped specimen cups.
>
> The overall effect might be called functionally erotic. That's better than some sperm banks, which offer little more than a bathroom and a box of tissues. Albert Anouna, the president of BioGenetics, concedes that dimmer lighting might be sexier, but he points out that at the critical moment, the men need to be able to see what they're doing, lest they miss the specimen cup. Some donors bring their girlfriends along for assistance (most sperm banks don't allow this), while others bring in briefcases that contain, Anouna assumes, private forms of stimulation.[99]

The directors of U.S. sperm banks have been quite concerned over the years about ensuring the anonymity of their donors. In fact, donor anonymity was an important consideration associated with artificial insemination for the past two centuries prior to the advent of commercial sperm banks.[100] Clinics outside the United States have also grappled with the anonymity question as discussed below. The most recent recommendations from the 1990 Ethics Committee of the American Fertility Society suggested that "a permanent record designed to preserve confidentiality should be maintained. It should include the genetic workup and other nonidentifying information and should be made available on request, on an anonymous basis, to the recipient and/or any resulting offspring."[101]

The most pressing concern about donor anonymity is whether eliminating it would significantly reduce the number of sperm donors. Several constituencies have expressed a stake in either maintaining or eliminating guidelines regarding donors' anonymity. Doctors, more than any other category of persons, have championed the need for anonymity. Over the years, they have been able to achieve this, in part, by keeping poor records. Furthermore, sperm banks have generally not made their records available even if they do exist.[102] In some settings, policymakers have also been staunch supporters of anonymity requirements. For example, 77 percent of the British Parliament in 1990 thought that donor anonymity should be preserved.[103] Some researchers, on the other hand, present a forceful argument for increasing the openness in donor insemination.[104]

Attitudinal research using the general population, recipient couples, and donors themselves has produced mixed findings about the desirability of disclosing information to children and maintaining sperm donors' anonymity. These studies have been conducted in a variety of countries, most notably, Australia, Great Britain, New Zealand, Sweden, and the United States. A survey of the general population in Australia found that 64 percent thought that children conceived through donor insemination should *not* be told about how they were conceived.[105] A few small-scale studies using established sperm donors in New Zealand and Australia found some support for allowing identifying information to be catalogued. Among the sample of 37 sperm donors in New Zealand, 68 percent thought anonymity was very important and 27 percent felt it was important.[106]

In Great Britain, a study of 52 sperm donors revealed a significant discrepancy in how established and potential sperm donors felt about donating sperm if identifying information were made available to offspring once they reached eighteen years of age.[107] Seventy-two percent of the established sperm donors but only 15 percent of the potential donors reported that they would be willing to donate sperm under these circumstances. Among the donor insemination patients who responded to a separate survey for this study, 60 percent indicated they would agree to the release of medical records that could identify the donor, but 85 percent said they would not tell their children about their unconventional form of conception. Findings from a multisite study of 799 donors, patients, and health care professionals in the United Kingdom confirm this latter finding since only 5 percent of recipient couples felt that the child should be told of his or her genetic origins.[108] All 91 donors in this study felt that confidentiality should be retained.

One frequently cited U.S. study of sperm donors was based on a survey of 79 sperm donors in two donor programs located in Texas and Louisiana.[109] This study examined how willing donors would be to provide in-depth medical and psychosocial information on their application forms. Furthermore, it considered whether donors would be willing to share this information with their offspring and the social parents. The researchers found that 90 percent of their sample were willing to complete lengthy forms providing in-depth information. Almost the entire sample, 96 percent, were willing to make this information available to recipient families if the information were presented in a nonidentifying manner. However, sperm donors were less receptive to the idea of donating sperm without an assurance of anonymity. Only 36 percent indicated that they would be donors if anonymity could not be guaranteed, and another 39 percent indicated that they were uncertain about their willingness to donate sperm under these circumstances. When asked a related question, respondents appeared to be somewhat less rigid about their concerns for anonymity. Forty-one percent indicated that they would not object to a meeting initiated by their offspring, although they would not seek out such a meeting. Another 19 percent wanted their offspring to know who they were through the exchange of a photograph or a meeting, while 37 percent reported they definitely had no interest in meeting children conceived through the use of their sperm.

The question of donor anonymity has important legal implications and has received attention from legal scholars in the United States. Anonymity offers distinct advantages; most importantly, it assures sperm donors that they will not be held financially accountable to the children who may be sired from their sperm. This has become a more pressing concern in light of the recent increase in court cases that have determined that men who are willing to donate sperm to their female friends are unable to sign binding contracts that relieve them of their financial obligations. In an Indiana case (*Straub v. B.M.T.*, 1994), a single woman bore a child using donor sperm from a friend in 1987. Prior to the insemination, they signed a contract stipulating that the man was consenting to donate sperm but was not interested in assuming any fatherhood responsibilities. In 1991 the woman sued for child support and the man was ordered to pay $100,000 in back child support. The court sided with the large body of family law that indicates that mothers and fathers cannot bargain away their child's rights. This type of case has profound implications because some experts in artificial insemination and family law contend that there may be more freelance sperm donors than men who make their donations to sperm banks.[110]

In 1993 Swanson challenged the utility of anonymity regulations in this area by arguing that the legal guidelines requiring anonymity in the use of donated sperm are outdated.[111] Although Swanson interprets findings from one small survey of sperm donors[112] as solid evidence supporting her proposal to drop anonymity guidelines, the fact that 36 percent of these sperm donors were unwilling to provide identifying information should not be ignored. Moreover, there is some evidence that the availability of donor sperm in Sweden declined after the government modified policies in order to weaken donor anonymity practices.[113] However, findings to the contrary have been reported by other researchers based on their experiences in their New Zealand clinic.[114] Eliminating the option of donors remaining anonymous at the beginning of 1993 did not adversely affect the number of potential donors at this particular clinic.

Although sperm donors have typically been unmarried medical students,[115] recent efforts to secure donations from married men has increased considerably.[116] Organizations such as the American Fertility Society (AFS) and the Australian Reproductive Technology Accreditation Committee (RTAC), as well as legislation like the Human Fertilization and Embryology Act in the United Kingdom, have sought to develop more effective strategies for recruiting married men while implementing more stringent screening procedures when securing sperm donations.

One consequence of the HIV/AIDS epidemic was that in 1988 the Centers for Disease Control, with the endorsement of the American Fertility Society, the American Academy of Obstetricians and Gynecologists, and the American Association of Tissue Banks, set forth recommendations for screening sperm donors to prevent HIV infection. As a result, donor insemination clinics now routinely require the use of frozen sperm that has been quarantined for six months by a donor who was subsequently retested and found to be seronegative for HIV.[117] In New Zealand, fertility specialists have recently initiated advertising campaigns with the intent of soliciting the assistance of married men, especially those with young children.[118] Married men are seen as desirable because they tend to have a lower incidence of sexually transmitted diseases, are thought to be more reliable donors who would be available to be tested for HIV, and are probably willing to donate without remuneration.

Reproductive specialists are concerned not only with developing recruitment strategies that will enhance their chances of securing sperm samples free of genital pathogens, they are also interested in developing procedures to improve their chances of acquiring very fertile sperm. Reproductive specialists in the United Kingdom have proposed several ideas along these lines. One promising strategy calls for the identification and recruitment of men whose partners have conceived within the past three months.[119] The success of this type of strategy depends upon the male partner's willingness to cooperate, and the female partner's willingness to condone his participation. In many instances, the female partner will be the donor's wife, or at least his cohabiting partner.

In at least one New Zealand fertility clinic, a married man's partner is required to sign a consent form before the man can make a donation.[120] This type of policy implicitly recognizes a normative code that establishes marriage as the legitimate context within which fertility should be experienced and controlled. It also recognizes that many women are distressed about their partner donating sperm and feel as though they have a significant stake in what their partner does in this respect. Ironically, some women may be more empathetic than men to infertile couples' frustrations. Given these patterns, some reproductive specialists are calling for advertisements to target women and/or couples with messages about the importance of sperm donations.[121] Recruitment strategies that focus on the couple, rather than just the man, implies that the production and use of donor sperm is a joint commitment whereby women's claims over the use of their partners' sperm are separate from their demands for sexual fidelity. In fact, some women might be willing to tolerate their partner's nonmonogamous sexual behavior but unwilling to grant him the opportunity to donate his sperm, although the reverse pattern is probably more common.[122]

If fertility specialists develop a better understanding of the needs men fulfill when they donate sperm, they will stand a better chance of improving their recruitment strategies. In this vein, one small-scale survey found that, when given the opportunity, 72 percent of the sample of donors left personal messages for their future offspring to read when the children turned eighteen. The sampling of messages presented below conveys sperm donors' thoughts about their contribution and their concern about their genetic offspring.

> Your parents wanted a child very much, but needed help. I wish you a long, good life. This chance to live is a singular gift, so strive to reach your best at everything you do.

> I am glad I could help in your conception, but your real parents are the ones who raised you and took care of you. I hope you find life beautiful. Be happy!

> Tell him that what's important is his present parents, who love him and went through the trouble of artificial insemination. I do think he should be informed of his situation.

> Be aware of the small sacrifices that your parents have made on your behalf. Artificial insemination is a difficult choice, and to have made it means your parents considered having you to be worth the struggle. Appreciate them. Also, pick a talent, focus on it. Stay away from rugby (it kills the shoulders) and strive for excellence.[123]

Although these messages do not explicitly clarify men's motivation for donating sperm, they seem to indicate that some sperm donors have at least partially altruistic reasons for donating sperm.[124] This may be particularly true for married fathers who have experienced the various phases of gestation and childbirth with their partner. Capitalizing on men's euphoria during the initial months after a child is born may prove to be an effective tactic to increase sperm donorship among married or cohabiting fathers. These men, if they recognize that they can help other men to have an experience similar to theirs, may be quite receptive to donating sperm.

The increasing use of ARTs has heightened concern in a number of countries about the legal relationships between social fathers, sperm donors, and the children conceived through the use of donated sperm. The most significant legislative response to these developments in the United States has been the Uniform Parentage Act (UPA). It stipulates,

> (a) If, under the supervision of a licensed physician and with the consent of her husband, a wife is inseminated artificially with semen donated by a man not her husband, the husband is treated in law as if he were the natural father of a child thereby conceived. The husband's consent must be in writing and signed by him and his wife. The physician shall certify their sig-

natures and the date of the insemination, and file the husband's consent with the [State Department of Health], where it shall be kept confidential and in a sealed file. However, the physician's failure to do so does not affect the father and child relationship. All papers and records pertaining to insemination, whether part of the permanent record of a court or of a file held by the supervising physician or elsewhere, are subject to inspection only upon an order of the court for good cause shown.

    (b) The donor of semen provided to a licensed physician for use in artificial insemination of a married woman other than the donor's wife is treated in law as if he were not the natural father of a child thereby conceived.[125]

One of the purposes of this legislation is to enable men to donate sperm without worrying about the possibility of being held legally responsible for any children that may result from the use of their sperm. Hence, a genetic relationship in this instance does not constitute paternal legal rights or obligations.

DNA Fingerprinting and Paternity Establishment

While technological and biosocial innovations have made it possible for individuals to have children in a variety of novel ways, modern technology has also left its mark on other aspects of the procreative realm related to paternity. It is now possible, thanks to modern DNA fingerprinting techniques, to determine whether two people are related genetically with almost perfect certainty. This new technology enables men to learn definitively whether they are the biological father of specific offspring whom they assumed they had sired, or perhaps the father of children whom they only suspected *might* be theirs, or in some cases the father of children whom they never even knew existed.

    Although this technology has been used rather sparingly, it is widely available. Thus far it has been used primarily to determine the validity of an unmarried mother's claim that a particular man is the biological father of her child.[126] As such, it has become a political asset for those who wish to increase the rate of establishing paternity for children born to single women, especially in the United States. The major policy objective behind the use of this technology is to increase children's chances of receiving adequate financial child support.[127]

    The threat of being forced to take such a test can prompt some men to acknowledge their paternity without contesting the matter further. In those cases where a man does not voluntarily acknowledge his paternity, this technology can only be used if a woman is willing to identify a particular man (or several men) as the genetic (or probable genetic) father to the proper authorities. The man must then be located and persuaded or forced to take the paternity test. If the test establishes the man as the biological father of the woman's child, he can be required to pay child support. However, not all women are willing to have paternity established in this fashion because many want to prevent the biological fathers of their children from having legal recourse to pursue paternity rights such as visitation.

DNA fingerprinting technology has intriguing legal implications for the definition of men as fathers. Should individuals be allowed to use this technology to challenge the marital presumption of paternity, the time-honored notion that children born to a married woman are assumed to be her husband's children?[128] Several legal issues dominate the debates being played out on both the federal and state level.

Legal analyses of paternity are often tied to the Uniform Parentage Act (UPA) mentioned earlier. The following represents an abbreviated description of the presumptions of paternity it lists:

A man is presumed to be the natural father of a child if
 1. he and the child's natural mother are or have been married to each other and the child is born during the marriage, or within 300 days after the marriage [ends];
 2. before the child's birth, he and the child's natural mother have attempted to marry each other . . . , although the attempted marriage is or could be declared invalid, and [the child is born during the attempted marriage or within 300 days after the marriage ends];
 3. after the child's birth, he and the child's natural mother have married, or attempted to marry, . . . although the attempted marriage is or could be declared invalid, and [he acknowledges his paternity of the child, is named on the birth certificate, or must support the child];
 4. while the child is [a minor], he receives the child into his home and openly holds out the child as his natural child; or
 5. he acknowledges his paternity of the child in a writing filed with the appropriate court or Vital Statistics Bureau.[129]

Eighteen states have adopted the UPA and many state paternity statutes integrate specific provisions from the UPA into their guidelines. Overall, there is still a considerable amount of variability among state statues, and this lack of legislative uniformity has complicated the process by which these statutes are interpreted and enforced.

As U.S. courts continue to deal with the different types of paternity actions, they will use various approaches to introduce the new genetic testing procedures into their deliberations. Basically, three types of paternity actions are associated with the marital presumption. First, a husband may wish to remain the legal parent of his presumed child when his wife challenges the presumption of legitimacy. This controversial scenario typically involves a mother who is going through a divorce and her ability to contest her spouse's paternity of a child that was born into (or lead to) the marriage. While most states bar paternity suits on behalf of a child when a legal father already exists, some states (e.g., Texas) permit a wife to request a paternity test even when the husband objects.

A second scenario includes an alleged biological father, not the husband, who wishes to assert his paternity for a child born into a marriage not his own. This second scenario is associated with the first because it, too, involves an attempt to circumvent a husband's paternity rights that are based on the marital presumption of paternity. In this instance, though, it is another man who is attempting to assert his paternity rights over the objections of the wife and husband. Considerable confusion exists within the legal system as to whether this type of paternity action is permissible. In 1989, the U.S. Supreme Court (*Michael H. v. Gerald D.*) upheld the California court's ruling that the Constitution is not violated by state statues that deny biological fathers the right to assert paternity when the marital presumption of paternity exists. In this case, the biological father was even denied visitation with his child despite the fact that they had had significant prior contact.

Some legal scholars have taken issue with this ruling, concluding that alleged biological fathers should have standing to assert their paternity when it is determined to be in the best interests of the child.[130] Ellingboe arrived at this conclusion after reviewing the amended Minnesota Parentage Act of 1989. This act, along with similar pieces of legislation in Colorado, North Dakota, and Ohio, has a provision that permits the presumption of paternity based on genetic tests. However, the Minnesota courts have yet to determine whether this amended statue permits biological fathers standing to pursue paternity actions in the face of a preexisting marital presumption. Courts in New Jersey and Maryland have recently ruled that an alleged biological father may be granted standing to attempt to establish paternity, even when the marital presumption exists, if it can be established in a pretrial hearing that efforts to establish paternity are in the child's best interests.

The third possibility for paternity action involves a husband who wishes to denounce his paternity rights and obligations toward a child he believes his wife conceived through an adulterous relationship. Hirczy, a legal scholar, recently addressed this issue and reasoned that "a child's interest in continuity of identity, parentage, and filial relationships should have greater weight than a nonbiological father's alleged right to remain or not remain a parent at his own discretion."[131] Thus, he recommended that a husband should be permitted to deny his paternity for a child he did not sire, but who was born within his marriage, only under very limited circumstances. If a husband does bring a nonpaternity action, he should be required to do so shortly after the child is born. While Hirczy did not specify the time frame, he argued for a provision that was shorter than California's two-year statute of limitations. In addition, this type of disavowal of paternity should be permitted only in the context of divorce.

This brief synopsis of how DNA testing has affected the legal processing of paternity actions illustrates the important role modern innovations can have in altering the way paternity is conceptualized within the legal system as well as by individuals. When used, this technology can fundamentally change men's procreative consciousness and sense of responsibility. It can inspire men to think about and negotiate their image of themselves as a procreative being and father. Even the knowledge of its potential use may influence the way some men experience and negotiate their paternal identity.

This technology, when viewed from a sociohistorical perspective, offers the possibility of eliminating the time-honored custom whereby men have been "forced" to trust women not to deceive them about their paternity status. While men in theory no longer have to accept their partners' word, and women need not rely simply on normative pressure to persuade former sexual partners to acknowledge their paternity and accept the accompanying obligations, the practical reality is that trust is likely to remain an essential feature of the social customs surrounding the reproductive process. The vast majority of males are not going to question their paternity status, and only a very small proportion of women who have multiple sexual partners but are in an established relationship are likely to request that several men take a paternity test to determine the child's progenitor. Other women may be reluctant to use DNA fingerprinting to establish paternity because they want to preserve their control over their child while minimizing their own involvement with the child's father. Notwithstanding these limiting factors, this technology opens up new possibilities for how men in the late twentieth century and beyond might experience different aspects of the procreative realm. This technology has also prompted a variety of new legal strategies that challenge the presumption of fatherhood that husbands have heretofore experienced, that is, the legal system has generally assumed that the spouse of a childbearing woman was the father of the child. Now individuals without a marital bond may attempt to establish or challenge paternity for children who may be currently living with, or had previously lived with, someone else.[132]

Adoptive Fathers and Stepfathers

The final two paths for men to experience social fatherhood include the formal adoption of a child and developing fatherlike roles through a romantic involvement with a single mother and her children. Formal arrangements and informal social psychological processes may provide men with opportunities to think of themselves as having a fatherlike identity to their stepchildren.[133]

Typically speaking, men who become fathers through adoption or a stepfather arrangement are not in a position to experience some aspects of the procreative realm because their involvement with the procreative process per se is limited to the postnatal period. There are exceptions to this pattern though, and the experiences of being a nonbiological father figure may also activate men's procreative consciousness by inspiring men to ponder aspects of their current or potential paternal identity that they otherwise might have left unexplored. In other words, being around children may inspire these men to think about siring a biological child who more closely resembles them in certain ways. They might also think about their desire to be involved in a child's life from the very beginning, including the pregnancy and childbearing processes. Part of men's interest in being involved from the outset of a pregnancy may reflect their desire to share the entire experience with their partner.

In the case of adoption or stepfatherhood, father figures may feel their experiences are limited in some areas, especially prenatally—but many still overcome their unconventional situation and develop a fatherlike identity. Are there particular social or cultural circumstances that lead some men to express a paternal commitment to their nonbiological children? What types of personality characteristics and interpersonal dynamics are related to men's willingness to devote themselves to caring and providing for "their" children without expecting immediate or direct reciprocation? To what extent is men's sense of procreative responsibility toward their nonbiological children contingent on their relationship with their partner? What type of differences, if any, exist between adoptive fathers' and stepfathers' perceptions?

These types of questions deserve attention since the formal adoptive route to becoming a father is chosen by thousands of men each year in the United States. While the National Adoption Information Clearinghouse in 1995 did not report the percentage of adoptive parents who were men, it is safe to assume that men were involved in a large percentage of the 127,441 adoptions that occurred in the United States in 1992. Forty-two percent of these adoptions involved stepparents or relatives. Many of the men who adopt children have never, to their knowledge, fathered biological children. Moreover, adoptive fathers in most cases do not experience aspects of the procreative realm, in relation to their adoptive child, during the prenatal period. Instead, they begin to develop their hands-on sense of being a father once the child has been placed with them. Some of these adoptive fathers may have thought about fatherhood issues extensively prior to becoming an adoptive father, but they have not personally experienced the pregnancy that led to the birth of a particular child. However, in a small percentage of cases, men may have an opportunity to develop a paternal identity that is "child specific" prior to their adoptive child's birth. Put differently, some men will first develop their sense of a paternal identity during the prenatal period when they think about a particular fetus that will be theirs once the child is born. Thus, adoptive fathers can develop a paternal identity during the prenatal period if they are aware of the woman's pregnancy that eventually ends with the birth of their adoptive child. This might be the case, for example, if a man has made a financial commitment to assist a woman with her unplanned pregnancy in exchange for the right to adopt her child. When prospective adoptive fathers are given the chance to anticipate and prepare for the birth of a specific child, they are probably more likely to develop a keener sense of their future paternal roles. These circumstances help distinguish this subset of adoptive fathers from all others. Unfortunately, the significance of this preparation period for adoptive fathers' future involvement with their children is not well understood. One key question is: Do fathers who are able to fantasize about a specific child during the prenatal period interact any differently with their children than do adoptive fathers who are not in a position to think about a specific child during the prenatal period? Though differences along these lines may be minor, if they exist at all, an informed conclusion about these types of issues must await more careful study.

Men's experiences in the adoptive process in some respects parallel the experiences of men who become fathers through ART. In both instances, men usually prefer to father a child whose physical appearance is relatively similar to their own, especially in obvious ways such as race and ethnicity. Not surprisingly, this desire probably stems from many men's ultimate preference for biological paternity. Men either explicitly or implicitly are likely to be concerned about their ability to feel a paternal affinity with a child that does not resemble them.[134]

Stepfatherhood, in both it traditional and more contemporary manifestations, represents an important path to social fatherhood that men increasingly experience in the United States.[135] Although the term "stepfather" has typically been used to refer to the husband whose wife has children from a previous relationship, the rapid increase in cohabitation has seemingly expanded the everyday use of this term. Now a man who lives with a woman with children may sometimes be viewed as a stepfather even if he is not married to the single mother with whom he coresides. This type of malleable definition is more likely to be embraced if the children in question feel comfortable perceiving the man in this fashion. When children in the home treat a man as though he were their father, a man is more apt to embrace a paternal identity and the associated roles.[136]

Men are typically first drawn into these stepfather situations because of their romantic interest in a woman. The man's commitment to the children is often therefore an outgrowth of his desire to please his partner, the children's mother. Depending upon the children's age, the man may act like a friend or a father toward them initially. In some instances, the man may learn to express a more fatherlike orientation over time; at other times, the man may never feel like a father figure although others may see him that way. In a study of 195 stepfathers from the first wave of the National Survey of Families and Households, I found that several factors were associated with stepfathers' tendency to develop a fatherlike identity.[137] Stepfathers who were involved with children who were younger when the parents married or began to cohabit and stepfathers who were happier with their relationship with their marital/cohabiting partner were more likely to develop a fatherlike identity. Stepfathers living with only stepchildren were less likely to develop a fatherlike identity than those living with a mix of biological and stepchildren.

Most of the romantic relationships single mothers experience never evolve into a situation where their male partner fully considers himself, or is viewed by others, as a stepfather. While some conditions may assist men, women, and children alike to perceive that something akin to stepfatherhood is being practiced, there are no definitive markers that designate a man as a stepfather.[138] Their absence may result from concerns about not making his partner and her child ineligible for public assistance.

Men who cohabit with or marry a single mother may be more likely to be perceived and perceive themselves as stepfathers than men who physically live apart from their partner. Unfortunately, the cohabitation criteria is a crude indicator because men's "permanent" presence in the household may be part of a dynamic process that changes from time to time.[139] Men may move in and out of a household in response to the ebbs and flows of their romantic relationship with their partner. They may also avoid coresidency so that women and their children will not be denied public assistance. Moreover, a man may spend a great deal of time around his partner's children, and care for them in a fatherlike manner, yet never formally live with them. Being married to a woman does not guarantee that a man is going to think of himself as a stepfather to her children, or that his "stepchildren" will perceive him in this fashion either.[140] The stepfather experience is further complicated by the diverse subcultural norms that emerge from specific sociocultural contexts, such as impoverished African American neighborhoods located in the inner city.

Because the stepfather concept is not easily defined and is no longer strictly tied to the formality of marriage, it is difficult to determine how the dissolution of a romantic relationship affects men in terms of their involvement with their former partner's children. At the one extreme, the dissolution of a romantic relationship can jeopardize an established stepfatherhood arrangement and consequently be detrimental for the stepfather and children. Former stepfathers must often face the grim reality that they will need to sever their attachment to their stepfather identity. Although many men are able to walk away from this situation without being traumatized, some men are emotionally distraught about being alienated from their stepchildren.

Despite many stepfathers' significant commitment to aspects of social fatherhood, stepfathers tend to have no legal recourse to demand visitation rights if their relationship with the children's mother dissolves. On the other hand, biological fathers, irrespective of how uninvolved they may have been with their children, can generally gain some visitation privileges, contrary to what happens with even the most devoted former stepfathers. A few exceptions to this pattern exist where courts have awarded paternity rights to men who had no biological connection to two small children.[141] These decisions may portend a more flexible legal approach toward defining the stepfather-child relationship.

From a pragmatic standpoint, questions about how men's procreative consciousness and sense of procreative responsibility are affected by either biological ties or their social experiences with their children may be largely irrelevant in instances where paternal behavior is unaffected. If fathers' level and type of behavioral commitment to their children is unaffected by whether or not they are genetically related to them, any potential differences in how men experience other aspects of the procreative realm are significant only from a theoretical perspective. An important question remains: Do children experience and treat their father differently if they are aware that they are not biologically related to him? While anecdotal evidence reveals that children are sometimes quite close with adoptive fathers and stepfathers, this does not negate the possibility that children may at times emphasize the presence or absence of a biological connection. Indeed, some adopted children devote a considerable amount of time and energy to locating their birth parents.[142]

Future Trends

Increasing numbers of men are likely to be affected by the recent trend toward greater variability in how fathers become biological and/or social fathers. This trend—with its ethical, legal, and social implications—will represent a distinctive feature of the procreative realm for years to come.

Obviously, most men will continue to become genetic and social fathers by impregnating their sexual partner who later gives birth to their child. Compared to their grandfathers, contemporary prospective fathers will also continue to have more opportunities to be involved in aspects of the pregnancy process leading up to their formal acknowledgement of paternity.

In recent years, some of the alternative pathways to paternity and social fatherhood, other than through sexual intercourse with one's partner, are becoming more commonplace due to the development and acceptance of ARTs, biosocial innovations, and stepfathering. As a result, more and more men will assume paternal responsibilities as a result of their use of one of the assisted reproductive methods or their involvement with adoption or stepfathering. Increasing numbers of men are also likely to become genetic fathers by donating sperm.

While financially comfortable middle-class men are likely to remain the principle users of IVF technology (sometimes in combination with surrogacy), increasing numbers of middle-class and less-affluent men may experiment with the relatively less-expensive AI procedure without surrogacy.[143] In some countries, such as the Netherlands, access to expensive reproductive technologies may be greater than in countries like the United States because individuals are eligible for a limited number of IVF treatments that are reimbursed by the state or private insurance companies.[144] In the United States, Massachusetts provides an excellent example of how greater insurance coverage is likely to increase the number of men who become fathers using asexual reproductive techniques. Insurers in Massachusetts have been required by law since 1990 to pay for fertility treatments. Consequently, activity at the Boston IVF clinic at Beth Israel Hospital is much higher than at any other clinic in the country. Three-quarters of the IVF patients are covered by insurance and 1,288 egg retrievals were performed at this clinic in 1992, 320 more than the next most active clinic in the country.[145]

In some instances, reproductive innovations will provide men with their only opportunity to experience biological paternity or their only chance to be a genetic father with a specific partner serving as the social mother. These innovations may serve many men quite well in the long run, but the use of these innovations may create difficulties as well. Many men will struggle with the expectations some fertility clinics place on their involvement. For many men, the personal anxiety they experience by attempting to use modern technologies to conceive a child may match the uneasiness they feel because they are part of a couple that is unable to reproduce a child through natural means.

When any of the reproductive technologies are used successfully, regardless of which of the eight permutations of fertility circumstances are present, they provide male participants with a chance to experience their social roles as fathers. As more men use alternative forms of reproduction, especially those that depart most radically from the natural reproductive process, the need for researchers to understand men's relationship to this aspect of the procreative realm will grow accordingly.

Several interrelated research questions come to mind when contemplating how men experience one of the eight specific forms of asexual assisted reproduction:[146] When are men most likely to feel financially and emotionally obligated to "their" children who are conceived using reproductive technologies? How are fathers' relationships with their children and partners affected by whether reproduction occurs through sexual intercourse or one of the artificial methods? Are there particular combinations of circumstances for asexual assisted reproduction that uniquely affect men's prenatal and postnatal perceptions and feelings about aspects of the procreative realm? What factors affect men's perceptions of their asexually conceived child and their own paternal roles when their relationship with the child's mother dissolves? Are nonresident fathers of ART children, especially those using donor sperm, even more detached from their children on average than nonresident fathers whose children were conceived naturally? Do men with a genetic tie to their children, irrespective of their partner's genetic relationship to their children, experience their paternal identity differently than men without such a tie?[147]

In addition to analyzing men and reproductive technologies at the micro-, or personal level, it is useful to think about some of the macrolevel implications of ART. Technologies associated with AI and IVF can affect how fatherhood is culturally constructed to some degree. If technologies using donor sperm were to receive even wider public acceptance, they could heighten the significance of the social dimensions to fatherhood and thereby expand the definition of fatherhood. These innovations could, therefore, indirectly influence aspects of fathers' procreative consciousness and sense of responsibility, as well as provide them with opportunities for experiencing their relationship to the procreative realm in novel ways. How fathers are influenced by these technologies will be based in part on some combination of individuals' perceptions (these may vary over the course of the pregnancy and the child's life), interpersonal dynamics, and the specific fertility circumstances associated with the application of the respective technology.

The indirect route that many fathers take in establishing their commitment to a paternal identity—linking it to their involvement with a romantic partner—represents another key issue related to men's paternity and social fatherhood experiences.[148] This issue is relevant to all men who are in a position to develop an identity as a social father. Hence, some men who use assisted reproductive techniques to become social fathers, not unlike fathers who reproduce children through natural means, may experience their paternal identity through their association with their partner and her pregnancy experiences. Likewise, men who adopt or become informal stepfathers are likely to confront this issue. To what extent do men's views about their paternal identity stem from their negotiated interactions with their partner rather than their own more general orientation toward procreation? Put differently, under what circumstances do men construct their sense of their procreative self in concert with their partner's expectations for them, rather than developing an identity that is generated by their own personal feelings about children or their feelings about a particular child? Questions about how, when, and why men rely on others to help them construct their paternal identity warrant careful study.

Research with men who become social fathers by using any of the nontraditional paths (e.g., ART, adoption, stepfatherhood), though fraught with methodological difficulties in some cases, will enable researchers to assess how men define fatherhood and experience unique aspects of the procreative realm. In particular, scholars will be able to examine the relationship between men's perceptions of biological paternity, social fatherhood, and their expression of their social roles as fathers. Though significant in their own right, these issues will take on greater importance if they are found to be related to children's well-being.

7

The Future of
Procreative Men

It should now be clear, having reviewed the intriguing gamut of experiences available to men as procreative beings, that men's lives in the procreative realm are profoundly affected by the social dimensions of gender and, perhaps to a lesser extent, their sexuality and gender-based reproductive physiology. That men's procreative lives will continue to be transformed by social initiatives and technological innovations should also be apparent, though the precise direction for some of these changes is not.

The politics of procreation and fatherhood will play a significant role in shaping the prospects for social change, as well as the research agendas relevant to it. As we look toward the future, it is helpful, then, to consider men's procreative lives within the larger sociopolitical context. This can be achieved by broadening the previous discussions about how ideologies, technological innovations, and social initiatives are likely to affect men as procreative beings, including their roles as fathers. Highlighting the politics of fatherhood is useful in this context because debates about fatherhood issues will influence how the general public thinks about men as procreative beings in ways distinct from their fathering roles with children.

Our intellectual journey has laid the groundwork for us to explore possible directions for future policymaking and program development aimed at improving men's experiences in the procreative realm, and indirectly benefiting women and children in many instances. Moreover, we can now identify some of the key avenues for future theory development and research that can inform debates about social initiatives targeted at men's experiences in the procreative realm.

Politics, Theory, and Procreation

A combination of unplanned social processes and planned initiatives, each influenced by the progressive and conservative ideologies I referred to in chapter 5, will affect the types of options men will face in the procreative realm in the future. These diverse ideological messages will be propagated by self-proclaimed feminists, the Christian Right and other religiously based organizations, as well as men's and fathers' rights groups. Proponents of these positions have a vested interest in altering men's experiences in the procreative realm. Men's procreative lives will also continue to be influenced by vestiges of the more pervasive patriarchal ideology.

Men's personal convictions about gender, family, and life in general will directly affect the way they think and feel about particular procreative issues. Consequently, the decisions men make in the procreative realm are often directly tied to their values and beliefs about a wider range of issues.

Ideologies will also shape the larger cultural, legal, and social context related to the procreative realm. Viewed from this perspective, ideologies can indirectly affect men's lives by determining many of the inducements and constraints men face in their procreative roles. This is significant because men may disregard their personal beliefs, or be unable to pursue them as they would like, if the larger social context does not accommodate them. For example, to the extent that liberal feminism played a role in revamping the legal system so that women once again were granted the legal right to seek abortions on their own, it has indirectly affected prospective fathers who prefer to bring a pregnancy to term.

The sociopolitical landscape surrounding men's procreative lives is distinguished by diverse and controversial ideologies associated with sexuality, reproduction, and parenting issues. Unfortunately, it is quite difficult to present a simple and tidy analysis of how these ideologies relate to men as procreative beings because of men's wide-ranging experiences. I have commented on men as contraceptive decision makers, men who assist their pregnant partners through the pregnancy process, men who go through an abortion procedure with their partners, sperm donors, male participants in clinical procedures designed to produce human life through artificial means, and fathers caring for their children. Admittedly, my inclusive approach complicates the process of showing how the various ideologies are related to men's changing lives in the procreative realm as well as the public debates about these changes. This type of approach is preferred, though, if we wish to fully appreciate men's varied and interrelated experiences.

For us to understand the hotly contested issues, as well as the common themes that define these ongoing debates, it is useful to place the current state of affairs within a larger historical context. Many of the political debates associated with men's lives as procreative beings can be viewed against a backdrop that accentuates notable twentieth-century social developments. Some of these developments have advanced women's reproductive and economic autonomy, others have fostered a more general cultural ethos of individualism among men and women alike. These developments are relevant to the conservative and progressive ideologies I mentioned earlier.

The stage for today's heated debates about men and procreative issues has been fashioned from the sweat of feminists who have struggled to give women control over their reproductive lives and, in turn, greater independence from men. Margaret Sanger and Mary Ware Dennett, two of the original feminist pioneers of the family planning movement that gained momentum in the early 1900s, sought to provide women with the knowledge and contraceptive devices necessary for them to avoid unplanned pregnancies.[1] Many of the other major spokespersons and foot soldiers for this movement were also feminists who wanted women to have the option of assuming nontraditional roles in society. The early feminists thus saw the concept of family planning, and the contraceptives that made it a reality, as indispensable vehicles for women's liberation. Because they viewed family planning as a critical innovation capable of dramatically enhancing women's lives in the United States and elsewhere, they enthusiastically attempted to educate women about the virtues of family planning. One of the unforeseen consequences of feminists' efforts during the first half of the century was that family planning was increasingly seen as a women's issue.

The introduction of the female pill and the I.U.D. in the United States in the 1960s further cemented this process, although the general sentiment about the family planning movement underwent significant revision. Previous feminist support for the family planning concept remained, but it was now tainted due to concerns about men's exploitation of women. Feminists were increasingly concerned with the health-related consequences of the new and medicalized birth control technologies. They expressed grave concern over how women were being exploited by a capitalist and patriarchal system that appeared to be more interested in making a buck than in women's well-being. In short, women were perceived to be guinea pigs in a research process sponsored by the male-dominated medical and scientific communities. Despite these serious concerns, the revised feminist perspective that emerged in the mid 1960s continued to support women's control over their reproduction.

Women's increased responsibility for contraception also meant that men were being pushed further into the background of the reproductive realm, especially in terms of contraceptive decision making. As mentioned previously, the contraceptive revolution of the 1960s fundamentally changed the context for partners' contraceptive decision making. Contraception was more likely to be perceived as part of the woman's domain than was previously the case.

While some feminists have taken issue with the disproportionate amount of funding being used to promote biomedical research on female-oriented birth control, feminists' main focus has been on the abortion controversy.[2] More than any other single issue associated with the family planning movement, the prospects for legal access to abortion symbolizes women's degree of reproductive freedom. With the Supreme Court ruling in the *Roe v. Wade* case in 1973, women's ultimate reproductive right to choose to terminate a pregnancy in consultation with their doctor was formally reestablished and became the law of the land, as it had been in the early 1800s. This decision has influenced the contemporary public discourse about men's participation in the reproductive realm. The parameters and tone of this discourse has also been shaped by other factors, most notably, high rates of divorce, unplanned childbearing, single-female-headed households, and the child support issues associated with these patterns.

Issues such as these are often linked to more general questions concerning the ethos of individualism thought to be so pervasive in our contemporary culture. The growth in this more egoistic philosophy of life, according to some critics, is directly attributable to the family planning and feminist movements. Conservative social commentators[3] have called attention to how these movements have enticed individuals to be more carefree in the way they think about and experience sex, reproduction, and family life. They warn us that traditional values of commitment, sacrifice, and family responsibility are no longer the central themes guiding the lives of growing numbers of teenagers and adults in the United States. They denounce what they see as a trend toward people making amoral sexual, reproductive, and parenting decisions based on their own selfish interests.

David Blankenhorn, one of the more vocal conservative critics, argues that a major consequence of these recent trends is that we now live in, as he entitled his book, a *Fatherless America*: "For when individual freedom becomes the reigning ethos not only of political life but also of sexuality and procreation, the primary result for children is the loss of their fathers."[4] From his perspective, the values and norms that once reinforced the cultural ideal of fatherhood have collapsed leaving the cultural expression of fatherhood fragmented and "decultured." Blankenhorn offers a stinging indictment of current social trends by asserting that

> a decultured paternity signals the growing detachment of fatherhood from the wider norms of masculinity. . . . In our elite discourse, masculinity is widely viewed as a problem to be overcome, frequently by insisting upon "new" fathers willing to disavow any inherited understandings of masculinity. In popular culture, the traditional male fantasy of sex without responsibility—the anti-father world view of the adolescent male, as emblematized in the philosophy of *Playboy* magazine, James Bond movies, and Travis McGee novels—is an increasingly accepted cultural model in our society, less an accusation than an assumption about male behavior. In addition, in what the sociologist Elijah Anderson calls the "street culture" of our inner cities, men's glorification of casual and even predatory sex, completely divorced from responsible fatherhood, now constitutes the core of what Anderson calls the "sex code" of young minority males.
>
> . . . Consequently, as paternity is decultured, the larger meaning of masculinity in our society becomes unclear and divisive. A decultured fatherhood thus provides a doubtful manhood. For without norms of effective paternity to anchor masculinity, the male project itself is increasingly called into question and even disrepute.[5]

Two basic assumptions appear to underlie Blankenhorn's analysis and the observations of other conservative thinkers on this topic. Men are assumed to possess some form of inherited masculine essence, a core that has implications for how men act socially and how a society should respond to them. Depending upon how this type of argument is formulated, the negative or positive aspects to this masculine essence may be emphasized. More specifically, many conservatives focus on what they see as men's biologically innate aggressive tendencies and their propensity to seek multiple sexual liaisons while avoiding making a commitment to their partners and children. Men's primitive predatory instincts are of critical importance from this perspective. Men, when left to express their instinctive nature, are perceived as being uncivilized "animals" who will pursue sex without commitment.

At the same time, from an evolutionary psychological perspective, some theorists stress the unique positive qualities that fathers, because they are men, tend to share with their children. For this reason, sociologist David Popenoe favors gender-differentiated parenting and underscores the important role fathers can assume in their children's lives.[6] He argues that fathers' biologically based and socially reinforced masculine qualities predispose them to treat their children differently than mothers do. Accordingly, children stand to benefit from being around their fathers because fathers are more likely than mothers to encourage their children to be competitive, independent, take risks, initiate their own activities, and demonstrate a willingness to challenge those around them.

Conservative theorists such as Blankenhorn also assume that society will only flourish if it effectively fosters the positive and deters the negative aspects to "inherited" masculinity. In other words, if men are left to their own vices, their actions will do untold harm to the larger society. More specifically, their behavior will endanger the social fabric of society by weakening the bonds between romantic partners as well as the attachments fathers have to their children. According to this logic, our society must provide men with normative standards and socially based incentives to act in a civilized and responsible fashion. Efforts must be made to link cultural images of masculinity with expressions of responsible fatherhood and presumably with responsible activities as sexual beings. Put simply, men need to be taught the value of embracing images of masculinity that elevate the status of being a good family man. While I tend to agree with Blankenhorn's conclusion that our culture needs to be more diligent in providing men with various incentives for being responsible parents and partners, given men's and women's disparate reproductive physiologies and biological predispositions,[7] I do not accept other aspects of his conservative philosophy.

Those who emphasize a social constructionist vision of social life are usually the most forceful critics of this conservative position. They are suspicious of arguments that highlight the notion of biological predispositions or dimensions to masculinity and fatherhood. The thought that social man, embedded in a complex sociohistorical and cultural context, would ultimately be driven by his primitive instincts, appears to be a foreign, if not abhorrent style of thinking for social constructionists. Their reasoning, in a broader context, is often based on feminist critiques of theory and research that address biological sex differences. Many feminists, for instance, are fearful that the growing body of biomedical research that documents distinctions between the "male" and "female" brain will be misused to set the clock back on women's rights.[8] Some feminists simply ignore or dismiss this research because it is seen as being antithetical to the feminist agenda of establishing gender equality.

I, too, am troubled by the thought that policymakers might try to use findings from biomedical research to justify policies that could potentially undermine the gains women have made during this century. However, I am equally convinced that it would be a grave mistake to ignore the emerging and intriguing insights generated by biomedical researchers. Instead of disregarding this research, scholars should figure out how our understanding of social life could be enriched if we were to expand our theoretical frameworks to take this research into account. The bottom line is that research on sex differences should be conducted irrespective of feminist or conservative politics.[9] The integrity of scientific inquiry should be preserved. At least in theory, research on biological differences between men and women need not jeopardize women's economic, social, and political advances.

Conservatives and feminists find themselves talking past one another because many of the debates about these controversial issues too often slip into simplistic, politicized, and unproductive arguments. These arguments juxtapose biological determinism against environmental influences in a predicable and largely uninformed fashion. Fortunately, more moderate voices can be heard in this debate. For example, we are reminded,

> A key tenet of sociobiology or behavioral ecology is that individuals are designed to maximize their fitness *in the context of the options available to them* given the physical, economic, and social ecology. The goal is individual inclusive fitness, not propagation of the family, group, or species. Behavior is only optimal (in terms of fitness) in the context of a specific environment (broadly defined), and thus it is necessary to consider the constraints or facilitators of behavior represented by the social and physical environment. (Italics in the original)[10]

When life is viewed from this type of sociobiological or behavioral ecological perspective, it is useful to focus on how the social organization of a species affects reproductive options and males' degree of certainty about their paternity.

The evolutionary goal referred to as "individual inclusive fitness" represents a theoretical concept drawn from evolutionary biology. This notion, when considered in the context of parents' caregiving efforts toward their children, suggests that evolution selects for behavior that enhances the sum of an individual actor's fitness in combination with a fraction of the recipient's fitness. In other words, evolution greatly values a parent's suitability for a particular environment (i.e., their chances of thriving), while rewarding, although to a lesser extent, behavior that enhances the offspring's fitness or well-being.

In some ways, my discussions of men's procreative consciousness and the way paternity is socially managed are relevant to theories about human males achieving inclusive fitness. I do not explicitly incorporate ideas from either the sociobiological or behavioral ecological models into my conceptual framework. Instead, my approach focuses on the social psychological processes related to men's lives as procreative beings, and it portrays the procreative realm as being socially constructed to a considerable degree. Nonetheless, by emphasizing men's identities as partners, fathers, and masculine men, I indirectly address issues associated with why men may or may not feel compelled to make and sustain commitments to their children, which in turn influence fathers' and children's chances of thriving in their particular environment, depending on the specific nature of fathers' involvement. Since the inclusive fitness concept manifests itself within a dynamic sociocultural context, it is necessary to understand the social psychological and larger social forces associated with men's lives as procreative beings.

It should be clear, then, that even though my framework emphasizes the social aspects to men's lives as procreative beings, I support research efforts that could unravel how a range of biological processes are related to men's perceptions and behavior in the procreative realm and how these factors might in turn be related to social structures and processes. My discussion of how men's reproductive physiology influences their procreative experiences is consistent with this general philosophy. It might even be possible to expand my framework in ways that would take into account issues associated with prenatal brain development and hormonal changes that occur during puberty and adulthood. For example, the fluctuations that men experience in their testosterone levels during puberty and middle years of life may affect their procreative consciousness and how they express their sense of procreative responsibility during these periods of the life course.

Unlike Blankenhorn and Popenoe, I am not convinced that one of the major reasons children need to have fathers in their lives is because children should be exposed to fathers' unique masculine qualities. Instead, I espouse a gender role philosophy that values androgyny for both men and women. This philosophy is much more likely to move us closer to gender equality, and enable us to sustain a society where it exists, than a more rigid gender role approach that tends to breed a gender-based division of labor in and out of the home.[11] In addition, I am not swayed by conservatives' claims that our society will suffer short- and long-term negative consequences if androgyny is promoted. In fact, I believe the reverse is true. We stand to lose a great deal more if traditional gender roles are resurrected.

Having said this, I am still persuaded by recent brain research that finds that males' and females' perceptual abilities and behavioral tendencies are shaped by prenatal and postnatal biological processes. What remains unanswered is to what extent and under what circumstances these sex-based differences affect the way individuals live their lives:

> If the world is a sexist world, it is because the men and women who created it before us behaved in what we would call a sexist way. To reconstruct the world on non-sexist lines takes a positive effort, because it is an unnatural act; it is a social and political precept, but political and social precepts do not organize brains. Only hormones do that.[12]

These biological sex differences should not thwart our efforts to dismantle our patriarchal system. Many conservatives disagree since they favor a gender-based division of labor. On the other hand, many social constructionists and feminists are obliged, generally out of political expediency, to discount the well-documented biological sex differences; I do not. With these thoughts in mind, the key questions would seem to be: Is it feasible, is it wise, and is it ethical to promote gender equality in the face of an escalating body of scientific evidence that points to fundamental, biologically based differences between males and females? On all three accounts the sensible answer is "yes." Differences in brain and hormonal function simply indicate that men are different from women. This fact does not mean that people living in a postindustrial society should strive to reinforce sex-based differences, nor does it mean that social behavior is completely or even primarily controlled by biological factors. We should instead acknowledge these differences, study them, and work toward structuring our society in ways that enlarge men's and women's opportunities. In other words, we need to find ways to adapt to our changing cultural, economic, and social circumstances.[13] It would be blatantly absurd to jeopardize the progress women and men have made in eradicating a patriarchal system by either exaggerating the significance of biological patterns, or overstating the role of culture in shaping gendered aspects of social life. Alice Rossi provides thoughtful commentary in this regard:

> Awareness of *both* social and biological processes adds a synergistic increment to knowledge that can then be used to provide the means for modification and change; it does not imply that we are locked into an unchangeable body or social system. Ignorance of biological processes may doom efforts at social change because we misidentify the targets for change, and hence our means to attain the change we desire. (Italics in the original)[14]

In addition to those ideologies directly relevant to gender and family issues, the general belief system that champions the wonders of medical science is likely to facilitate social changes in selective areas of the procreative realm. The medicalization of reproduction in recent decades has meant that social science researchers have begun to focus on the social and psychological facets of men's and women's perceptions of, and experiences with, new technologies associated with different areas of reproduction. A number of legal issues have also been raised in connection with these technologies.

Some of the sociopolitical critiques of the new assisted reproductive technologies suggest that men's procreative experiences continue to be privileged in the sense that women are medically exploited to accommodate men's needs (e.g., their need to be genetically related to their child). More generally, women's gestational and birthing experiences from a legal perspective are not considered to be as significant as men's genetic contribution to a child. This legal pattern is reinforced by innovations in medical science and ideological developments that make it increasingly likely that life can be maintained outside the womb and babies can be removed through cesarean section.[15] One consequence of these patterns is that men (and women) will continue to receive informal and formal advice to pursue artificial means of becoming parents while receiving subtle messages to pursue adoption only as a last resort. In some situations, men will have an opportunity to be related genetically to their child; in other instances, only their partner will have this chance. In either case, framing infertility as a medical problem with technological solutions will continue to shape many men's experiences in the procreative realm by emphasizing the genetic rather than the social dimensions to parenthood.

In addition to the new asexual reproductive technologies (e.g., IVF) and new ways to apply old technologies (e.g., artificial insemination), DNA fingerprinting techniques, modern prenatal-monitoring devices, and futuristic forms of male hormonal and nonhormonal birth control will also influence the way some men experience aspects of the procreative realm. These developments are likely to have implications for how men express their father, partner, and masculine male identities. The potential and actual use of DNA fingerprinting technology and modern male birth control will raise important ideological issues about how men and women negotiate their respective interests. A relatively small proportion of men and women will find themselves at odds with one another as they attempt to use, or threaten to use, DNA fingerprinting technology to resolve biological paternity disputes. Feminists also argue that the side effects of using modern contraception should be shared equally by men and women in committed relationships.

Social Movements and Social Change

Ideologies and social movements will either foster or constrain men's personal experiences in the procreative realm. While some of the major social movements in this area (e.g., Promise Keepers, fathers' rights) tend to focus on men's involvement with their children, these movements, as well as new ones, may eventually develop more explicit messages about a wider range of issues associated with men as procreative beings. The men's rights, pro-choice, and pro-life movements already address aspects of men's lives as procreative beings prior to men being legal or social fathers. I defer my discussion of the latter two movements to a subsequent section devoted to ongoing and future social initiatives.

Men and Religious Social Movements

The religiously based social movement, the Promise Keepers, has gained national acclaim during the 1990s for its involvement in mobilizing men. The Promise Keepers is a Christian-based social movement founded in 1990 by the former University of Colorado football coach, Bill McCartney.[16] It promotes men's commitment to being responsible fathers, husbands, and friends to other men. This movement also promotes racial reconciliation and challenges homosexuality.[17]

The basis for this movement has grown from a collection of 72 men who participated in a weekly prayer and fellowship group to a well-financed, rapidly expanding organization that had a $120 million budget, a staff of 500, and thirty-eight regional offices in 1996.[18] The Promise Keepers sponsored thirteen events attracting more than 700,000 men in 1995 and fielded twenty-two events drawing more than a million men in 1996. This social movement's strength is evidenced by the upcoming rally, "Stand in the Gap," to be held in Washington, D.C., in the autumn of 1997. This movement is projected to involve over a million Christian men. One of the stadium events of 1996 that may ultimately have the greatest impact was a gathering of 43,000 pastors in Atlanta's Georgia Dome in February. This is thought to be the largest gathering of religious leaders ever held in the United States. In addition to these stadium events, the Promise Keepers publishes its own glossy covered magazine, *New Man: For Men of Integrity*, and the organization began a Saturday morning, hour-long radio show broadcast on 100 stations in May 1996. There can be little doubt, then, that this social movement has gathered a tremendous amount of momentum while establishing a solid and well-financed organizational base.

Men who participate in these evangelical-like rallies are challenged to make a personal pledge to uphold seven specific commitments over a twenty-five-year period. The fourth commitment, which is particularly relevant to my discussion, has received the most media attention and political critique. It requests that men make a conscientious effort "to build 'strong marriages and families through love, protection, and biblical values.'"[19] This commitment is one of the more dominant themes at the mass gatherings. Although Promise Keepers' speakers address a variety of topics, including God's holiness and racial reconciliation, there is an underlying tone to most of the messages that assumes that the audience is predominately married fathers. According to one survey, about 90 percent of the Promise Keepers attending rallies in 1994 were married.[20]

While many observers praise the Promise Keepers' motives as well as the role it has played in fostering men's positive involvement with their families,[21] some feminists are alarmed by what they perceive to be its patriarchal philosophy and traditional agenda for marital relations. At the very least, these feminists see the Promise Keepers' message as "patriarchy-lite."[22] These feminists are adverse to promoting a traditional family form where husbands are encouraged, based on biblical teachings, to be the leaders and heads of households. Feminists are alarmed by statements such as those made by movement spokespersons Tony Evans and Bill Bright. On giving advice to men about how they should reclaim their manhood, Evans writes in the *Seven Promises of a Promise Keeper*, the founding text of the Promise Keepers movement,

> I can hear you saying, "I want to be a spiritually pure man. Where do I start?" The first thing you do is sit down with your wife and say something like this: "Honey, I've made a terrible mistake. I've given you my role. I gave up leading this family, and I forced you to take my place. Now I must reclaim that role." Don't misunderstand what I'm saying here. I'm not suggesting that you *ask* for your role back, I'm urging you to *take it back*. (Italics in the original)[23]

Similarly, Bright, the head of the Campus Crusade of Christ, told the crowd at the Syracuse rally that wives should be treated with love and respect and included in decision making but the man is "the head of the household and women are responders."[24]

Promise Keepers' president, Randy Phillips, responds to feminist criticism by arguing that the male leadership role in the family is not the same as male chauvinism. Instead, he retorts,

> It comes down to whether you understand what it is to be a spiritual leader, which we define in the person of Jesus Christ. . . . What did Jesus do to respond to the needs of others? He gave his life for others. So, from a biblical perspective, a spiritual leader is not one who lords authority over others; spiritual leadership is the absolute commitment to serve and to honor. It means involving yourself in the life of your wife, hearing her needs and responding to those needs, just like Jesus responded to our needs. . . . There is responsibility in providing spiritual initiative and there is authority in carrying out those responsibilities, but it is expressed through a servant's heart.[25]

Irrespective of how the Promise Keepers' mission is perceived, this movement clearly attempts to promote some form of responsibility among fathers. Their willingness to do so is noteworthy and should give self-proclaimed male liberals good cause to consider why they, collectively as men or at least in collaboration with women, have not done more to promote this cause.[26]

Despite the Promise Keepers' efforts to promote its vision of "responsible fatherhood," it has been far less vocal about men's responsibilities as they relate to prenatal issues. However, this movement does stress the moral righteous of abstaining from premarital sex and is firmly aligned with the pro-life movement. The Promise Keepers have received strong public support from such fundamentalist groups as the Campus Crusade for Christ, Christian Coalition, Christian Men's Network, and the Focus on the Family.[27] Bill McCartney has also given pro-life speeches to Randall Terry's anti-abortion group, Operation Rescue. The Promise Keepers' strong support for school-based abstinence messages for unmarried teenagers precludes it from encouraging unmarried men to demonstrate contraceptive responsibility directly. At the same time, though, abstinence messages can be considered pleas for young men to engage in responsible birth control.[28] To my knowledge, the Promise Keepers has not expressed a position on married men's role in contraceptive decision making or their participation in using assisted reproductive technologies.

The Promise Keepers' basic philosophy encourages men to be beneficent household leaders who devote themselves wholeheartedly to taking care of their partner and child in a manner consistent with biblical teachings. However, the bottom line is that when major issues are contested, men's leadership role in the household translates into their views being privileged. Furthermore, notwithstanding Phillip's point that men should listen to and respond to women's needs, his argument has a conditional clause when applied to pregnant women. Phillip's position is predicated on pregnant women making pro-life decisions. Presumably, the Promise Keepers would support men's "right" to prevent their partners from having abortions.

In the future, it will be fascinating to follow the Promise Keepers to see whether this organization addresses men's procreative roles other than those dealing with paternal behavior. With time, the Promise Keepers may begin to address a wider range of issues affecting men as procreative beings.

The Nation of Islam represents another highly visible and influential religiously based organization that is affecting how large numbers of men are thinking about procreative issues. For example, one of the important messages conveyed at the Million Man March, which was held in Washington, D.C., in 1995 and organized by Louis Farrakahn, leader of one of the major factions of the Nation of Islam, was that African American fathers needed to be a more positive force in their children's lives. The Nation of Islam has emphasized this point in other contexts as well. At an event called *For Men Only* held at Madison Square Garden in New

York City earlier in the year, Farrakahn had lectured 20,000 African American men about their responsibilities to their families.[29] Like the Promise Keepers, the Nation of Islam has focused little explicit attention on men's roles in other aspects of the procreative realm to date, although Farrakahn has forcefully voiced his disapproval of premarital sex. While sociologists would categorize Farrakahn's organization as a religious organization rather than a social movement per se, its impact on many African American men may be very similar to how the Promise Keepers influences its followers.

Men's Rights and Fathers' Rights Groups

Two other highly visible social movements that address issues related to men's lives as procreative beings are the men's rights and fathers' rights movements. These movements aggressively drive home the message that men should have procreative and parental rights that are, for the most part, comparable to the rights of women.

As noted earlier, some men's rights groups (e.g., the National Center for Men) have tried to institute legal safeguards to protect men from being forced to accept formal fatherhood roles against their will. The ideological views that guide their efforts are consistent with the cultural ethos of individualism. Moreover, their basic ideology is compatible, in some ways, with a school of feminism that rejects the victimization philosophy and supports a theme of individual accountability.[30] It therefore seems misleading, and simplistic, to label men's rights groups as "male backlash groups," categorically opposed to women's reproductive rights. The activities of men's rights groups in other areas may indeed justify this label, but these groups by and large do not wish to control women's reproductive options and should not be confused with more conservative efforts to restrict women's access to abortion. Men's rights groups are interested, instead, in changing laws that require unmarried men who impregnate women to assume fatherhood responsibilities irrespective of their desires. Unmarried men's willingness to have intercourse, they argue, should not be treated as their formal commitment to become fathers. In addition, these groups oppose a conservative patriarchal philosophy that expects unmarried men, as a matter of principle, to marry their pregnant partner and become responsible fathers to their children conceived out of wedlock.

A related, though more narrowly defined movement consisting of fathers' rights organizations emerged from the 1970s' men's liberation movement. These groups represent an organized response to the perceived injustices of child custody awards.[31] The fathers' rights movement flourished to the point where there were over 200 local organizations around the country by the end of the 1980s. These organizations have struggled to bring about change by combining the equal rights theme from feminism with the notion of nurturing fatherhood. Thus, this movement is not only a reform movement, but part therapy group. The movement's main objectives have been to eliminate the assumption that mothers are the more capable parent while ensuring that fathers are given the opportunity to maintain close contact with their children.[32]

Assessing the activities and rhetoric of the fathers' rights movement is a complex task, largely because this movement taps into highly charged emotional issues. Two distinct positions have emerged out of the fierce debate over the activities of fathers' rights groups. Since historian Robert Griswold has competently summarized the key issues elsewhere, and the issues in question deal with only one aspect of men's lives as procreative beings, only a brief comment is warranted. My intent is not to resolve the ongoing and complex debates about child custody here, but merely to highlight the role the fathers' rights movement plays in shaping the public discourse about men as procreative beings and fathers.

One side of the debate focuses on the emotional crises many fathers experience because of the formal and informal impediments they must deal with as they struggle to maintain close relationships with their children after the dissolution of a romantic relationship—often marriage:

> Their stories reverberate with tales of vindictive ex-wives, uncooperative, obstructionist social workers, and inattentive, insensitive judges. They tell, too, of children turned against them by maniacal former spouses, of specious sexual abuse allegations that destroyed peace of mind, of their dawning sense that they would be forever alienated from their children.[33]

For many men, the pain is real and long lasting. Despite the obvious anguish some fathers feel in this area, harsh critics of the fathers' rights movement present the other side of the debate in compelling fashion. Two of the more severe critics, Carl Bertoia and Janice Drakich, have few kind words to say about participants in the Canadian fathers' rights group they studied:

> Although fathers' rightists portray themselves as caring, loving fathers who have been denied their rights to equal custody and access to their children,

they are more concerned about the equality of their legal status than their equality in everyday parenting. [Fathers' rightists'] . . . self-disclosures point to the essentially economic and hegemonic underpinnings of their disclosure. Although equality is the organizing principle of their rhetoric, a closer examination exposes a notion of equality that conforms to the gendered familial division of labor. The fathers' rightists are not lobbying for joint, equal responsibility and care of children after divorce; they want equal access to their children, to information, and to decision-making. The individual, self-disclosed accounts reported here unveil a masculinist construction of equality that obfuscates the gendered differences and experiences of mothers and fathers. Fathers' rightists have co-opted the language of equality but not the spirit of equality. The fathers' own words, reported here, tell us that they do not want sole responsibility for children, nor do they want an equal division of child care and responsibility. What they want, they tell us, is to have equal status as legal parents, which would give them equal access opportunities to their children and to information. The rhetoric of fathers' rights gives the illusion of equality, but, in essence, the demands are to continue the practice of inequality in postdivorce parenting but now with legal sanction.[34]

As is often the case in debates such as these, there is an element of truth associated with each position. What must not be forgotten is that all of the processes being debated have occurred within a preexisting, gendered society. It may therefore make sense for feminists such as Nancy Polikoff to criticize the sex-neutral standard for resolving child custody disputes:

> But the only appropriate purpose of a sex-neutral standard is to require evaluation of who is providing primary nurturance without automatically assuming it to be the mother; its purpose should not be to eliminate the importance of nurturance from the custody determination and equate the provision of financial support with the provision of psychological and physical needs.[35]

Likewise, it's reasonable to criticize judges who devalue mothers' caregiving activities while granting custody to fathers, simply or primarily because they have demonstrated economic superiority. Those who share this criticism recognize the importance of caregiving in children's lives and wish to reward parents who perform these everyday parenting roles. Fair enough.

Fathers' rightists are correct in pointing out, though, that this scenario often evolves because mothers and fathers make certain types of decisions in the context of their relationship about parenting and work. Partners make these decisions, in part, because they are confronted with the realities of a gendered occupational system and because they assume that they will remain together indefinitely. For a society to encourage fathers to be responsible providers for their children while they are living together and, then, to devalue their contribution to the family system when child custody decisions are being made seems, at best, unfair. No doubt many members of the fathers' rights movement try to use child custody procedures to retain a sense of control over the lives of others without wanting to devote a sufficient amount of time and energy to their children's everyday needs, but not all fathers associated with this social movement should be judged by this stereotype. In addition, most nonresident fathers are not even involved in this movement, and many have legitimate complaints about being denied access to their children.[36]

The Marketplace of Ideologies

Despite their stark differences, liberal feminist, religiously based, and fathers' rights ideologies are similar in principle because each, in varying degree, supports efforts to promote what they perceive to be men's greater positive involvement in family life, most notably their children's lives. Concerns about gender issues and family responsibilities are at the heart of these value-laden positions. However, there should be no mistake that the nature of these social movements' goals, the manner in which they attempt to accomplish them, and the primary reason for pursuing such goals tend to be quite different.

Although the ideologies in question share the common objective of encouraging fathers' positive involvement in family life, those who espouse a given set of beliefs may or may not explicitly support men playing an active role in areas of the procreative realm other than paternal conduct (e.g., contraception, abortion, activities associated with assisted reproduction). Many feminists want to see men take a more active role in contraception, though they are discouraged by the current mix of available, reliable contraceptives. As noted earlier, many feminists favor more biomedical research on modern male methods so that couples eventually will have a wider range of highly effective methods from which to choose. Can individuals with feminist values make a significant difference in altering the funding process for contraceptive research? If feminist women and profeminist men are able to move into key decision-making positions in the organizations associated with the funding and scientific development of contraceptives, the prospects for developing modern male methods would probably improve. Ultimately though, scientific and business concerns are likely to dictate the research and development process for bringing new contraceptives to the marketplace.

Many feminists' orientation toward abortion is likely to be quite different than it is for contraception. While they may encourage men to make themselves available to their partners for emotional and financial support if this is what their partners want, they typically oppose men being able to interfere with their partners' decision to abort a pregnancy. From this view, men's involvement in resolving a pregnancy should be by invitation only. Depending upon the circumstances, if pregnancies are brought to term and mothers retain custody of their children, men might be expected to provide financial and perhaps emotional support. Recall, though, that some feminists disagree about whether men should be held financially accountable for children conceived out of wedlock, especially when men make it known very early on that they have no interest in becoming a father at this point in their life.

Unlike feminists, members of the Christian Right tend to favor men's active involvement in the abortion process so long as they attempt to prevent the abortion. Their support of men's more active role in this area is therefore conditional on men's pro-life motives. Meanwhile, they have little to say about contraceptive issues. Single men should not be having sex; thus, questions about men's contraceptive use are not addressed because they are inappropriate. The more salient issue is birth control in the form of abstinence. Men, as well as women, should take it upon themselves to refrain from sex outside of marriage.

Advocates for men's rights and fathers' rights groups tend to hold views on selective issues that fall somewhere between those of feminists and Christian Right activists. Contraception, for example, has not been a major issue for men's rights groups thus far, yet they want to insure that men avoid becoming legal fathers against their will. Fathers' rights groups have been, and are likely to remain, much more interested in issues associated with fathers' involvement with their children than they are with contraception.

Although it is difficult to predict in many instances how these ideologies will affect men's birth control and abortion experiences, the leading versions of liberal feminist thought will probably be the most consequential because of their role in maintaining women's autonomy over abortion decisions. The other voice of the gender debate, as represented by men's and fathers' rights groups, may affect some legal reforms in the areas of child custody, visitation, and child support involving nonresident fathers. However, these groups are unlikely to produce significant institutional changes in the area of birth control or abortion anytime in the near future.

Social Initiatives

When assessing social initiatives relevant to men's involvement in the procreative realm, it is helpful to consider how the sociocultural context shapes the nature of their development as well as their viability. Of particular importance, as I have alluded to repeatedly throughout this book, is the notion that men's experiences within the procreative realm are fundamentally shaped by gender role norms and gender-based social patterns.

Gender-based social patterns are reflected in women's greater likelihood of making regular visits to physicians and other health care professionals. Men's greater reluctance to seek medical attention is consistent with traditional masculine norms that underscore the virtues of independence and stoicism. So, too, the mix of contraceptive methods is partly responsible for this pattern because women are, for practical purposes, more likely to be in the position of seeking a consultation and prescription for birth control. As a result, the family planning clinic system, which originated in 1965 and was founded primarily to address women's reproductive health needs, continues to service a predominately female clientele.

Institutional Responses

The obvious consequence of this pattern is that there are fewer institutional resources directed at men's sexual and reproductive concerns than there are for women.[37] In fact, a 1995 Urban Institute survey of public family planning clinics recently found that in only 13 percent of these clinics do males represent more than 10 percent of the clientele.[38] Overall, men represent merely 6 percent of all clientele in these clinics and represent an even smaller fraction of the clients who receive assistance from family planning services subsidized by the federal government. Despite males' low participation rates, 31 percent of the clinic managers who responded to the Urban Institute survey indicated that the number of men using their services had increased during the last five years.

In recent years, clinics appear to be more motivated to reach out to male clientele because of greater public awareness of STDs and HIV. These clinics are interested in lowering the incidence of STDs among female patients, and they are trying to provide primary health care services to low income men who have few health care alternatives.[39]

At least four major barriers appear to hinder family planning clinics' ability to service more men. First, the most significant of these impediments is the commonly held perception that family planning clinics are organizations run by and for women. This perception is largely due to the fact that the clientele and staff are generally female. Some clinics have tried to address this image issue by recruiting more male staff and altering the appearance of their waiting rooms (e.g., more male-oriented magazines and pictures). Unfortunately, it is not always easy to find men willing to work in this type of setting. A second condition involves men's unfamiliarity with the health care system. Clinic managers have had little success in altering men's views or practices in this regard. While the recent success of men's health magazines suggests that more men are demonstrating an interest in their physical well-being, this does not necessarily mean that more men will participate in the health care system. The third factor involves the lack of sufficient funding. Securing adequate funding is quite difficult and the funding that is obtained is seldom continuous. Funding for outreach programs is particularly important because of men's reluctance to frequent family planning clinics. The fourth barrier results from the fact that male clients are as likely as female patients to be from low-income backgrounds, but men are less likely than women to be eligible for Medicaid because the program is associated with AFDC. Males from lower-class backgrounds are thus separated from many of the resources that might make a difference in the way they think about and experience their procreative consciousness and sense of responsibility.[40]

Revamping the family planning clinic system so that it will attract and accommodate significantly more male patients is likely to be a difficult and protracted process. To the extent that growing numbers of heterosexual men in our society become HIV infected and the public grows more at ease with promoting condom use, males may avail themselves more regularly to the expanding services offered by many family planning clinics.

One way in which men's participation in family planning clinics is likely to be affected appreciably is if modern forms of male contraception that require a health care provider's intervention are marketed. However, the prospects for an immediate revolution in male contraception are not good, even though scientists are cautiously optimistic that modern methods of male birth control will be developed eventually. When this occurs, many men, especially those in committed relationships, are likely to undergo a transformation in their procreative consciousness and sense of procreative responsibility. But until this next contraceptive revolution occurs, most men are likely to remain alienated and indifferent toward institutional supports for their reproductive health unless profound changes occur.

If men do become more involved in family planning clinics, some will benefit by developing a keener sense of their body and reproductive physiology. Some may even feel a greater sense of control if they know they are making a concerted effort to assume responsibility for protecting themselves from initiating an unplanned pregnancy or acquiring a STD. These types of opportunities could provide men with personal growth experiences, as well as access to the types of relevance structures described in chapter 1. These relevance structures would enable men to sharpen their awareness of themselves as procreative beings.

Schools represent another important vehicle for disseminating information about reproductive health and paternity issues to young men. In fact, a handful of school-based clinics already service male students, and it is possible that additional school-based clinics will work more extensively with young men. Unfortunately, it's unlikely that a dramatic change in this regard will occur in the foreseeable future, even though school-based efforts to institutionalize young men's involvement in the health care system are clearly warranted.[41] This is especially the case with respect to sexual and reproductive health issues. Providing young men with convenient, comfortable, and private opportunities to interact with a school-based health care provider might encourage them to be more open to visiting family planning clinics later on in life.

The distribution of condoms in schools could also encourage young men to be more aware of procreative responsibility issues, especially those related to contraceptive use. Condom distribution programs, though quite controversial, may become more commonplace in the future.[42] School districts interested in developing these types of programs received good news when the U.S. Supreme Court in January 1996 decided not to review or comment on the Massachusetts' Supreme Judicial Court case of *Curtis v. School Committee of Falmouth.* The Massachusetts court had earlier upheld the Falmouth School District's condom availability program, which provides students in grades 7 to 12 access to condoms upon request. While the long-term consequences of condom distribution programs have not yet been assessed, institutionalized efforts to reduce the negative images some people associate with using condoms may influence the way many young men experience their procreative consciousness and sense of responsibility. Such efforts will continue to meet with stiff resistance from conservatives who believe that schools should not be promoting sex.

Today, while many young men are exposed to biologically based information about the male reproductive system, it often occurs in narrowly defined sex education courses.[43] Young men seldom learn about how gender and family-related issues are associated with sexuality and procreation. In addition, their knowledge about abortion issues is quite limited and in many cases inaccurate.[44]

Classroom instruction needs to deal more explicitly with the range of issues involving young men's sexuality, procreative consciousness, and procreative sense of responsibility. To the extent that sex education and family life programs can instill in young men a greater appreciation for the responsibilities associated with being sexually active, a father (ideally prior to becoming a father), a romantic partner, and a masculine young man, it is possible that these young men will reduce their risk of impregnating their partners. Young men need to develop a better sense of how their masculine and partner role identities are related to their sexual and procreative feelings. If responsibility is defined broadly, without moral overtones concerning premarital sex, young men may learn that careless sexual behavior and disrespectful treatment of their female partners are unattractive behaviors. This process is likely to be enhanced if young men can be persuaded to redefine masculinity in terms of adulthood status rather than the rejection of femininity and homosexuality, as is currently the case.[45] Campaigns to revise young men's perceptions of masculinity to include notions of adulthood responsibility may, in the process, fundamentally alter the way young men think about and express themselves as procreative beings.

Innovative school programs might even provide young men with supervised opportunities to provide daycare for young children and to learn indirectly about parenting responsibilities.[46] The Germantown Friends School in Philadelphia has already introduced this type of program.[47] Students as early as the fourth grade are taught about human growth and development. In addition to their traditional book learning, fourth graders learn about caregiving through their hands-on experiences teaching kindergarten and first-grade students. These types of experiences during early and late adolescence might influence the way young men experience their procreative consciousness and think about their future procreative responsibilities.

One novel program that can heighten young males' appreciation for their future fatherhood roles was recently introduced statewide in Minnesota. In 1992, school authorities began work on a project to promote the importance of fatherhood to young people. This work culminated with the program "Dads Make a Difference," which is tailored to middle school students enrolled in health and family life courses. The centerpiece of this four-week, four-lesson curriculum revolves around a set of exercises and simulated games that require students to think about fatherhood responsibilities, the consequences of uninvolved fathers, and the ways students can shape their future parental roles. Students are given the opportunity in one game, for example, to see what difference a father can make in a family's financial status, the prospects for children going to school, the care of a baby, and the solving of a personal problem. An eighteen-minute video discussing why fathers are important in children's lives is also a component of this program.[48]

Another example of a school-based program on fatherhood is the Paternity/Parenthood Program (PAPA) in Texas. This curriculum is distributed to every middle school, junior high, and high school in the state and includes teacher instructions, student exercises, and an adaptation to a video, *Think About It*, being used in California schools. The program does not deal with sex education, rather it focuses on the legal rights and financial responsibilities associated with parenthood. The main objective is to show teenagers that parenthood is at least an eighteen-year commitment.[49]

Efforts that capitalize on the mass media's ability to influence young men's views about their sexuality and procreative responsibilities also need to be emphasized, particularly since many young and older men involved in high-risk sexual behaviors are not attending school. Important initiatives along these lines emerged during the past decade. For example, the National Urban League initiated an aggressive advertising campaign ten years ago to promote young men's responsible sexual and parental behavior within the inner city.[50] Likewise, the Greater New York March of Dimes successfully started a public education campaign in 1991 to alter men's expectations about their fatherhood roles. This campaign was expanded to the national level in June 1993. The New York chapter bombarded adolescent and adult men with television ads, radio spots, and subway posters promoting the ways in which they could prepare themselves for fatherhood. This organization also prepared a booklet, *A Guide for Fathers-to-Be*, which outlined specific steps men could take to demonstrate their interest in being responsible fathers, such as accompanying their partner during her prenatal checkup; avoiding harmful substances like cigarettes, alcohol, and drugs while encouraging their partner to do the same; and persuading their partner to eat well. While no formal evaluation of this campaign has been conducted, men's calls to the city's pregnancy hotline increased, more men accompanied their partners to prenatal visits, and thousands of requests were made for the booklet.[51] Similar types of programs should be promoted in other locations and efforts to coordinate these programs with school programs should be pursued.

An exemplary model program that promotes responsible fatherhood to those men in need who cannot be reached through the school system is the rapidly expanding Men's Services Program in Baltimore, Maryland.[52] Participants in this program, which began operating in 1993, are on average about twenty-five years of age, primarily African American, and for the most part biological fathers to their partners' children. The parenting curriculum for this program, *Life After Planting the Seed*, encourages prospective fathers to reflect upon their perceptions of their own father's role in their lives. Detailed practical advice is also shared, and participants are asked to sign a Prenatal Participation Pledge to be an active participant during various facets of the pregnancy process.

Getting larger numbers of young prospective fathers involved in some type of prenatal education intervention is a worthy goal for social service agencies. While one small-scale study of 15- to 18-year-old African American prospective fathers found little evidence that exposure to a particular intervention affected young men's supportive behavior toward their partner and child, continued program development and evaluation research is needed in this area.[53]

For many men, being involved with their partners during the entire pregnancy is not an option because their partners terminate their pregnancies. These men could still feel involved in an aspect of the procreative realm if abortion clinics did a better job of accommodating their participation in the various phases of the abortion process. Unfortunately, there are no data to suggest that abortion clinic practices have significantly changed since the early 1980s.[54] Many men's needs during the abortion ordeal are still not being met. From my vantage point, there is little, if any, evidence indicating that this pattern is likely to change in the near future.

The prospects are also not good that pro-choice men will collectively lobby abortion clinics to expand men's opportunities for involvement. Compared to women, men have been less motivated to identify family planning and reproductive health care as central issues affecting their lives.[55] The women's movement was instrumental in instituting the family planning clinic system initially because its followers had a vested interest in improving the availability of reproductive health care. Similarly, the women's movement helped to establish and preserve institutionalized abortion services. Men, on the other hand, have not aggressively tackled family planning and certain abortion issues[56] aggressively because they have not, as a group, perceived that their rights have been abridged or that they have been deprived of a valuable resource. While men's rights groups have not been very aggressive in these areas, it is possible they will assert themselves more forcefully in the future.

Meanwhile, there is little chance that large numbers of abortion clinics will voluntarily alter the services they offer without being pressured into doing so. Some administrators may modify their clinic's practices because of their personal preferences, but they are likely to be in the minority, especially if they do not perceive that their female clients are demanding these changes. In short, so long as abortion remains legal, most pro-choice men will not feel compelled to pressure abortion clinic administrators into revamping their practices to better accommodate men's needs.

Men's primary objective, to the extent that they actively get involved in the abortion issue, will be to make sure that abortion either remains legal or, on the other side of the debate, is eventually defined as a criminal act. Although some men are currently involved in the pro-choice and pro-life movements, their participation pales in comparison to women's involvement.[57] Whereas most of the current leaders of the pro-choice movement are female, men appear to play a more prominent role in the leadership of the pro-life movement, even though the rank and file membership consists predominately of unemployed women.[58] As of April 1996, 12 percent of the affiliate executive directors, and 27 percent of the affiliate board presidents for the Planned Parenthood Federation of America were men.[59] In contrast, 38 percent of the board of directors for the National Right to Life board were men as of June 1996.[60] Unfortunately, there is a paucity of empirical research on either the male leaders or male activists associated with these two movements.

One consequence of this lack of information is that popular press publications,[61] and those based on newspaper and magazine articles as well as interviews with journalists,[62] have played a significant role in creating public stereotypes of male pro-life activists. Take, for instance, Susan Faludi's description of participants in Randall Terry's Operation Rescue organization. She comments that most were

> men who belonged to the second half of the baby boom, who had not only missed the political engagement of the '60s but had been cheated out of that affluent era's bounty. . . . [They were] hurting from severe economic and social dislocations in their lives—changes that they so often blamed on the rise of independent and professional women. As they lost financial strength at work and private authority at home, they saw women gaining ground in the office, challenging their control of the family at home, and even taking the initiative in the bedroom. As resentment over women's increasing levels of professional progress became mixed with anxiety over the sexual freedoms women had begun to exercise, they developed a rhetoric of puritanical outrage to castigate their opponents.[63]

Because portrayals such as these have found their way into the public consciousness, it is possible that a distorted and poorly documented portrait of the subpopulation of males involved in the pro-life movement has been accepted. One study, based on interviews with thirty-two male pro-life activists, found no support for the popular notion that "prolife direct action represents the retaliatory backlash of young, disenfranchised males" or that activists are "compensating for 'status anxiety,' 'social dislocation' or the like."[64] Most men saw their activism as an expression of their Christianity as well as a desire to belong to a group that would enable them to act on their beliefs. Men tended to use masculine themes associated with bonding in groups and war imagery to describe their activism—they felt as if they were waging battle against a national threat.

While these types of characterizations may depict pro-life men's general approach to the abortion issue, they tell us nothing about whether men's own procreative consciousness is influenced by a pro-life ideology. How do pro-life activists' values and beliefs influence the way they experience their own procreative consciousness? Are these men likely to think about themselves as procreative beings in ways that differ significantly from men who do not share their views?

Turning to the future, more men may play an active role in either the pro-choice or pro-life movements if they perceive that their vital interests or values are being threatened. Although it is possible that men will become more involved in pro-choice activities as the federal and state governments continue to accelerate child support enforcement efforts, it is by no means guaranteed. Abortion activists were predominately male during the 1960s prior to the *Roe v. Wade* decision, when abortion became more accessible.[65] Thus, any significant changes to this decision might intensify pro-choice men's activism. Pro-life men, on the other hand, may increase their involvement in activities that are designed to disrupt clinic operations so long as abortion remains legal. In addition to men's pro-life activism, groups such as Fathers United Against Abortion and Fathers of Aborted Children Together as One suggest that some pro-life men are also attempting to cope with their disdain for abortion by joining all-male support groups. Pro-choice and pro-life activities such as those mentioned above may not directly heighten men's procreative consciousness to any great extent, but some men may personalize their involvement in these movements and, in turn, think more often and intensely about themselves as procreative beings.

Men's views about the legalization of abortion and abortion clinic practices are formed within a larger social context where social norms about sexuality and reproduction influence individual- and institutional-level responses. The decisions people make about how to resolve a pregnancy, as well as abortion clinic rules about men's involvement, originate from within this larger sociocultural context. It appears for now that the majority of the population still defines abortion as a women's issue, so women's needs are emphasized in these matters. But abortion is obviously not simply a women's issue. In many cases, couples and sometimes other family members agonize over the decision whether or not to bring a pregnancy to term. Moreover, there are those who argue that men should have as much say as their partners in how a pregnancy is resolved. Men should, from this perspective, have the veto power to prevent a pregnancy from being terminated. This position is stressed in situations where men are willing to care for their newborn children. Strategies clearly need to be developed to encourage men to feel more connected to their procreative identity, but ultimately these efforts must *not* curtail women's reproductive freedom nor jeopardize children's well-being.

A Contractual Approach to Abortion and Child Support

When it comes to individuals' abortion rights and child support actions, it is exceedingly difficult to establish gender equity. Several complicating factors are at play. The differences in men's and women's reproductive physiology may be the most notable. Nonetheless, in the spirit of attempting to establish gender equity and increase men's interest in reproductive issues, it seems appropriate to seriously ponder the pros and cons of innovative options. Such options might enable *some* adult men and women the chance to negotiate their rights and responsibilities as they pertain to abortion and child support.

One possible first step in this direction would be to institutionalize a more formal approach that enabled partners to identify and negotiate their concerns in this regard. While some features of the National Center for Men's proposal previously described in chapter 5 are appealing because they encourage sexual partners to think about their intentions, it is too simplistic. It does not take into account children's best interests. As an alternative, I offer a brief and preliminary sketch of a hypothetical document that would address children's financial needs and at the same time represent the cornerstone of a more formal and legal approach to *some* men's involvement in the sexual and procreative realms. In suggesting this tentative proposal, I hope to provoke a sober discussion of its key features and the basic ethical issues it addresses.

This document, ideally signed prior to partners having sex, would delineate the negotiated rights and responsibilities of the parties involved. The rationale for this approach is that it would ensure that consenting sexual partners understand how they and their partner would want to resolve an unplanned pregnancy prior to becoming sexually involved with one another. This approach could also prompt some men to be more attentive to the potential consequences of sexual relations. Ideally, more men would voluntarily fulfill their child support obligations if they had signed a contract prior to having sex which stipulated their commitment to support their child financially. Finally, it would help to establish a more equitable balance of power between the subset of partners eligible to pursue this contract, while reinforcing women's autonomy to abort or carry their pregnancy to term.

I leave to other scholars the formidable task of analyzing the numerous legal aspects to this type of formal agreement. My comments are merely suggestive of what such an arrangement might entail and the logic behind it, although I do highlight several of the key concerns raised by contractual arrangements of this sort.[66] The exact terms of such an agreement are likely to vary from one couple to the next, and couples involved in ongoing relationships might need to update their agreement as circumstances dictate. At minimum, the document would deal with two of the key areas related to pregnancy resolution decisions: abortion and child support. Partners' abortion preferences may or may not be compatible, and this would have implications for their willingness to assume responsibility for or to request child support.

The format of what I call the *Pregnancy Resolution/Child Support (PRCS)* contract builds upon one of the four general templates or scenarios illustrated in figure 2. The four versions represent the logical permutations that result from combining partners' basic views about abortion and child support. Dichotomizing individuals' views in this manner, in order to reflect either their clear support or rejection of a position, may oversimplify individuals' preferences in some instances. However, most individuals should be able to state their preferences using this scheme if they are challenged to think about and negotiate these issues. No doubt some individuals will change their minds when faced with an actual preg-

FIGURE 2
Pregnancy Resolution and Child Support Contract

	Version 1	Version 2	Version 3	Version 4
	Abortion Preference			
Man	Yes	Yes	No	No
Woman	No	Yes	Yes	No
	Child Support Commitment			
Man	No	No[*]	Yes[*]	Yes
Woman	Yes	Yes	No	Yes

[*]If woman changes her mind about abortion preference.
The versions of the PRCS contract presented above assumes that the mother (or father) would keep the child so the adoption option is not included.

nancy; stipulations in the document would need to take this into account.

In situations where couples do not use this contract and the woman gets pregnant, partners would still be subject to the prevailing laws regarding abortion and child support. The contract would therefore be used only in special cases because most people would either be ineligible to use it on financial grounds or would not feel comfortable planning their personal matters in this fashion. My proposal clearly does *not* represent a comprehensive solution to the various issues associated with unplanned childbearing and child support. Its overall impact, given the limited number of persons who might avail themselves to it, would actually be rather modest in scope.

The PRCS contract would stipulate partners' preferences for resolving a pregnancy in the event a pregnancy occurred. Four possible combinations of partners' abortion views exist, as illustrated in figure 2. The man might prefer to abort a pregnancy and his partner may disagree (version 1) or agree (version 2) with him. In other instances, the man might prefer to bring a pregnancy to term while his partner disagrees (version 3) or agrees (version 4).

Versions of the document, in addition to having partners explicitly stipulate their preferences for resolving a pregnancy, would also ensure that the respective partners clarify how they planned to provide financially for a child born out of their sexual involvement. Version 1 would enable a man to state his preference to have a pregnancy aborted while his partner could assert her preference to bring the pregnancy to term. This version also indicates that the woman agrees to accept sole financial responsibility for the child if she decides to maintain custody. The father would therefore not be liable for child support. Versions 2 and 3 are similar in that they address the possibility that the woman who initially asserts her desire to abort a pregnancy may change her mind. In version 2, as in version 1, the woman agrees not to hold the father financially responsible for a child she bears despite the father's objections to bringing the pregnancy to term. The situation is reversed in version 3 because the man agrees to provide financially for the child, while indicating his willingness not to hold the mother financially responsible even though she changed her mind about the abortion. The man in this situation has already asserted that he does not want the pregnancy to be aborted. In those scenarios depicted by version 3, the man might opt to pursue legal custody of the child. Finally, version 4 indicates that because both partners reject the idea of having an abortion, they will both be responsible for the financial support of the child if a pregnancy is brought to term. The conditions outlined in version 4 are, in effect, consistent with current legislation. Thus, couples who chose this version would simply be reaffirming their commitment to their current legal obligations as parents.[67]

Numerous issues will need to be resolved prior to making PRCS contracts available to the public, and other concerns will emerge as these documents are scrutinized in the courts. At the outset, partners should be required to have separate legal counsel when they sign these types of contracts to ensure that both partners fully understand the legal and financial implications of their decision. The document will also need to have provisions for the possibility that a woman might not be able to have an abortion because of medical or legal reasons (e.g., pregnancy discovered too late during gestation). Another critical issue that will need to be addressed involves whether married couples should be permitted to use these contracts. It would be judicious, especially in the early stages, to limit these contracts to unmarried couples so as to minimize the disruption to current policies and practices concerning abortion and child support issues.

As a controversial, novel, and formal approach, this type of contract will undoubtedly encounter firm opposition from social policy analysts, the courts, and the public at large. Many social policymakers will object to this approach on the grounds that it is seemingly inconsistent with the state's goal of protecting children's welfare and keeping people from becoming wards of the state. They will argue that children will suffer if this goal is ignored and some biological fathers (or mothers) are given the legal means to relinquish their financial obligations to their children prior to their child's conception (or birth). This objection is deeply rooted in our court system and will be difficult to overcome, especially without a viable alternative financial strategy to care for unplanned children.[68] A well-established body of case law stipulates that parents cannot negotiate away their children's rights to child support.

The legal and ethical reasoning underlying these cases is quite persuasive; consequently, attempts to reduce the asymmetry between men's and women's power in the reproductive realm should be limited in scope. PRCS contracts might be restricted, for instance, to couples in which the female partner (or the male partner if he plans to assume custody of the child) is economically autonomous and the interests of the child can be assured.[69] Such a restriction would probably require legislators to make a fundamental exemption to the Equal Protection clause of the U.S. Constitution. This clause states that individuals should be subjected to laws in the same manner unless doing otherwise is in the public's best interests. Legislators have the power to make this type of exemption, but they would need to demonstrate that it was the least obtrusive way to advance a basic social policy objective. In this situation, the principle objectives would be to further gender equity in decisions involving abortion and child support, encourage larger numbers of sexual partners to recognize explicitly what their rights and responsibilities are in this area prior to conception, reduce or at least simplify civil litigations stemming from an unplanned pregnancy/birth, and improve child support compliance among men who agreed to support their children.

Assuming that policymakers were willing to take this type of bold action sometime in the near future, which unfortunately is highly unlikely, they could establish a threshold income level that women and men would need to earn in order for them to enter into a PRCS contract with their partner. Thus, PRCS contracts could be initiated (or perhaps could only be honored at a later date) if women and men were able to demonstrate that they had access to some predetermined level of income. Stipulations would also need to be made to account for potential changes in a person's financial status over time. For example, what happens in those situations where a woman's financial status falls below some threshold level because she loses her job or elects to discontinue her employment to take care of additional children she subsequently has with another partner(s)? Should biological fathers who negotiated an earlier arrangement that released them from child support responsibilities be held financially accountable at a latter date because of women's involuntary or voluntary unemployment circumstances? These are obviously important and perplexing questions. Progress in establishing clear guidelines and procedures will clearly be a slow and incremental process because there are a variety of complex issues, political considerations, and possible mitigating circumstances to consider.

An additional impediment to the widespread adoption of PRCS contracts includes the prevailing images of romance and sexuality in our society. Critics will caution that only a relatively small percentage of couples will follow through with the pragmatic steps necessary to prepare a PRCS contract. They will argue that because many partners loath talking about their sexual history and contraception prior to initiating a sexual relationship, it is unrealistic to think that people will be willing to express their views about how they would resolve a pregnancy that has not yet occurred, or share their thinking on child support issues. History has shown that individuals are often reluctant to think about the long-term consequences of their sexual and contraceptive behavior.

For all of these reasons, achieving any degree of public acceptance of PRCS contracts is likely to be a lengthy process. Efforts to promote this concept and educate the public will be essential. There is historical precedent, though, that innovative social policies (e.g., welfare policies, civil rights), despite initial negative reactions, may eventually receive some level of public acceptance and be incorporated into the social fabric. The degree of public acceptance, whatever it is, will most likely vary considerably among different types of individuals. Individuals' initial and subsequent acceptance of PRCS contracts will probably vary considerably based on personal and relationship characteristics, including age, social class, religiosity, previous pregnancy scare, abortion, ongoing child support payments, marital status, and partners' level of commitment to one another.

An optimistic view of the long-term consequences of PRCS contracts is that the availability of these contracts could foster a significant shift in how many men (middle-class men in particular) experience aspects of the procreative realm. These contracts, for instance, could heighten some men's procreative consciousness if they spent more time thinking about their procreative abilities and considering if and when they would like to become a father. The process of thinking seriously about specific scenarios prior to them occurring is likely to affect how men will respond emotionally to a pregnancy, abortion, or birth experience. Likewise, these contracts will force some men to think about what obligations, if any, they feel they have toward children they beget. Compared to men who make no prior formal agreement, child support compliance will likely be greater among those men who agree in writing to help financially support a particular child. Similarly, those men who have talked with their partner about possibly terminating a pregnancy if it were to occur, and who have similar views, may be more likely to accompany their partner during an abortion procedure.

Despite the widespread availability of modern contraceptives, each year millions of individuals in the United States are directly involved in an unintended pregnancy.[70] These pregnancies often lead to undesirable consequences for men, women, and children. Unfortunately, efforts to balance the oftentimes competing interests of the affected parties are extremely difficult. The PRCS contract represents one innovative approach that could in a limited fashion redress men's lack of power in this area.

Ideally, this type of contract would be available to all unmarried couples irrespective of a woman's or man's socioeconomic standing. However, the state's vested interest in children's well-being supersedes the ideal of trying to balance men's and women's power in those situations where they are attempting to resolve a pregnancy. Making sure that a child is financially provided for takes precedence over worrying about whether each of the child's parents will have an equitable stake in decisions about resolving a pregnancy and child support obligations. Consequently, in order to maintain its political viability and moral legitimacy, this proposal should be restricted to couples in which the female partner (in some cases, the male partner) is economically self-sufficient.

The ideological rationale for this proposal is based on a progressive view of family life, relationships, gender roles, and sexuality. According to this view, partners in committed relationships are encouraged to maximize their joint benefits while engaging in equitable decision making.[71]

My argument is also consistent with the emerging view among the general public, scholars, and policymakers that concerted efforts should be made to acknowledge men's roles in the procreative realm. On a practical level, it is unrealistic in a society where many basic feminist principles have taken root, and men are simultaneously denied without exception any legal rights concerning how a pregnancy should be resolved, to expect a high percentage of single men to be committed to financially supporting their nonresident children born out of wedlock. Many women, as well as men, oppose efforts to enhance men's involvement in decisions about how a pregnancy should be resolved. Their major fear is that such efforts will curtail women's autonomy over their bodies. However, my proposal is designed to preserve women's autonomy, while extending greater responsibilities to women who have the financial means to assume sole financial responsibility for their unilateral decision to bring a pregnancy to term, so long as they agreed to these responsibilities prior to conceiving a child.

Many individuals will either be ineligible or uninterested in using the PRCS contract. Nevertheless, the PRCS contract may provide a growing number of middle-class couples the means to negotiate their sexual relationship in a rational and equitable manner. Those couples with progressive family values and gender role attitudes are most likely to discuss these matters. Such discussions do not preclude a couple from having a passionate sexual relationship; in fact, they can heighten the level of intimacy two partners share. The PRCS contractual approach will be beneficial if it encourages partners to discuss their pregnancy resolution and child support preferences more explicitly, ideally prior to their first sexual experience together, or at least before a conception occurs. Moreover, these contracts will prove useful if they minimize partners' disputes when they discuss how to resolve a pregnancy and, in the process, raise men's awareness of the potential consequences associated with their sexual activity. PRCS contracts may even improve contraceptive diligence among many men and women.

An alternative, and potentially disturbing, pattern could emerge if these agreements induce some men to become more careless about practicing contraception. Men who have an understanding that they will not be held financially responsible for their offspring in a particular situation may be less diligent about their contraceptive practices. Thus, it is important that evaluation research be conducted to consider whether these contracts increase or decrease individuals' risk of pregnancy due to their contraceptive practices.[72]

Individuals' reactions to formalizing sexual relations along the lines dictated by the PRCS contracts will be accentuated because sex and abortion are such highly volatile issues. Many believe that individuals' willingness to have heterosexual intercourse represents prima facie evidence of their willingness to accept the financial consequences associated with a pregnancy and possible birth. This traditional view of sexuality is inconsistent, though, with a progressive view of consensual sex as an opportunity for personal expression and development, independent of reproductive needs. Sex, seen in this contemporary light, does not excuse men and women from acting ethically. It merely implies that individuals who are capable of financially supporting their own children should be given the opportunity to make personal and informed decisions about how they wish to express their sexuality, while at the same time stipulating their preferences about parenthood. Moreover, the alarmingly high rates of abortion, out-of-wedlock pregnancies and births, delinquent child support payments among nonresident parents (especially fathers) in the United States, and the reality that contraception sometimes fails are sufficient reasons for experimenting with novel approaches that address pregnancy resolution, child support, and related issues. The fact that my proposal, by necessity, would be restricted to persons with above average financial means should not preclude its adoption given its potential to address gender equity issues in the reproductive realm. Providing the means to promote gender equity in one area of the reproductive realm for at least some people is better than ignoring everyone's situation.

Support for Reproductive Technologies

A final group of men who will continue to have an interest in procreative issues includes those who are thinking about, or are actively involved with, some form of assisted reproductive technology. Unlike men who address abortion issues that have been framed to some extent by the *Roe v. Wade* case, those men who attempt to become social fathers by using some form of assisted reproductive technology have no landmark piece of legislation to capture their attention. Instead, they must confront the policies and practices of individual fertility clinics. For instance, fertility clinics will generally require individuals to be married if they are going to use an artificial reproductive technique, or they will at least require that a male partner designate himself as the legal father. These criterion generally prevent gay men and lesbians from having a child by using asexual reproductive means. Sometime in the near future more individuals will probably support the drafting of legislation (similar to the Massachusetts law described in chapter 6) that will provide a broader array of individuals with access to assisted reproductive technologies. While some individuals have begun to pressure their congressional representatives, men are unlikely to collectively pursue new legislation to address reproductive technologies. Rather, to the extent men get involved at all, it will probably be through their joint efforts with women (probably pairs of romantic partners). Moreover, if new legislation is passed, it is unlikely to have a dramatic impact on a large proportion of men anytime in the near future, given the relatively small percentage of men who are involved with artificial forms of reproduction.

Research Initiatives

During the past fifteen years, researchers have clearly enhanced our understanding of the way men think, feel, and act as procreative beings and have contributed to the ongoing debates about social change relevant to the procreative realm. Despite these efforts, many important questions about men and procreative issues still remain unanswered.

The conceptual framework I introduced in chapter 1, in combination with the theoretical themes I emphasized throughout the book, provide the basis for identifying some of the many important research questions that should be addressed. I alluded to some of these questions as I dealt alternatively with men's attitudes regarding paternity and their involvement in contraceptive use, abortion, reproductive technologies, and the prenatal process. Research on these topics will have both theoretical and social policy implications.

If researchers are able to clarify how men are affected by the three interrelated levels of phenomena I depicted in chapter 1, they will learn a great deal about men's experiences within the procreative realm. Regardless of whether the focus is on men's views about begetting children, their contraceptive behavior, their experiences using reproductive technologies, their involvement in resolving a pregnancy, or their active participation in their partner's pregnancy, men's experiences are influenced by cultural and subcultural phenomena, interpersonal exchanges, and intrapsychic activities. The biological and social dimensions of gender fundamentally affect the way these three levels of activity shape men's experiences as procreative beings. Likewise, the ways in which men experience the cultural, interpersonal, and intrapsychic dimensions to the procreative realm will be conditioned by features of the larger social structure other than gender. In particular, men's social class will affect their access to various types of cultural messages and resources that will color their experiences in the sexual and procreative realms.

Thus, one of the basic goals of future research should be to document the parameters of the cultural and subcultural scenarios men face as procreative beings. Researchers should attempt to clarify more precisely the prevailing norms and cultural images that are commonly applied to a wide range of men's procreative situations. Some of the more important categories of men in this regard include those who are biological fathers, those who are very involved or uninvolved in their children's lives, men who adopt children, men who become social fathers by way of donor sperm, sperm donors themselves, men who discuss birth control and pregnancy issues with their partner, men who personally negotiate with their partner how a pregnancy should be resolved, and those who are unable to sire children. The public's view of men who are fathers-in-waiting should also be documented to assess how the public thinks about men's prenatal status as fathers. Although distinctive cultural and subcultural images are likely to be associated with some of these situations more than others, they each warrant attention.

Efforts to document the mainstream collective images and norms associated with each of these areas, though important, should be supplemented with research on how social class, race, age, and religious factors affect subcultural scenarios. Discerning these types of differences is vital because many men will be influenced primarily by their perception of images emanating from specific reference groups, many of which will be quite different from mainstream images. It is critical to develop a better understanding of the processes by which men are exposed to these messages and then incorporate them into their strategies for adapting to their surroundings.

Thus, at the interpersonal level, it will be informative to examine how men construct and negotiate their roles as father, partner, and a masculine man. Role identity theory can guide analyses that focus on these interpersonal issues. How are these roles interrelated? Under what circumstances do men's roles as partner and a masculine man influence the way they experience their paternal identity? The most important avenue of research in this vein will be to explore the ways in which female partners affect men's images of themselves. This will be particularly important during pregnancy because of men's physiological inability to experience the fetus directly, and it will take on added importance postnatally. Questions dealing with how men negotiate various issues with their partners concerning abortion, contraception, and assisted reproductive technologies should also be addressed.

This line of research is consistent with research on the role women play in mediating fathers' involvement with their children.[73] In their informal roles as gatekeepers, mothers of men's children often shape the ways and extent to which fathers interact with their resident and nonresident children. Women's impact on men obviously transcends the area of childrearing. They can affect how men experience aspects of the procreative realm, including abortion, gestation, childbirth, and the procedures for asexual assisted reproduction.

The interpersonal level is also important because it is here that men's decisions about forming and dissolving unions with romantic partners are linked with their sexual, contraceptive, and fertility behaviors. Aside from sperm donorship, men typically express themselves as procreative beings within the context of some type of sexual relationship or intimate union. Consequently, it is essential to explore the links between the way men express themselves as procreative beings and their negotiated interactions with their female partners.

At the intrapsychic level, there is much to learn about how men perceive themselves as procreative beings and how they would like others, especially their partners, to perceive them. Since the way men perceive themselves is based on how they interpret cultural and subcultural scenarios, as well as their interactions with others, it will be useful to explore aspects of men's procreative consciousness through a social psychological lens. This perspective, with its emphasis on people's perceptions, focuses attention on the processes that lead men to view themselves in particular ways in relation to their salient identities.

Identity theory provides possible directions for developing this line of research. One direction is informed by a version of identity theory that suggests that men's (and women's) salient identities operate on the basis of a cybernetic control system.[74] According to this view, men use dissonance-reduction techniques to alter their role behavior in response to the reflected appraisals they receive from others. As men contemplate these appraisals, they often attempt to modify their behavior to make it consistent with the internal identity standards they have created for themselves. In this respect, much can be gained by exploring the intrapsychic processes men use to express their procreative consciousness as it relates to their roles as father, partner, and masculine male.

Future research should consider how men develop salient identities that are connected to procreative experiences and how their commitment to these identities shapes their experiences. In general, this type of research should consider how men learn to define and express themselves in various areas of the procreative realm. Researchers will need to identify some of the key factors that impinge upon men's ability to enact behaviors consistent with their salient identities. For example, unemployed men may have a difficult time fulfilling the traditional provider role for their pregnant partner or the mother of their child. Or, men interested in being with their partner throughout the abortion process may be prevented from doing so because of clinic policy. Or, nonresident fathers may face obstacles to developing or maintaining a full-fledged and engaged father identity if the legal system and their partner's informal tactics restrict their ability to enact key aspects of their father roles.[75] Men may therefore be hindered, through no fault of their own, in their efforts to enact certain roles and experience their procreative consciousness in particular ways. Identifying these factors and revealing how men think, feel, and act in these situations are important avenues for future research.[76]

It will be useful, then, to study the way salient identities affect men's sense of self-worth and their psychological well-being.[77] In a related vein, researchers should consider how intensely men feel about maintaining particular identities that involve their procreative lives and their father, partner, and masculine male identities. Moreover, efforts are needed to explore the ways in which men organize their identities.[78]

More needs to be known about how men's religious convictions and identities affect their involvement in personal and social movement activities associated with the procreative realm, abortion in particular. Extreme efforts to encourage men to take an active role in the pro-life movement, for example, sometimes appeal to men's masculine identity. Paul Hill, a leading spokesperson for the relatively small faction of pro-life supporters who advocate lethal violence to stop abortion, tried to recruit men through a direct mailing of his position paper, "Should We Defend Born and Unborn Children with Force?" Hill tried to mobilize pro-life men to protest legalized abortion by challenging their masculinity:

> This calls for men who love the truth and are willing to swim against the tide. . . . For less duties than stopping abortion men have left their families and occupations to fight and die in World War II and the Civil War. . . . Indeed, all able-bodied men who *are men* indeed should rise to serve the cause in one form or another . . . isn't sacrifice and suffering in doing our duty to protect life the honorable way to serve our God? (Italics added)[79]

These activities raise the question: How do extremist groups (e.g., Operation Rescue), as well as more mainstream pro-life organizations (e.g., Pro-Life Action Network [PLAN]), try to appeal to identity themes to solicit men's involvement in activities related to the procreative realm?

Since men's identities associated with their lives as procreative beings are likely to change over time, additional insights can be gained by considering men's procreative lives from a developmental perspective. This perspective informs discussions about how men's perceptions of procreative issues evolve over the life course. What factors lead men to change their perceptions and beliefs? Why are some perceptions more stable than others? How do key life course transitions affect the way men experience themselves as procreative beings? These are just a few of the questions that can be raised by applying a developmental perspective to men's lives as procreative beings.

In addition, the phenomenological perspective, given its emphasis on the subjective aspects of social life, can guide analyses that address some of the intrapsychic issues associated with men's experiences within the procreative realm. When viewed in the context of what Alfred Schutz refers to as a "domain of relevance,"[80] men's experiences within the procreative realm represent a range of typifications (i.e., patterned ways of organizing or grouping events and objects), intersubjective understandings, and personal motivations that shape the ways in which men experience their procreative self. My purpose in selectively drawing upon this approach is not to propose a full-blown analysis of men's procreative consciousness consistent with Schutz's process model of consciousness. Instead, I suggest that a phenomenological approach can be used to frame questions about how men's experiences in the procreative realm are shaped by men's activities in various subworlds of reality including sex, dreams, and fantasies. It complements the scripting and symbolic interactionist perspectives because it, too, addresses questions about the way in which men draw upon their previous experiences and knowledge base to shape their sense of self as a procreative being.

It focuses attention on what I referred to earlier as men's situational procreative consciousness as well as their global procreative consciousness. With respect to the former, it emphasizes, in a rudimentary sense, the process by which men come to think about and express their subjective views about procreative issues in specific situations. This perspective acknowledges that men possess meaningful thoughts about experiences and relevance structures even though they may not be an active part of men's procreative consciousness at any given point in time. In other words, men will move in and out of a state of consciousness where procreative themes are relevant to them either because they have been forced into this awareness, have drifted into it, or have actively attempted to think about procreative issues that are relevant to them. Studying these types of processes, though difficult, is essential if we are to understand more fully how men experience themselves as procreative beings. Understanding these subjective processes will require us to become more sensitive to the ways in which men's sexual and procreative lives overlap.

The phenomenological approach also informs the study of men's *global* sense of self as a procreative being, which is represented by those more enduring dimensions to self-concept. As noted earlier, these relatively stable expressions are generally associated with the more long-lived phases of men's lives as procreative beings. These are likely to be fostered by men's use of the prevailing typifications related to specific procreative roles (e.g., prenatal caregiver, single man who uses condoms with multiple partners). These typifications enable men to organize their own sense of self as a procreative being around a set of meanings over an extended period of time. Determining how men experience themselves as procreative beings at this global level, and examining the consequences when they do, are important avenues for future research. Moreover, exploring how men's global procreative consciousness informs and is shaped by their experiences in particular situations will enhance the depth of our understanding of men's lives as procreative beings.

Procreative Men in the Twenty-first Century

When the twenty-first century arrives, it will earmark an intriguing and potentially tumultuous era for men as procreative beings. The tone for this period will be set by debates about a variety of policy-relevant issues, ranging from defining the meaning of family to delineating men's paternity rights. Social, legal, and technological developments will continue to reshape the way many individuals think about and experience their varied roles within the procreative realm. These developments have captured the attention of scholars, policymakers and political activists, the media, the scientific and medical communities, and the public at large. All indications suggest that this enthusiasm is likely to flourish well into the next century. The new and evolving reproductive era will be defined in no small measure by the interplay between these segments of society as they address numerous, and in some cases volatile, issues related to men's procreative roles. While it is impossible to predict the exact nature of these transformations, men will, on average, encounter significant changes along the way.

There will be meaningful opportunities for policymakers, program personnel, and researchers to work together to alter men's experiences in the procreative realm. Unfortunately, there is little hope that a large-scale, integrated effort will emerge to heighten men's procreative consciousness and sense of procreative responsibility. The more likely scenario is that the majority of changes will occur piecemeal and haphazardly, often in isolation from one another.

Ideally, my conceptual framework, with its emphasis on the procreative consciousness and responsibility themes, should entice scholars and policymakers to see men's lives as procreative beings from a more holistic perspective. This expectation is admittedly far removed from current reality. Policymakers are unlikely to use one coherent framework to guide their decisions, and the political divisions over the ideological underpinnings of my framework are quite entrenched. Moreover, policymakers tend to emphasize the practical value of making decisions one issue at a time. Nevertheless, I believe my general framework has merit because it treats men's prenatal and postnatal experiences as part of one larger domain. It also draws attention to the ways in which men's sexual and procreative lives are intertwined due to the gendered dimensions to social life.

Seeing men's individual procreative experiences as part of a larger reproductive and fatherhood realm has theoretical and policymaking significance. From a theoretical point of view, this approach enhances our understanding of men's lives as procreative beings because it highlights how various aspects of men's lives in this broadly defined area are interrelated and connected to their romantic relationships. In addition, while many policymaking strategies isolate one reproductive issue at a time for practical purposes, a more integrated social policy might encourage men to develop a heightened procreative consciousness and be more responsible in this area as well. This will, in turn, influence men's roles in contraception, abortion, the gestation process, and facets of asexual reproduction, as well as other areas. The process of defining responsibility, and the inherent controversies that go along with this labeling process, will definitely make this venture a precarious one.

The politicized nature of reproduction and parenthood is accentuated by the ongoing debates about the responsibilities and rights of those involved in the reproductive realm. A diverse mix of groups, including feminists and profeminists, Promise Keepers and other religious groups, men's and fathers' rights activists, pro-life and pro-choice advocates, will continue to struggle in their efforts to shape the way men think about and experience aspects of the procreative realm. Because these groups often establish rotating and sometimes unconventional alliances depending upon the issue in question, making reliable predictions about how these struggles will resolve themselves is not possible. However, it is clear that the struggles over these highly politicized issues will persist for the foreseeable future and have profound consequences for men, women, and children. Serious challenges therefore await those researchers, social activists, and policymakers who intend to study men's procreative lives and enhance fathers' involvement with their children.

Notes

1. Interest in how fathers can affect children's quality of life is also based on reviews of data that conclude that children in single-mother (as well as single-father) homes have a greater chance for emotional, educational, and developmental problems than children from two-parent households (Annie E. Casey Foundation, 1995; McLanahan and Sandefur, 1994). Moreover, there is a growing body of health care and biomedical literature that speculates that men may affect, either directly or indirectly, the prenatal and postnatal status of their offspring through their interaction with their partner or because of their own health circumstances due to smoking, alcohol consumption, or exposure to hazardous materials (Cicero, 1994; Dobkin et al., 1994; Lindbohm er al., 1991; Sable et al., 1990; Savitz and Chen, 1994).

2. Edwards, 1991; McNeil, 1990; Ragoné, 1994; Rothman, 1989; Whiteford, 1989.

3. Ragoné, 1994; Robinson, 1993; Rothman, 1989; Whiteford, 1989.

4. This case pitted Dan and Cara Schmidt against Jan and Roberta DeBoer in their struggle to either establish, or retain, legal custody of Baby Jessica. This case was unique in that Dan Schmidt, a truck driver living in Iowa, fought to obtain custody of a child that he learned was his biological child nineteen days after the child's birth. By then the child had already been given to the DeBoers, who were living in Ann Arbor, Michigan. (The DeBoers had sought to adopt a child in Iowa since Michigan law did not provide them the option of pursuing a private adoption in their own state.) Cara, Dan's former girlfriend at the time, had lied to him about his paternity status. Dan had been under the impression that Cara's child had been fathered by another man, who had relinquished his paternal rights. Upon learning the truth, Dan immediately initiated a legal effort to regain his paternal rights and custody of his child on the basis that he had never relinquished his rights. This case illustrates the significance that some men, and the general public, place on the biological aspects of fatherhood—or parenthood more generally. Furthermore, it has prompted public scrutiny of the relative importance of biological paternity versus social fatherhood ties.

5. Levine and Pitt, 1995.

6. A number of scholarly and journalistic publications and reports have re-

cently explored the historical, political, psychological, and social aspects of fatherhood, see Coltrane, 1995; Ehrenreich, 1983; Furstenberg, 1988; Gerson, 1993; Griswold, 1993; Hawkins and Dollahite, 1997; Marsiglio, 1995a; Lamb, 1987; 1997; LaRossa, 1997; Levine and Pitt, 1996; Parke, 1996; Pleck, 1987; Working Group on Conceptualizing Male Parenting, 1997; Working Group on Male Fertility and Family Formation, 1997.

7. Some of these include the National Center on Fathers and Families at the University of Pennsylvania in Philadelphia; the Center on Fathers, Families, and Public Policy in Chicago; the National Center for Fathering in Shawnee Mission, Kansas; the National Fatherhood Initiative in Lancaster, Pennsylvania; and the Fatherhood Project in New York City.

8. Bertoia and Drakich, 1995; Coltrane and Hickman, 1992.

9. Clatterbaugh, 1997; Gilbreath, 1995; Hackett, 1996; Murchison, 1996; Swomley, 1996; Wagenheim, 1996; Woodward and Keene-Osborn, 1994.

10. Levine and Pitt (1995) provide an invaluable resource for scholars, community leaders, social service providers, and social policy advocates who want to learn more about the various types of ongoing community strategies to promote fathers' positive involvement in their children's and partners' lives.

11. Sonenstein, Holcomb, and Seefeldt, 1993.

12. Crowell and Leeper, 1994.

13. Greene, Emig, and Hearn, 1996, p. 3; Greene, Hearn, and Emig, 1996; Greene and Emig, 1997. A report on the March 1997 conference was in the process of being produced as this book went to press. The purpose of the Working Group on Male Fertility and Family Formation, as summarized by Bachrach (1997), was to explore the processes that are associated with men's fertility behavior and that help shape the context for men to become fathers and express their paternal roles. A high priority for future research is to understand how male fertility and relationship processes (union formation and dissolution) are linked to men's fathering experiences.

14. Throughout this book I attempt to present the available evidence that explores African American and Hispanic men's experiences as procreative beings. Unfortunately, the data are simply not available to provide a thorough and scholarly analysis of these issues in most cases. For instance, the research on men's involvement with assisted reproductive technologies (ART) deals primarily with white middle-class men. The men who use ART and the sperm donors who help support fertility clinics around the country (and internationally) tend to be white men, including a disproportionate number of medical students. To my knowledge, no study on ART addresses race issues. Likewise, the literature on men's involvement in the pregnancy and childbirth processes tends to use samples of white men and does not address social class issues. There is also little research that addresses the differences in black and white men's use of male sterilization, other than references to whites being more likely to use this technique. Future re-

search efforts, where appropriate, should consider how a wide range of procreative issues are affected by race and ethnic factors.

15. My approach also selectively focuses on men's sexual and family roles. See Grady et al., 1996, for a recent study of some of the relevant issues.

16. As a participant in the Working Group on Male Fertility and Family Formation that evolved out of the Fatherhood Initiative, I discovered at the January 1997 meeting held at the Urban Institute that scholars are interested in a variety of questions dealing with the interrelationships between male fertility and relationship processes. The formation and dissolution of stable unions are two of the more important processes. Many of these issues were addressed at the March Conference on Fathering and Male Fertility: Improving Data and Research.

17. Given the breadth of topics relevant to my book, I try to integrate an eclectic assortment of materials. These include the biological, cultural, historical, psychological, social, and technological factors relevant to men's involvement in procreative issues. I am particularly intent on showing how men's procreative experiences are shaped by a combination of biological and gender role influences. I do not claim, however, to address every aspect of men's lives in this area. For example, I do not specifically address issues associated with gay men and procreation. While some of the issues I address are equally applicable to gay and heterosexual men, the unique aspects to gay men's lives as procreative beings and fathers are beyond the scope of this book.

18. While a great deal of the fatherhood literature is relevant to my objectives for this book, much of it is tangential to my main focus. In addition, numerous cogent discussions about fatherhood issues currently exist (see note 6), so I will focus primarily on men's experiences that do not deal specifically with fathers' active paternal involvement. I will, however, clarify how the topics I consider can be conceptualized as being related to paternal involvement or conduct issues in some cases. These issues are central to much of the growing interdisciplinary literature on fatherhood dealing with how resident and nonresident fathers are involved in their children's lives.

19. Swidler, 1986.

20. I discuss the different paths to paternity and social fatherhood at length in chapter 6.

21. I am grateful to Nicky Albert for providing me with this clever phrase to refer to prospective fathers.

22. Blumer, 1969; Stryker, 1980.

23. See Sullivan's (1995) discussion of the role played by subcultural factors in shaping experiences in the procreative realm of teenage and young adult males from several poor, New York City neighborhoods.

24. Sullivan, 1995.

25. Sullivan, 1995.

26. Laumann et al., 1994; Simon and Gagnon, 1986.

27. The three levels of activity I describe as contributing to men's experiences in the procreative realm are embedded within a dynamic sociocultural context that features interrelated cultural, demographic, health care policy, historical, social structural, and technological changes. I discuss ongoing and potential changes throughout this book.

28. Subcultural scenarios emerge because specific groups or classes of people may have different views about how a particular role should be played. Racial and class factors often shape people's views in this regard. While I attempt at times to shed light on how race and social class affect men's experiences in selected areas of the procreative realm, the limited research on these issues restricts my ability to analyze these topics in depth.

29. Identity theorists differ in the way they treat role-related variables such as gender, which actually represent categorical attributes rather than interpersonal roles per se. For ease of presentation, I will use the role concept in a broad fashion to include gender.

30. Since people seldom share the exact same beliefs, the general scenarios reflect a somewhat muddled and dynamic representation of individuals' perceptions. These beliefs contribute to an obscure type of collective consciousness. To further complicate matters, there are often competing cultural scenarios from which individuals can choose and these scenarios are likely to change over time. For these reasons, it is difficult to define cultural scenarios precisely. Despite these limitations in defining cultural scenarios, individuals seem to be aware of the different clusters of normative guidelines that define the parameters of particular roles.

31. Some men's religious beliefs will shape their roles as they relate to being a romantic partner, father, and masculine man in the procreative realm. Although it is possible to perceive men as having separate religious roles, I restrict my analysis by considering religious factors only in combination with one or more of the three primary types of roles listed above.

32. Engle and Leonard, 1995.

33. While the general public continues to expect men to work and help support their families, people are less likely today to feel that men should solely assume this role while their partner takes care of the home and family. Whereas 62 percent of women and 68 percent of men in a 1977 national survey felt that family members were most likely to benefit if the man were the sole provider, these figures declined by 1994 to 32 and 37 percent, respectively (Mitchell, 1996, p. 313).

34. When men think about their personal needs and expectations which they associate with being a partner or father figure, they often draw upon general cultural or subcultural scenarios related to gender and adult roles. They learn about these scenarios through a variety of sources including family, friends, the media, and social programs. On occasion, men refer to these scenarios to develop spe-

cific ways of interacting with others that enable them to confirm their self-images in the procreative realm. For instance, those men who typically are emotionally detached from their partners may also be somewhat removed from them when their partners are pregnant. When these men express their masculinity by being inexpressive around their partners, they have little opportunity to experience the pregnancy process indirectly through them. As I discussed earlier, men's involvement with one or more of the areas of the procreative realm sometimes reflects their concerns about their role performances, and others' assessments of them, in their related roles as a romantic partner and masculine adult male.

35. Men's prior experiences are likely to influence the types of questions they ask themselves and the way they think about them. This intrapsychic process can be clarified by considering it in light of the role identity orientation I discuss in the text.

36. Burke, 1991; Burke and Reitzes, 1981; 1991; Hogg, Terry, and White, 1995; Stryker, 1980; 1987; Stryker and Serpe, 1982; Thoits, 1991. Several scholars have specifically discussed how identity theory can be used to interpret fathers' conduct with their children (see Ihinger-Tallman, Pasley, and Buehler, 1995; Marsiglio, 1995a; 1995b; Pasley and Minton, 1997).

37. Stryker (1980) refers to this structure as a salience hierarchy.

38. Pasley and Minton's (1997) exploratory research suggests that, compared to fathers, mothers may be more apt to prioritize their identities and experience less overlap between them. They note that some fathers' perceptions of themselves as fathers incorporates their views about their martial relationship. Thus, they recommend that scholars pay more attention to the potentially integrative aspects to men's identities because "our failure to recognize the inclusive or integrative nature of fathers' self-definitions may cloud our understanding and interpretation of how self-definitions translate into fathering behaviors and how behaviors, in turn, affect self-definitions" (p. 120). I concur. Future research along these lines should also consider not only men's fathering behaviors, but their varied expressions as procreative beings.

39. Stryker (1980) argues that several factors determine individuals' commitment to a role identity. I illustrate his interpretation by using fathers as an example.

40. Marsiglio, 1995c.

41. See Peter Burke's work (1980; 1991; Burke and Reitzes, 1991); see also Hogg, Terry, and White, 1995.

42. The transitions men make in how they prioritize and perceive their work, family, and gender roles sometimes coincide with developmental stages connected to the aging process, for them or their partners. For example, young men may begin to develop the urge to sire and care for children as they simultaneously begin to shift away from a self-centered egoistic orientation to one that is more other-orientated and compassionate. Older men, meanwhile, may undergo sig-

nificant changes in their procreative self as they move into their middle and later years of life because their partners become postmenopausal.

43. I view both of these concepts as exploratory or sensitizing concepts given the paucity of information about men's experiences in this area (Blumer, 1969). Consequently, I do not attempt in any rigorous fashion to delineate the numerous dimensions of these concepts or suggest how the basic concepts or dimensions should be measured.

44. The fact that I use the phrase "procreative consciousness" warrants comment, given the political significance of language and the importance this concept has for my analysis of men's experiences. My initial use of this phrase (Marsiglio, 1991; 1993) was influenced by O'Brien's (1981) work. She used the phrase "reproductive consciousness" in her historical analysis of men's discovery of biological paternity to emphasize men's awareness of their ability to procreate. In my previous works I used "procreative" rather than "reproductive," in part, to be consistent with Cutright's (1986) phrase "responsible male procreative behavior." It also seemed more appropriate to think of men as being involved in "procreation" rather than "reproduction" even though these two terms are typically thought to be synonymous. The image that procreative conveys is one of autonomous, creative action, whereas reproduction implies a type of duplication process in which creativity is less central. It is beyond the scope of my purposes here to debate whether this language reflects larger social issues or is intrinsic to what has been labeled patriarchal "male-stream" thought (O'Brien, 1981). For simplicity's sake, I retain my usage of the procreative term and submit that it could be used interchangeably with the term reproductive. I am indebted to Goldie MacDonald for bringing these issues to my attention.

45. Schutz, 1970a; 1970b; Schutz and Luckmann, 1973.

46. Webb, 1976.

47. Schutz, 1970a; 1970b. I am aware that it is imprecise to say that those experiences and feelings that men may not be fully aware of at a specific point in time are, in a strict sense, part of their consciousness. Nevertheless, inactive or subconscious experiences may come to represent important factors that influence how men actually attend to particular experiences, whether men are aware of them or not. I have therefore chosen to comment briefly on the significance of previous experiences that may eventually affect men's procreative consciousness as it is expressed at a given time. By incorporating the inactive dimensions to procreative consciousness into my discussion, I am able to underscore men's ability to draw upon their reservoir of untapped knowledge and feelings to apprehend a particular situation more fully.

48. Men's experiences in these situations are likely to be affected by their interactions with their partners as well as others (e.g., drug store clerks, health care professionals, social movement participants, parents).

49. While these middle-aged men may not perceive the procreative realm as

being directly relevant to them anymore, they may still be quite concerned about procreative issues if they have adolescent children.

50. Shostak, McLouth, and Seng, 1984, pp. 99–100.

51. The importance of recalling information about previous experiences can be illustrated by imaging men who have children with other women and are then asked by their current partners to have children with them. Another example would include those men who have had previous abortion experiences and are then told by their current partner that she is planning to terminate the unplanned pregnancy.

52. Wilson, 1987.

53. Levine and Pitt, 1995; Venohr, Williams, and Baxter, 1996.

54. Marsiglio, 1993; Mott, 1983; Seccombe, 1991.

55. Gilmore, 1990; Hill, Stycos, and Bach, 1959. See also anthropologist Matthew Gutmann's (1996) nuanced interpretation of how working-class Mexican men living in Colonia Santo Domingo, Mexico City, during the early 1990s are changing the way they construct their gender role identity. Based on his extensive ethnographic study, Gutmann concludes that many of the Mexican men he studied did not fit the stereotypical macho image often associated with them. In particular, his analysis of male domesticity reveals that many men's experiences with paternity and male parenting issues are inconsistent with the stereotypical image of Mexican men. The portrait of having lots of genetic offspring, preferably boys, and displaying a distant style of fathering is becoming increasingly less representative of Mexican men.

56. Anderson, 1989; Gagnon and Simon, 1973; Marsiglio, 1993; see also Majors and Billson, 1992.

57. Pleck, Sonenstein, and Ku, 1996.

58. Marsiglio, 1993.

59. While respondents' self-reported academic grades were not related to the likelihood that impregnating someone would make them feel like a real man, controlling for other background factors, parental education was negatively associated with this variable. That is, young men with parents who had completed fewer years of school were more likely to report that impregnating someone would make them feel like a real man.

60. Lipkin and Lamb, 1982; see also May and Perrin, 1985.

61. Dawson, 1929; Malinowski, 1966.

62. May and Perrin, 1985; Munroe and Munroe, 1973; see also Paige and Paige, 1973.

63. There is also a great deal of anthropological research that clearly documents the wide-ranging social customs and rituals that give men in nonindustrialized countries opportunities to play significant roles in the procreative realm. One of the more "ingenious" rituals along these lines used to be practiced among the Huichol Indians of Mexico during childbirth. The father, with ropes attached

to his scrotum, squatted in the rafter above the mother who was accompanied by attendants who assisted in the childbearing process. The mother pulled on the ropes when she had contractions so the father could share the overwhelming sensations of the childbearing experience.

64. In my first attempt to delineate the basic definitions for procreative consciousness and procreative responsibility, I presented these concepts as being completely distinct from one another (see Marsiglio, 1991). For this book, I have revised my conceptualization of these concepts because it is intuitively more appealing to think of procreative consciousness as the larger, more encompassing concept. Note, too, that there may be other dimensions of procreative consciousness that are related to men's sense of procreative responsibility (e.g., the intensity with which men feel bonded with their genetic offspring).

65. Cutright, 1986.

66. Levine and Pitt, 1995, pp. 5–6.

67. Cutright, 1986.

68. Lamb, 1987; 1997.

69. Miller and Pasta, 1995.

70. Men in this situation probably have their most focused thoughts about procreative responsibility during sex when they suspect their partner is ovulating. However, if men are intent on impregnating their partner, they may regularly think about these issues even though their chances are low for siring a child during particular times in their partner's cycle.

71. Situations such as these illustrate how aspects of the sexual and reproductive realms sometime overlap as I discuss in chapter 3.

72. Rosenwasser, Wright, and Barber, 1987; see also Newman, 1987; Overall, 1987.

73. Shostak, McLouth, and Seng, 1984.

74. May and Perrin, 1985.

75. Marsiglio, 1987.

76. Ventura, Martin, et al., 1995.

77. Johnson and Sum, 1987; Marsiglio, 1988a; Sullivan, 1989.

78. Marsiglio and Menaghan, 1990.

79. A separate analysis with these data revealed that young black and white men were equally likely to report that they would like to live with their partner and child (46 percent). Whites' responses, however, varied appreciably based on the educational level of their parents, whereas blacks' responses were essentially unaffected by their parents' education (Marsiglio, 1989).

80. Ehrenreich, 1983.

81. In chapter 7, I discuss more fully how these organizations are attempting to change men's family roles.

82. While 34 percent of a national sample of women responding to the General Social Survey in 1977 disagreed with the statement "It is much better for

everyone involved if the man is the achiever outside the home and the woman takes care of the home and family," 63 percent of women disagreed with this statement when asked in the 1994 GSS (see Mitchell, 1996, p. 313).

83. Men can also be encouraged to become social fathers without being a genetic father. Women can ask their partners to consent to adoption or some form of asexual reproductive technology that uses donor sperm. These requests, and the ensuing discussions, are still likely to affect men's procreative consciousness, although they may do so in decidedly different ways.

84. Nonresident fathers may be encouraged, at the very least, to pay child support.

85. Men develop their views and accumulate their experiences in various ways. Some have few partners, encounter only a handful of dramatic events, and associate most of their experiences with the same partner over a period of many years. Others, though, have many partners and experience a wide variety of situations relevant to the procreative realm, including some combination of conceptions, pregnancy resolution processes, prepared childbirth classes, abortion, adoptions, births, condom use, fertility tests, use of ART, and sperm donations.

86. The meanings men attach to their experiences both at the individual and interpersonal levels in the procreative realm are affected, in part, by cultural and subcultural norms concerning the appropriate patterning of key life events such as marriage, education, work, and fertility. Some of these normative expectations are connected to men's life course positions. For example, an adolescent, unemployed young man will be expected to experience the procreative realm much differently than a middle-aged, employed father of four children.

NOTES TO CHAPTER 2

1. Pinchbeck, 1996; Lemonick, 1996; Wright, 1996; Carpenter, 1996.

2. I discuss these issues more fully in chapter 6 when I consider the different ways men can become fathers.

3. See Howe, 1993; Jackson, 1989. DNA fingerprinting technology can be used to determine with near certainty whether a particular man is a specific child's biological father. This technique examines DNA (deoxyribonucleic acid), which can be found in all living cells with a nucleus. DNA is the chemical structure of a molecule that carries the body's genetic code. According to Jackson, "When a person is conceived, his or her DNA is formed by the combination of the chromosomes in the father's sperm and the mother's ovum. . . . Since a person's DNA is derived half from [each parent] the question of whether a man is the father of a particular child can be resolved by comparing the 'bar codes' of the man, the child, and the child's mother." This technology is being used more regularly even though it is a bit more expensive than earlier, less precise methods for establishing biological paternity.

4. Tannahill, 1980.

5. Freud, 1927.

6. Reiss, 1986.

7. Fisher, 1982.

8. Fisher, 1982, p. 91.

9. Fisher, 1982, p. 94.

10. Fisher, 1982, p. 95.

11. Graves, 1955.

12. Kraemer, 1991, p. 384.

13. O'Brien, 1981.

14. Kraemer, 1991.

15. Lerner, 1986.

16. Kraemer, 1991.

17. Engels, 1972 [1884]; O'Brien, 1981.

18. McLaren, 1990.

19. Glick, 1989; Hernandez, 1988; Larson, 1992; Marsiglio, 1992.

20. Mintz, 1996.

21. Marsiglio, 1995c; see also LaRossa, 1988.

22. See Bahr and Bahr, 1996; Berscheid, 1996; Beutler et al., 1989; Delaisi de Parseval and Hurstel, 1987; Edwards, 1989; Jurich, 1989; Marks, 1996; Menaghan, 1989; Seligman, 1990; Scanzoni and Marsiglio, 1991; 1993; Scanzoni et al., 1989.

23. March, 1995.

24. O'Brien, 1981.

25. Akerlof, Yellen, and Katz, 1996, p. 281.

26. Delaisi de Parseval and Hurstel, 1987; Edwards, 1991.

27. Rothman, 1989, pp. 36–37.

28. Baldwin and Nord, 1984; Bloom and Trussell, 1984; Thornton, 1989; 1995.

29. Blake, 1966; 1974; Gallop Report, 1986.

30. Mott, 1983.

31. This pattern is likely to be most pronounced among whites because African American women have historically been more likely to work outside the home.

32. Nock (1987) suggests that women today are more likely to weigh the costs and benefits of childbearing in much the same way they think about purchasing durable household items (e.g., cars and major appliances).

33. Pleck, 1987.

34. See Bernard, 1981; Ehrenreich, 1983; Furstenberg, 1988; Griswold, 1993; Rotundo, 1985.

35. Coltrane, 1995; Gerson, 1993; Griswold, 1993.

36. LaRossa, 1988.

37. Cutright, 1986; Stokes, 1980; Swanson, 1985.

38. Lewis, 1986; Pleck, 1985; 1994; 1997; O'Connell, 1993.

39. The same can be said of the comparatively low levels of fathers' "mental labor" with respect to childcare. Walzer (1996, p. 219) introduces this concept to "distinguish the thinking, feeling, and interpersonal work that accompanies the care of babies from physical tasks." This concept is also meant to capture "aspects of baby care that involve thinking or feeling, managing thoughts or feelings, . . . that are not necessarily perceived as work by the person performing it."

40. DeVault, 1987; Hochschild, 1989; Hood, 1983; Pyke, 1994; Thompson, 1991.

41. This pattern of greater male involvement may be restricted to some extent though because of the increasing proportion of unmarried women who are giving birth to children conceived outside of marriage, many of whom will never cohabit with their biological father.

42. Men's awareness of and reaction to reproductive issues may be affected indirectly by the increased political clout of child advocacy groups such as the Children's Defense Fund. These groups can affect men's views and behaviors if they can marshal public and legislative support to hold fathers accountable for their children's financial well-being.

43. Cutright, 1986.

44. Achatz and MacAllum, 1994; Kiselica, 1995; Klinman et al., 1986; National Urban League, 1987.

45. Cutright, 1986; Pirog-Good, 1993; Savage, 1987; Sonenstein, Holcomb, and Seefeldt, 1993.

46. Levine and Pitt, 1995.

47. Child Support Report, 1996.

48. Cutright, 1986; Moore, 1987.

49. Jackson, 1989. Ironically, this development has surfaced during an era when the practical value of social fatherhood is being accentuated by many persons because the rates of divorce, single parenthood, cohabitation, and child poverty are so high.

50. I am personally familiar with one case in which a man in his early thirties is currently thinking about taking the DNA test in order to establish whether a man he suspects may be his biological father is in fact related to him. The man's mother apparently has never been certain which of two men were responsible for her son's conception and she only recently informed him of this dilemma. Until recently, the son had viewed his "potential" father as a friend of the family and uncle figure.

51. Weaver and Cranley, 1983.

52. Rothman, 1989.

53. Whicker and Kronenfeld, 1986.

54. Marsiglio, 1985; Swanson, 1985.

55. Djerassi and Leibo, 1994; Swanson, 1985.

56. Henshaw, 1991; 1992; Henshaw, Forrest, and Blaine, 1984; Henshaw and O'Reilly, 1983; Henshaw and Van Vort, 1990.

57. In some cases, their responses have probably come on the heels of their partner having a legal abortion without their consent. In others, their concern may have been expressed at a more general level, perhaps through their involvement in the pro-life movement.

58. Shostak, McLouth, and Seng, 1984.

59. Shostak, McLouth, and Seng, 1984.

60. Levine and Pitt, 1995.

61. Heggenhougen, 1980; May and Perrin, 1985.

62. Ernst, 1975.

63. May and Perrin, 1985.

64. See, DeGarmo and Davidson, 1978; Leonard, 1977; Levine and Pitt, 1995; Lewis, 1986. These relatively recent developments can be viewed within a longer historical perspective. While it is difficult to know precisely the extent to which husbands attended the births of their children during earlier centuries, Suitor (1981, p. 289) concludes that,

> examination of midwifery/obstetrics books and marriage/health guides published prior to 1911 suggests that American husbands began participating in their wives' childbirth experiences sometime around 1830. The employment of male practitioners as birth attendants for normal labors, beginning around 1750, was probably a necessary but insufficient condition for the emergence of husbands' participation.

She further speculates that changes within the family system during the late 1700s and early 1800s affected husbands' rate of participation in the birth process. These included the emergence of the compassionate marriage, the growing cultural concern over children and the acceptance of childhood as a unique developmental stage, and the decrease in family size. Many husbands were apparently present at the birth scene until hospital births became popular during the early 1900s.

65. I explore men's condom use in more detail in chapter 4.

NOTES TO CHAPTER 3

1. DeLamater, 1987; Gaylin, 1992; Leigh et al., 1994; Udry, 1988.

2. Scanzoni, 1996, personal communication.

3. Some of this shift is evidenced by the fact that social scientists increasingly want to include biological markers (e.g., blood and saliva samples) in their data collection efforts. See Udry's (1988) work based on blood samples for a discussion of biologically based gender differences in adolescents' sexual experiences. In chapter 7, I briefly discuss the potential relationship between biological factors and parenting behavior (see Rossi, 1987).

4. Gaylin, 1992.

5. The 1994 Hollywood movie *Junior,* starring Arnold Schwarzenegger as a male scientist who allowed himself to be impregnated through an experimental technique and later gave birth to an infant daughter, satirized many of these differences. The movie made light of the stereotypical images we often associate with how men and women experience the reproductive process; differences that could, according to the plot, be minimized through innovative medical procedures and pharmacological strategies.

6. The popularity of *Junior* was predicated on the idea that Schwarzenegger's character allowed himself to be experimented upon for the expressed purpose of seeing whether a man could become pregnant.

7. Davis, 1983.

8. Men who use condoms primarily as a means to minimize their risk of contracting a sexually transmitted disease, rather than to prevent a pregnancy, may still reflect upon their procreative self at times since the condom is often thought of as a birth control technique.

9. Some cultures provide men with alternative strategies for experiencing pregnancy-like symptoms, known collectively as the couvade syndrome.

10. Abbey, Andrews, and Halman, 1991; Greil, 1991; Miall, 1986.

11. Gaylin, 1992.

12. Marsiglio, 1993; Zilbergeld, 1992.

13. Poynor, 1996, personal communication.

14. DeLamater, 1987; Marsiglio, 1988b.

15. Hochschild, 1979.

16. Much of this activity occurs within established groups, such as fraternities, sports teams, gangs, and the military. The violent excesses that are produced by this form of male bonding have been well publicized and documented (see Boswell and Spade, 1996; Kirshenbaum, 1989; Martin and Hummer, 1989; Sanday, 1990).

17. Listings on the Internet reveal that pro-life supporters have established some support groups for men who encounter selective reproductive experiences (DWILSON@FACT1.SURF.TACH.NET).

18. Cooke, 1986.

19. In some cultures, such as that of the Sambia of New Guinea, rituals do exist that emphasize same-gender bonds around male reproductive issues. The common practice of encouraging young males to engage in receptive oral sex on a regular basis with older males is not merely a facet of this culture's sexual customs, its fundamental purpose is to enhance younger boys' masculinity and their ability to reproduce a child when they become men. The Sambia believe that this practice affords younger boys the opportunity to strengthen their own semen supply for their future life as adult males (see Reiss, 1986).

20. The prevalence and exact nature of these group activities in the erotic realm probably varies due to individuals' social class and race/ethnic back-

ground. Future research should explore the ways in which persons from different social environments are exposed to these group activities, and the extent to which gender remains an overriding factor that distinguishes individuals' experiences in this area above and beyond other variables.

21. I am indebted to Goldie MacDonald and Janet McNellis for bringing to my attention these female-oriented bonding experiences that deal with sexuality in a less explicit fashion.

22. Ragoné, 1994.

23. Ragoné, 1994, p. 136.

24. Ragoné, 1994.

25. Ragoné, 1994, pp. 129–130.

26. A possible rare exception to this pattern would involve cases where men might be able to request that the body of a woman who is brain dead be kept alive artificially in order to deliver their child.

27. Axelrod, 1990; Stetson, 1991; Walters, 1989.

NOTES TO CHAPTER 4

1. From a medical perspective, the term "contraception" is generally applied to technologies that prevent a fertilized egg from implanting in a woman's womb because the medical community views the implantation of a fertilized egg as the defining moment for a pregnancy. Pro-life supporters, on the other hand, typically define pregnancy as occurring at the moment of conception. In medical terms, then, technologies such as the I.U.D. or the application of "morning-after pills" would be considered contraceptives, but pro-life advocates would probably refer to them as abortifacients. In either case, these technologies could still be broadly defined as forms of birth control.

2. McLaren (1990) provides an insightful historical account of contraception beginning with the ancient Greeks and Romans. I restrict my discussion here to the latter half of the twentieth century.

3. McLaren, 1990, p. 244.

4. Edwards, 1994; Westoff and Jones, 1979.

5. Rogow and Horowitz, 1995.

6. Grady et al., 1996. This study found that black men, controlling for a variety of background factors, were significantly more likely than their white counterparts to view decisions about contraception as a woman's responsibility. Likewise, men living with their partners and those with more educated partners were more likely to see women as having more responsibility for contraception compared to unmarried, noncohabiting males and those with less-educated partners.

7. O'Campo et al., 1993. For focus group studies of the interpersonal dynamics associated with sexual and contraceptive decision making and behavior among African American as well as Hispanic youth, see Sugland, Wilder, and

Chandra, 1996, and Gilmore, DeLamater, and Wagstaff, 1995. Data from the Kaiser Family Foundation's national Survey of Men's Role in Preventing Pregnancy, which were released initially as this book was going to press, are also relevant to discussions about men's involvement in contraception (Stewart, 1997). Preliminary results show that 72 percent of men (and 73 percent of women) feel that men in general need to play more of a role in making sure that contraception is always used in situations where couples are trying to avoid pregnancy. However, only 32 percent of men agree with the statement that men feel left out when it comes to using birth control and preventing pregnancy.

8. The condom when used correctly and consistently is, in fact, rather effective, although less effective than the hormonal female-oriented methods (Tse, 1980, p. 442).

9. These exchanges would be affected by numerous factors, including participants' gender role preferences. I develop this thesis further in a subsequent section.

10. Comhaire, 1994; Djerassi and Leibo, 1994; Liskin, Benoit, and Blackburn, 1992; Lissner, 1992; Waites, 1993.

11. Bialy and Patanelli, 1981; Balswick, 1972; Gough, 1979; Jaccard et al., 1981; Laird, 1994; Marshall, 1980; Marsiglio, 1985; Marsiglio and Menaghan, 1987; Ringheim, 1993; 1995; WHO, 1982.

12. Grady et al., 1993. This study also found that those who had completed more than twelve years of education were more likely to have used a condom (91 percent) than those who had not completed high school (84 percent). Blacks and whites were almost equally likely to have used a condom (91 percent versus 88 percent). Another study of 242 sexually active black adolescent males between the ages of 13 and 19, conducted in 1985 and 1986 in an adolescent clinic in Washington, D.C., found that 67 percent had used condoms at some point in their life. Among this sample, current concerns about contracting sexually transmitted diseases was related to condom use, but previous experience with a STD or impregnating a partner was not (Wilson, Kastrinakis, and D'Angelo, 1994). My research with the first wave of the NSAM duplicated this latter finding (Marsiglio, 1993). See Leigh et al., 1994, for a racial comparison of condom use among a national sample of 12- to 17-year-olds.

13. Sonenstein, Pleck, and Ku, 1989. Analyses using both the NSAM-1 and NSAM-2 found no change between 1988 and 1991 in the condom use rate for similarly aged cohorts (17.5 to 19 years of age) of young men (Pleck, Sonenstein, and Ku, 1993).

14. Peterson, 1995.

15. Crain Communications, 1994; Green, 1995; see also Moran et al., 1990.

16. While increases in condom purchases partly reflect men's buying patterns, condom purchases are also affected by women's buying patterns. According to a study conducted by Frost and Sullivan Inc., women today are more likely to pur-

chase condoms than earlier cohorts of women, and they account for about 20 percent of the market (Crain Communications, 1994). In addition, one recent study of college students found that 70 percent of male respondents and 48 percent of female respondents reported that they had bought condoms at some point in their lifetime (Stringfellow, 1994). However, 91 percent of the male respondents but only 21 percent of the female respondents indicated that they had provided a condom at last intercourse (see also Rickert et al., 1989). Thus, men continue to be primarily responsible for introducing condoms into a sexual episode, even though a significant number of women report having experience in purchasing condoms. Irrespective of who provides the condom, if a condom is used, men will need to be involved. Hence, their procreative consciousness can be affected regardless of who provides the condom.

17. Conservative legislation and advertising policies have no doubt inhibited health educators' efforts in this regard.

18. Ku, Sonenstein, and Pleck, 1994.

19. Tanfer et al., 1993; see also Landry and Camelo, 1994; Langer, Zimmerman, and Katz, 1994. In addition, Anderson, Brackbill, and Mosher (1996) use data from the 1990 telephone reinterview of participants in the 1988 National Survey of Family Growth (aged 15 to 44) to analyze sexually experienced unmarried women's reports of condom use for disease prevention. Forty-one percent of these respondents indicated that they had used condoms at least once for disease prevention during the last three months in which they were having sex.

20. Tanfer et al., 1993.

21. Grady et al., 1993.

22. Ku, Sonenstein, and Pleck, 1994.

23. Ku, Sonenstein, and Pleck, 1992.

24. Pleck, Sonenstein, and Ku, 1991; see also Pleck, Sonenstein, and Swain, 1988.

25. Tanfer et al., 1993.

26. Pleck, Sonenstein, and Ku, 1993.

27. Leigh, Temple, and Trocki, 1993; Marín, Goméz, and Hearst, 1993.

28. Weisman et al., 1991.

29. Ku, Sonenstein, and Pleck, 1994.

30. Pleck, Sonenstein, and Ku, 1991.

31. See Pleck, Sonenstein, and Ku, 1990; 1991.

32. Pleck, Sonenstein, and Ku, 1990. My own research with the NSAM has also shown that attitudes toward contraceptive responsibility are positively associated with actual condom use (Marsiglio, 1993).

33. Marsiglio, 1993.

34. Sullivan, 1995.

35. Ross, 1992.

36. Peterson, 1995.

37. Office of Population Census and Surveys, 1990.
38. Althaus, 1995; Djerassi and Leibo, 1994.
39. Chandra, 1995.
40. Forste, Tanfer, and Tedrow, 1995.
41. Stokes, 1980.
42. Djerassi and Leibo, 1994, p. 11.
43. Humphrey and Humphrey, 1993.
44. Waites, 1993, p. 212.
45. Lissner, 1992.
46. In one study of 1,469 cases where attempts were made to reverse vasectomies in Britain, researchers reported a 76 percent pregnancy rate for those who had undergone the initial operation within the past three years (Belker et al., 1991). The pregnancy rate declined significantly, however, to only 30 percent when the operation was performed 15 years or more after the vasectomy.
47. Cale et al., 1990; Guess, 1990; McDonald, 1990; and Tang et al., 1988.
48. Healy, 1993; Waites, 1993.
49. Rogow and Horowitz, 1995.
50. Zelnick, Kantner, and Ford, 1981.
51. Rogow and Horowitz, 1995.
52. See Clark, 1981; Free and Alexander, 1976; Pudney et al., 1992; and Ilaria et al., 1992. After reviewing this literature, Rogow and Horowitz (1995, p. 146) concluded,
> The generally accepted wisdom that the presence of sperm in pre-ejaculatory fluid makes withdrawal an ineffective method of contraception—an opinion repeatedly cited in the literature and echoed by clinicians worldwide—has little scientific support.
53. *Contraceptive Technology Update*, 1993; Lethbridge, 1990; Potts, 1985.
54. Rogow and Horowitz, 1995.
55. Free and Alexander, 1976.
56. Lissner, 1992.
57. Djerassi, 1980; Benditt, 1980; Nieschlag, Wickings, and Breuer, 1981.
58. Waites, 1993.
59. Comhaire, 1994; Nieschlag, Behre, and Weinbauer, 1992; Swerdloff, Wang, and Bhasin, 1989; Waites, 1993; WHO, 1990; 1992; 1995.
60. Researchers have been exploring LHRH (luteinizing hormone-releasing hormone), a brain hormone critical to reproductive physiology and the use of drugs, vaccines, and artificially made LHRH analogues to suppress gonadotrophin secretion and sperm production. Androgens, male sex hormones, are a necessary part of these methods of fertility control because the drugs that reduce the production of spermatozoa also decrease testosterone production. Hormonal birth control for men must therefore include some form of androgen replacement in order to maintain libido and the metabolic effects of testosterone

(Sundaram, Kumar, and Bardin, 1993). Researchers have been studying whether androgens alone or in combination with progestogens could achieve azoospermia (total absence of sperm in the ejaculate) in healthy fertile men (WHO, 1990; 1992; 1995). Some researchers have also been studying the utility of providing men with supplemental, synthetic androgen preparations (e.g., 7 _-methyl-19-nortestosterone, MENT) through implants (Sundaram, Kumar, and Bardin, 1993). These researchers propose that MENT implants could replace the frequent (1 to 3 week intervals) intramuscular injections generally associated with some male hormonal birth control methods currently being studied. The National Institute of Child Health and Human Development has conducted studies on synthetic androgens for over fifteen years. One androgen, testosterone enanthate, was studied extensively among 160 men in the United States and Germany. Azoospermia was not obtained in a considerable number of men (one-third to a half) and the recovery time for regaining normal sperm counts was a year or longer in most cases.

61. Schearer, 1978.

62. The ICCR studied seven progestins (synthetic hormones that exert action similar to the female sex hormone, progesterone) in thirty-five clinical studies among more than two hundred men from 1971 to 1977. None of the twenty-five regimens tested were fully effective in bringing about azoospermia.

63. Waites, 1993; Ringheim, 1993; 1995.

64. Ringheim, 1995.

65. Pangkahila, 1991.

66. Ringheim, 1995; Waites, 1993.

67. Bialy and Patanelli, 1981, p. 103.

68. Ringheim, 1995, p. 124.

69. Cited in Stokes, 1980.

70. Djerassi, 1981.

71. Jaccard et al., 1981.

72. Djerassi and Leibo, 1994, p. 11.

73. Cited in Nevid, Fichner-Rathus, and Rathus, 1995, p. 375.

74. Waites, 1993, p. 219.

75. Waites, 1993, p. 219.

76. Seaman, 1972, p. 243.

77. Segal, 1972; see also Djerassi, 1980; Liskin, Benoit, and Blackburn, 1992.

78. Perry and Dawson, 1985.

79. Stokes, 1980.

80. U.S. House of Representatives, 1990, p. 212.

81. The process of developing and marketing a contraceptive drug is time-consuming and arduous, particularly in the United States (Djerassi, 1980; Klitsch, 1995; Mastroianni, Donaldson, and Kane, 1990; Smith, Potts, and Fortney, 1991). A major reason for this situation is the stringent requirements of the Food

and Drug Administration (FDA). Clinical testing of contraceptives in other countries is also frequently delayed by a long series of clearances imposed by regulatory agencies (Bialy and Patanelli, 1981).

82. Service, 1994.

83. Results from the 1997 Kaiser Family Foundation survey found that many men, aged 18 and older, reported that they would be willing personally to use hormonal methods if they were available (Stewart, 1997). When alternatively asked whether they would be willing to use "birth control pills," "Depro-Provera, or the shot," and "NorPlant, or implants," 66, 43, and 36 percent, respectively, of this national sample indicated that they would. Only 29 percent said they would not use any of these methods.

These companies are also concerned with the prospects of liability litigation. In the late 1980s, the National Academy of Sciences sponsored a series of meetings on the impediments to conducting contraceptive research. It was concluded that the climate to conduct contraceptive research was adversely affected because of recent product liability litigation and the impact this litigation had on the cost of liability insurance and companies' ability to secure it (Klitsch, 1995; Mastroianni, Donaldson, and Kane, 1990). One effect of this less than ideal funding situation for contraceptive research is that fewer talented scientists elect to pursue career research paths in this type of high-risk environment, which in turn serves to thwart the development of new methods, including potential male contraceptives.

84. Klitsch, 1995.

85. Djerassi, 1980, p. 119.

NOTES TO CHAPTER 5

1. For a poignant narrative about these issues, see Darryl's extensive comments—the twenty-eight-year-old man we first met in chapter 1 (Shostak, McLouth, and Seng, 1984, pp. 97–100)

2. Figueira-McDonough, 1989.

3. Harris, 1986; Shifman, 1990.

4. One example of this gender distrust can be seen in the comments of 15- to 19-year-old, black focus group participants in Milwaukee (Gilmore, DeLamater, and Wagstaff, 1995, pp. 16–17; see also Sugland, Wilder, and Chandra, 1996; Furstenberg, 1995). These participants reported that it was common for young women to try and trick their peers into becoming unwilling fathers, or "hooked up." Speaking of a recent partner, one participant said, "Yeah, she think, she wanted to be pregnant so I could be for her for the rest of her life. 'Til the end, 'til I'm old and grey, something like that." Others mentioned that they did not trust some partners because they feared that they might intentionally put a hole in a condom to get pregnant, or they might lie about taking birth control pills be-

cause, as two participants combined to report: "She's settin' you up for somethin'." "She just, she want to hook you up."

5. See Jencks, 1992; Mare and Winship, 1991; and Wood, 1995, for analyses that challenge the magnitude of the effect decreasing employment has had on marriage rates among blacks.

6. Anderson, 1990; Braithwaite, 1981; Franklin, 1984; Lichter et al., 1992; Wilson, 1987.

7. Hall and Ferree, 1986.

8. Lynxwiler and Gay, 1995.

9. Lynxwiler and Gay, 1994; 1996.

10. Marsiglio and Shehan, 1993.

11. Marsiglio, 1989.

12. Zelles, 1984.

13. Shostak, McLouth, and Seng, 1984.

14. Ryan and Plutzer, 1989.

15. Seltzer and Brandreth, 1995.

16. Major, Cozzarelli, and Testa, 1992; Shostak, McLouth, and Seng, 1984.

17. Major, Cozzarelli, and Testa, 1992.

18. Shostak, McLouth, and Seng, 1984. This sample is obviously not representative of all men whose partner chooses abortion because it excludes men who do not accompany their partner to a clinic as well as those men whose partners visit a private physician. Nevertheless, the directors of the participating clinics confirmed that the sample reflects the composition of those men who typically attend one of the selected sites.

19. These researchers drew tentative conclusions about differences they observed in the 100 African American and 900 white males they surveyed. Their impression was that the black men who accompanied their partners to the abortion clinic viewed themselves as more "moralistic, traditional, abortion-leery, fetus-concerned, pronatalist, and solemn" than the white men attending the clinic (Shostak, McLouth, and Seng, 1984, p. 97).

20. Shostak, McLouth, and Seng, 1984, p. 108.

21. Shostak, McLouth, and Seng, 1984, p. 121.

22. Furstenberg, 1988; Furstenberg and Cherlin, 1991.

23. Scanzoni, 1989.

24. They do so by influencing the content of formal sex education programs, media campaigns promoting responsible male contraceptive behavior, school policies regarding the distribution of condoms and other forms of birth control, abortion clinic policies designed to encourage male partner involvement, pro-life organizations' information pamphlets and demonstrations against abortion clinics, and laws involving partner notification in cases of abortion.

25. Bauer, 1986; Bellah et al., 1985; Francoeur, 1983.

26. Rue, 1986.

27. Scanzoni et al., 1989.

28. A vocal collection of women have historically identified themselves as both feminists and pro-life (MacNair, Derr, and Naranjo-Huebl, 1996). These types of women tend to represent only a small segment of the feminist movement today.

29. DeCrow, 1982.

30. Morse, 1995/96.

31. DeCrow, 1982.

32. Kapp, 1982, p. 376.

33. Newman, 1987.

34. Axelrod, 1990; Stetson, 1991; Walters, 1989.

35. Kimmel and Kaufman, 1994.

36. See Ryan and Plutzer, 1989.

37. Aron, Barnow, and McNaught, 1988; Family Impact Seminar, 1990; Meyer, 1992; Nicholas-Casebolt and Garfinkel, 1991; Wattenberg, 1993.

38. Lacay, 1992; see also Shifman, 1990.

39. Marsiglio and Shehan, 1993.

40. Adebayo, 1990, see also Shostak, McLouth, and Seng, 1984.

41. *People in the Interest of S.P.B.*, 1982.

42. Newman, 1987.

43. In the final chapter, I present a preliminary proposal that attempts to address these gender conflicts for a select category of persons.

NOTES TO CHAPTER 6

1. My discussion focuses on men in heterosexual couples even though more gay men (and lesbians) may attempt to overcome stiff political resistance and avail themselves in the future to these alternative means of reproducing children (Bradley, 1995).

2. Gerson, 1993; Griswold, 1993; LaRossa, 1988; Marsiglio, 1995c.

3. Ahlburg and De Vita, 1992; Da Vanzo and Rahman, 1993; Hollander, 1996.

4. Larson, 1992.

5. See Bahr and Bahr, 1996; Berscheid, 1996; Beutler et al., 1989; Delaisi de Parseval and Hurstel, 1987; Edwards, 1989; Griswold, 1993; Jurich, 1989; Marks, 1996; Menaghan, 1989; Seligman, 1990; Scanzoni and Marsiglio, 1991; 1993; Scanzoni et al., 1989.

6. Anderson, 1992. At the same time, gays and lesbians have recently been spearheading a movement to gain formal public acceptance of gay/lesbian marriage. With or without these formal ties, many gays and lesbians in serious relationships tend to see their partner as family.

7. See Seligman, 1990. When I ask students in my introductory sociology

courses to define "family," many intentionally prepare definitions that go beyond the conventional definition that is restricted to blood, marriage, and adoption.

8. Quoted in Ragoné, 1994, p. 118.

9. Delaisi de Parseval and Hurstel, 1987; Edwards, 1991; Macklin, 1991.

10. This technique, of course, still requires individuals to either step forward and request testing or be singled out and then tested.

11. Anderson, 1992, p. 865.

12. Anderson, 1992, pp. 870–871.

13. Hawkins et al., 1995.

14. There has been a voluntary shift in New Zealand in recent years toward identifying sperm donors that was prompted by this country's poor experiences with closed adoption (Purdie et al., 1994).

15. In some instances, these views may be differentiated along the lines I suggested in chapter 1 when I introduced the concepts global and situational procreative consciousness. See Stycos, 1996, for a brief summary of the recent growth in the international family planning literature that explores male's fertility goals and views about contraception.

16. My comments here draw heavily on Miller's (1992) extensive discussion about childbearing motivations.

17. I draw upon Jacob's (1995) conceptualization to talk about men's "wish" for children. He, like Miller, distinguishes between latent and manifest representations of concepts dealing with paternal motivation.

18. Jacobs, 1995; Miller, 1992.

19. See also Mitchell, 1996, for attitudinal data based on the 1994 General Social Survey (GSS), which sampled noninstitutionalized adults 18 years of age and older. In the GSS, 52 percent of men reported that having two children was "the ideal number of children for a family to have" and 54 percent of women reported two as the ideal number. Meanwhile, 20 percent of men and 17 percent of women agreed with the statement that "people who have never had children lead empty lives." On a related matter, 72 percent of men and 70 percent of women agreed that people should get married if they want children. Presumably, white men are more likely to support this view than African American men because 74 percent of whites but only 54 percent of blacks agreed with this statement, and there were only minor differences based on educational attainment.

20. Seccombe, 1991.

21. Kaufman, 1995.

22. Davis, 1987; Neal, Groat, and Wicks, 1989; Nock, 1987; Ryder, 1979.

23. Miller, 1992; Seccombe, 1991.

24. Contrary to some parents' perceptions, some research from the 1980s suggests that the cost of raising children did not actually increase during the twenty-five years prior to the study (Espenshade, 1984).

25. Neal, Groat, and Wicks, 1989, p. 325.

26. Miller, 1992. The sample for this study included 363 husbands and 354 wives from Santa Clara County, California.

27. Both of these studies were based on data from the National Survey of Families and Households.

28. Seccombe, 1991.

29. Kaufman, 1995.

30. Mackey, White, and Day, 1992.

31. Mott's (1983) analysis of the youth cohort of the National Longitudinal Survey of Labor Market Experience showed that young men in their teens and twenties were much less accurate than young women in reporting their fertility. Misreporting of one sort of the other was so pervasive that of the 728 male respondents who reported a live birth, 341 were found to have at least one discrepant record. While many of these discrepant records dealt with children's birth dates, it was surprisingly common for children to "appear" and "disappear" from men's fertility histories during various waves of the NLSY panel survey. About 25 percent of fathers of children who were *not* living with them acknowledged their child for the first time in 1982, even though the child had been born prior to the 1981 survey. Overall, Mott found that men's reporting inconsistencies were not random; those men who had never married, did not live with their child, or were African American were more likely than their counterparts to have inconsistencies in their birth histories.

32. Bachu, 1996.

33. This report presents extensive tabular fertility data by gender, age, race, Hispanic origin, educational attainment, labor force status, occupation, income, geographic region, and marital status. One of the important contributions of this research is its analysis of nonresponse rates. Demographers have long been concerned about the quality of men's fertility reports because men are thought to intentionally and unintentionally misreport their fertility experiences more often than women. Some types of men are thought to do this more often than others (see note 31).

The Survey of Income and Program Participation (SIPP) documents that 8.3 percent of men did not report on a "children ever born" question, compared to a rate of 6.9 percent rate among women. Nonresponse rates were higher for African American (12.8 percent) and Hispanic (10.7 percent) men than for white men (7.8 percent). Part of the nonresponse rate for blacks can be attributed to the higher proportion of black men who were never married. Never married men, compared to their married counterparts, were more likely not to answer this question, 14.3 to 6.4 percent, respectively.

See Kaplan, Lancaster, and Anderson (1996) for another recent analysis of male fertility patterns. Their study, based on a clever sampling strategy that obtained respondents from a Motor Vehicle Division office in Albuquerque, New Mexico, resulted in a large sampling of Hispanic men.

34. Henshaw, 1992; Institute of Medicine, 1995.

35. Gerzi and Berman, 1981; Heinowitz, 1982; Herzog, 1982; May, 1980; Sherwen, 1987; Soule, Stanley, and Copans, 1979.

36. Klein, 1991.

37. Bogren, 1984; Clinton, 1987; Munroe and Munroe, 1971; Strikland, 1987; Trethowan and Colon, 1965; Trethowan, 1968.

38. Klein, 1991; see also Munroe and Munroe, 1971, 1973; Munroe, Munroe, and Nerlove, 1973; Meigs, 1976.

39. Conner and Denson, 1990.

40. Klein, 1991.

41. Bogren, 1984.

42. Clinton, 1987; Curtis, 1955.

43. Strikland, 1987.

44. Quill, Lipkin, and Lamb, 1984.

45. Herzog, 1982.

46. Herzog, cited in Sherman, 1987, pp. 165–166.

47. Siegel, 1982; Zayas, 1988.

48. Zayas, 1988, pp. 292–293.

49. May, 1980.

50. Given the rise in out-of-wedlock childbirth, a growing number of single women are participating in these prepared childbirth classes. As a result, some instructors have noted that an increasing number of expectant mothers are bringing female friends and family members to serve as their labor coach. One instructor in Gainesville, Florida, Elizabeth Poston, commented that she has made a conscious effort to refer to these helpers in a gender-neutral way—generally referring to them as the pregnant woman's helper.

51. Bowen and Miller, 1980; Myers, 1982; Peterson, Mehl, and Leiderman, 1979.

52. Manion, 1977; Rodholm, 1981.

53. Westreich et al., 1991.

54. Mosher and Pratt, 1990.

55. Peterson, 1995. Estimates vary due in part to differing ways of defining infertility and the time period being studied.

56. Menning, Wentz, and Garner, 1993.

57. While artificial insemination has been practiced in human beings since 1799 and can be accomplished without medical intervention, I have chosen to discuss this asexual form of reproduction alongside the more recent technological innovations in assisted reproduction because the medical community gradually gained control over this practice during the mid and late twentieth century. Moreover, the procedures have been perfected during this time and artificial insemination has increased dramatically during the middle and late twentieth century (Curie-Cohen, Luttrell, and Shapiro, 1979; Issacs and Holt, 1987; McNeil,

Varcoe, and Yearley, 1990; Office of Technology Assessment, 1988; Shalev, 1989; Stolcke, 1988). There are three forms of artificial insemination: AIH, artificial insemination by husband (or partner); AID, artificial insemination by donor; and AIC, which represents a combination of the first two types.

58. Many authors refer to this technology as ovum transfer (OT), but technically the ovum is fertilized outside the woman's body and a five-day-old embryo is then transferred to the woman. Another technology, gamete intrafallopian transfer (GIFT), enables fertility specialists to place through laparoscopy sperm and eggs directly into one or both fallopian tubes of the gestational mother, the normal site of human fertilization. A third variation, zygote intrafallopian transfer (ZIFT), is a hybrid of IVF and GIFT and involves egg retrieval and the incubation of the eggs and sperm. After fertilization has taken place, the zygotes are transferred to the fallopian tube(s) (see Edwards, 1991; Issacs and Holt, 1987; Partridge-Brown, 1993; Asch and Marrs, 1992). Finally, intracytoplasmatic sperm injection (ICSI) is a new and promising technique that enables a single sperm to be injected into one ovum (Velde, 1994; Wolinsky, 1994). This technique could have profound implications because it enables men with extremely low sperm qualities to experience biological paternity and thereby reduce the proportion of children conceived with donor sperm. The first pregnancies using this technique were reported by Dr. Gianpiero and his colleagues at the Center for Reproductive Medicine in Brussels, Belgium, in 1992. Since then, numerous embryologists from around the world, including the United States, have visited Belgium to learn this technique.

59. While I list the practice of surrogacy as a biosocial innovation, and in the process implicitly acknowledge that its practice is typically associated with the medical community, this process (in combination with self-insemination) can and has at times been used by individual women without the assistance of the medical community (Issacs and Holt, 1987; McNeil, 1990; Ragoné, 1994; Whiteford, 1989).

60. Society for Assisted Reproductive Technology, 1994, personal communication; Laborie, 1988. The development and increasing use of innovations in reproductive technology overlaps the recent development of contraceptive technology, the second major moment in the history of reproduction according to O'Brien (1981). These earlier (and ongoing) technological developments have provided women (and men) a greater opportunity to exert control over their reproductive potential without abstaining from sexual intercourse.

61. Begley, 1995b.

62. Office of Technology Assessment, 1988.

63. Edwards, 1991.

64. See Pinchbeck, 1996; Wright, 1996. Healthy men typically produce about 100 million sperm per milliliter. When sperm counts fall below 20 million per milliliter, men have reduced fertility and those with counts below 5 million are

frequently sterile. Several early studies conducted in the 1970s reported U.S. data based on men from several cities that was consistent with the thesis that sperm counts were declining. However, additional research in this area did not appear in the scientific literature after John MacLeod, a prominent anatomist who had retired from Cornell University Medical College, published a negative critique in 1979 of these early studies thereby discouraging other researchers from conducting additional studies (cited in Wright, 1996). In 1992 several Danish scientists published studies of sperm counts from around the world that suggested that sperm counts had, in general, declined (Carlsen et al., 1992; see also Keiding and Skakkebaek, 1995; McDonough, 1995; Olsen, Ross, Bodner, Lipshultz, and Ramlow, 1995; Olsen, Ross, Bodner, and Lipshultz, 1995).

In *The Children of Men*, P. D. James (1992) develops an intriguing fictional account of the potential cultural, political, and social ramifications resulting from a world crisis in which all men are rendered infertile in 1995. Set in the year 2021, this novel explores the dire consequences of a world without viable sperm.

65. Keoun, 1996.

66. Greil, Leitko, and Porter, 1988; McGrade and Tolor, 1981.

67. Corney, 1990; Koman, 1991.

68. Meerabeau, 1991; see also Rothman, 1986.

69. Newton et al., 1992.

70. See Blaser, Maloigne-Katz, and Gigon's (1988) study of Swiss men.

71. Humphrey and Humphrey, 1988.

72. Cited in Mahlstedt, 1994, p. 560.

73. Jequier, 1990.

74. Hinting et al., 1990; Horbay, Cowell, and Casper, 1991; Meacham and Lipshultz, 1991; Sigman, 1991; Tournaye et al., 1991.

75. Marsiglio, 1988b.

76. Carmeli and Birenbaum-Carmeli, 1994, p. 673.

77. Harrison, Callan, and Hennessy, 1987; Kentenich et al., 1992.

78. Carmeli and Birenbaum-Carmeli, 1994.

79. Carmeli and Birenbaum-Carmeli, 1994, pp. 671–672. This study is based on observations from two fertility clinics, one in Israel and the other in Canada. When the authors single out Israel in their comments, they are therefore suggesting that their observation is not as relevant to Canada.

80. Bresnick and Taymor, 1979; Collins et al., 1992; Link and Darling, 1986; McGrade and Tolor, 1981; Greil, 1991; Greil, Leitko, and Porter, 1988; McEwan, Costello, and Taylor, 1987; Wright et al., 1991.

81. Adler and Boxley, 1985; Weltzien, 1984.

82. Berg, Wilson, and Weingartner, 1991.

83. Greil, 1991; Nachtigall, Becker, and Wozny, 1992.

84. Nachtigall, Becker, and Wozny, 1992, p. 118.

85. Nachtigall, Becker, and Wozny, 1992, p. 120.

86. While it is important to consider individuals' views about and responses to these technologies, it is also useful to look at the significance of these technologies from a larger sociopolitical perspective. Numerous scholars have assessed the implications reproductive technologies are likely to have for women (Blankenship et al., 1993; Rothman, 1989). Many feminists are highly critical of those who praise the innovative birth technologies that supposedly expand women's reproductive choices. Some make the point that these reproductive innovations induce the exploitation of women, who are swayed by pronatalistic ideologies and submit themselves to the medical community's interventionist techniques. In addition, feminists have been concerned with the way court decisions, as they relate to the use of reproductive technologies, have increased the government's control over women's reproductive lives (Blankenship et al., 1993). An important adage of feminist ideology is that discussions about reproductive choices are meaningless unless they take into account the conditions under which women make those decisions (Gertner, 1989; Gimenez, 1991; Petchesky, 1980).

This debate, though vital, goes beyond my more narrow focus on men's involvement with reproductive technologies. I therefore do not attempt to resolve it here. Women who undergo some forms of assisted reproduction are typically subjected to more intrusive and extensive treatments than their male partners. However, men must deal with the infertility stigma that is based on societal perceptions of the interrelationship between masculinity, sexual prowess, and virility. Men must also cope with treatment processes that tend to marginalize them (Carmeli and Birenbaum-Carmeli, 1994). Some men report concern over being excluded from treatment decisions and procedures that are focused more directly on women; for example, in some clinics men are not allowed to be present when their partner's ovum are being retrieved or when she is being artificially inseminated. Some men may also feel pressured by their partner to demonstrate repeatedly that they are committed to the treatment process since the treatment is typically not directly focused on them.

87. See Crowe, 1985; Overall, 1987.

88. Snowden, Mitchell, and Snowden, 1983.

89. Snowden, Mitchell, and Snowden, 1983, p. 128.

90. Snowden, Mitchell, and Snowden, 1983.

91. Klock and Maier, 1991.

92. Humphrey and Humphrey, 1988; Snowden, Mitchell, and Snowden, 1983.

93. Snowden, Mitchell, and Snowden, 1983.

94. See, Kanter, 1994; Kovacs, Clayton, and McGovern, 1983; Nicholas and Tyler, 1983.

95. Fletcher, 1988.

96. Frankel, 1976.

97. Gaines, 1990.

98. Holbrook, 1990.

99. Hill, 1992, p. 209.

100. Beck, 1984.

101. Cited in Mahlstedt and Probasco, 1991, p. 752. For an extensive discussion about the anonymity issue with respect to sperm donation, the interested reader should review the series of international commentaries that were written in response to Daniels and Taylor's (1993a) international roundtable article (Achilles, 1993; Bielawska-Batorowicz, 1993; Burfoot, 1993; Cooke, 1993; Haimes, 1993; Holmes, 1993; Knoppers, 1993; Lansac, 1993; Lasker, 1993; Lauritzen, 1993; McWhinnie, 1993; Raboy, 1993; Rowland, 1993; Snowden, 1993; Triseliotis, 1993; Turner, 1993; see also Daniels's [1993] response).

102. Baran and Pannor, 1989.

103. HMSO, 1990, cited in Robinson et al., 1991.

104. Daniels and Taylor, 1993a.

105. Rowland and Ruffin, 1983.

106. Daniels, 1987. In Daniels's (1989) subsequent small-scale survey of twenty-three current sperm donors in Australia, 86 percent reported that they would be willing to provide identifying information. Meanwhile, 42 percent of active sperm donors in another Australian sample reported that they would continue to donate if identifying information were registered (Rowland, 1983).

107. Robinson et al., 1991.

108. Walker, Gregson, and McLauglin, 1987.

109. Mahlstedt and Probasco, 1991.

110. Meyers, 1994.

111. Swanson, 1993.

112. See study conducted by Mahlstedt and Probasco, 1991.

113. Bydgeman, 1989.

114. Purdie et al., 1994.

115. Chauhan et al., 1988; Mahlstedt and Probasco, 1991; Noble, 1987.

116. Purdie et al., 1994.

117. Barratt, Chauhan, and Cooke, 1990.

118. Purdie et al., 1994.

119. Barratt, Chauhan, and Cooke, 1990.

120. Purdie et al., 1994.

121. Purdie et al., 1994.

122. I receive a wide range of responses when I ask my female university students about how they might feel if their potential spouse wanted to donate sperm. Some report that they would not tolerate it, others say they would permit it reluctantly, and still others indicate that they would leave it up to their husband and that they would support whatever decision he made.

123. Mahlstedt and Probasco, 1991, p. 751.

124. Daniels, 1989.

125. Uniform Parentage Act, 1973, p. 301.

126. It is far less common, though not unheard of, for older children and sometimes adults to request that a paternity test be performed if they are curious about their origins.

127. Wattenberg, 1993. For general discussions about paternity establishment efforts, see also Sonenstein, Holcomb, and Seefeldt, 1993.

128. Ellingboe, 1994; Filhiol, 1990; Hinnant, 1990; Hirczy, 1993; Mallon, 1989; Runner, 1989–90; Secor, 1990; Stranger, 1989; Sylvain, 1990.

129. Uniform Parentage Act, 1973, pp. 298–299.

130. Ellingboe, 1994.

131. Hirczy, 1993, p. 99.

132. Anderson, 1992.

133. Marsiglio, 1992.

134. Adoptive mothers and women who use ART may have similar feelings. However, some women who use ART with donor ova may actually not feel as strongly about dissimilarities in appearance between them and their child because they, unlike men, can establish a type of psychic connection with a child because of the physiological bond that occurs during the gestation process. This type of maternal connection may compensate for differences in physical appearance between mothers and their children conceived with donor ova.

135. Larson, 1992.

136. This observation is consistent with Cooley's (1902) classic ideas about the looking-glass self concept.

137. Marsiglio, 1992.

138. Men may feign their interest in children at times in order to convince their partner early on in their relationship that they have androgynous, care-giving qualities. These qualities are consistent with more modern versions of masculinity (Knijn, 1995).

139. Mott, 1990.

140. Marsiglio, 1992.

141. Shoop, 1993.

142. March, 1995.

143. Issacs and Holt, 1987. IVF technology in countries like the United States is extremely expensive and can involve tens of thousands of dollars in some cases (Beck, 1984). In comparison, the AI procedures, though expensive, are much more affordable. It was estimated, on average, that women in the United States had to spend $953 during 1986 to 1987 to become pregnant through artificial insemination. Physicians reported that 51 percent of these women had insurance to cover this procedure, and insurance defrayed about 48 percent of the total cost (Office of Technology Assessment, 1988). Insurance coverage of IVF treatment procedures is typically not available in the United States (Fox, 1993).

144. Velde, 1994.

145. Brownlee et al., 1994.

146. For related questions, see Edwards, 1991.

147. On a more theoretical level, questions can be asked about how studying men's responses to asexual reproductive methods may reveal connections between aspects of men's procreative consciousness and their sense of procreative responsibility?

Although I have focused on fathers' perceptions and experiences, reproductive innovations may also have consequences for children's development. A smaller proportion of children than fathers will be affected directly, though, because many more children than fathers will be unaware that ART played a role in their conception and birth. An important factor that needs to be taken into account when discussing the development of these children is whether or not they are aware of the circumstances surrounding their conception. The types of questions that researchers can address will obviously vary depending upon whether children have been informed of the nature of their conception and birth. To date, these children (and their families) have not been subjected to careful study, so it is only possible to speculate about their socioemotional development (see Snowden, Mitchell, and Snowden, 1983; Iizuka et al., 1968). Children conceived through asexual methods, especially methods involving the use of donated sperm and/or ova, might have different familial experiences and self-perceptions if they were compared to children who were conceived naturally. This would be consistent with evidence that shows that adoptive and foster families often have different familial dynamics than those traditional families where a husband and wife live with their naturally conceived children (Humphrey and Humphrey, 1988).

While it might be possible to draw some conclusions about these children's feelings by extrapolating from studies using adopted children, the comparison is confounded by the fact that adopted children will probably have a greater tendency to feel that they were abandoned as infants by a genetic and gestational mother, as well as by a genetic father in many cases. Children born with the aid of noncoital reproductive technologies will not experience this anxiety and may even feel special because their parents went to such great lengths to have them. Snowden, Mitchell, and Snowden, (1983, p. 81) concluded, based on their small, nonrepresentative study of AI couples using donor sperm, that all of the spouses

> appeared to have accepted the children willingly and happily; indeed some of the fathers had a particularly close relationship with their children and appeared to be deeply involved in child care and family life. Because their children had been achieved after considerable heartache, and after much effort, they were particularly valued and loved and the couples tended to find parenting particularly rewarding and satisfying.

148. Furstenberg, 1988; Furstenberg and Cherlin, 1991.

NOTES TO CHAPTER 7

1. Back, 1989.

2. Faludi, 1991.

3. Bellah et al., 1985; Blankenhorn, 1995; and Gilder, 1981; 1986.

4. Blankenhorn, 1995, p. 167.

5. Blankenhorn, 1995, p. 17.

6. Popenoe, 1996, personal communication.

7. Another feminist who would agree with Blankenhorn's conclusion is Alice Rossi (see Rossi, 1987).

8. See Moir and Jessel, 1989, for a readable description of this literature.

9. While useful, models that emphasize gender differences should be supplemented within the research community by models that look for similarities between men and women. Researchers sometimes run the risk of exaggerating the practical significance of gender differences. At the same time, they should not ignore them. In short, each of these approaches have their respective strengths and limitations in the kinds of knowledge they produce about individual behavior and social life.

10. Lamb et al., 1987, p. 115.

11. Rossi, 1987.

12. Moir and Jessel, 1989, p. 66.

13. Whatever these efforts may be, they should take into account the complex issues Barbara Whitehead (1996) raises in connection with women, fatherhood, and marriage. Policymakers and the general public must grapple with the competing images of marriage (or a committed union) as either a setting for "egalitarianism and emotional fulfillment" or a context where two people maintain a relationship infused with the responsibilities associated with raising children.

14. Rossi, 1987, p. 65. As we contemplate strategies for promoting men's and women's opportunities respectively, we should be mindful of the fact that biomedical research has shown that social experience can, in fact, influence brain functioning (see Begley, 1995a). While the short-term gains are likely to be minuscule, the long-term evolutionary possibilities are intriguing.

15. Rothman, 1989.

16. See chapter 9 in Clatterbaugh, 1997. For journalist accounts of this movement, see Clarkson, 1996; Gilbreath, 1995; Murchison, 1996; Novosad, 1996; Swomley, 1996; Wagenheim, 1996; and Woodward and Keene-Osborn, 1994. This movement has a number of similarities to the Muscular Christianity men's movement of the late nineteenth century (Hackett, 1996).

17. In October 1996, I witnessed these messages firsthand during my participation in a two-day rally held in the Jacksonville Municipal Stadium in Florida. Bill McCartney, who is white, made an impassioned plea for racial reconciliation in his closing address to the conference. Despite McCartney's zest for promoting

racial reconciliation, the Promise Keepers is still very much a white, middle-class, male movement. While half of the speakers at the Jacksonville rally were racial minorities, at least 95 percent of the general audience appeared to be white. My experience is consistent with those reporting on other rallies (see Clarkson, 1996), although official Promise Keeper literature reports that 16 percent of the membership is not white (cited in Hackett [1996] and based on an article, "Picture of a Promise Keeper," in *New Man*, 2, 1996). While it is not surprising that relatively few minority men attend these rallies given the high ticket prices of $60, the Promise Keepers' leadership has recently been making a concerted effort to sponsor poor men's participation in the rallies.

Given the organization's strong ties to conservative religious groups, it is also not surprising that a strong undercurrent of this movement is its antigay sentiment. The antigay viewpoint was recently expressed by Tony Evans, a black Dallas evangelist and popular speaker at Promise Keepers' rallies, who proclaimed to a Detroit audience in 1995,

> I am here to serve notice on you today, if black homosexuals can get together with white homosexuals, and if yellow homosexuals can get together with Hispanic homosexuals and produce immorality in the name of *hell*, then black and white Christians can get together and bring the kingdom of God in the name of *heaven* (cited in Novosad, 1996, p. 26).

This dogmatic attitude toward gays was also expressed on several occasions at the Jacksonville rally by some of the speakers and attendees.

18. Novosad, 1996.

19. Murchison, 1996, p. 6.

20. Gilbreath, 1995; I also witnessed these types of messages at the 1996 Jacksonville rally.

21. The two wives I spoke to about their husbands' participation in Promise Keepers' rally were both pleased several weeks after the event with the way their husbands were treating them. The husbands apparently made a conscious effort to compliment their wives at least three times a day and they made sure that they ate at least one meal with their wives. Unfortunately, my more recent discussions with these women reveal that these changes were relatively short lived.

22. I chose this term after learning of Mary Stewart Van Leeuwen's characterization of Promise Keepers' message as "soft patriarchy" in her unpublished manuscript "Servanthood or soft patriarchy? A Christian feminist looks at the Promise Keepers movement."

23. Evans, 1994, p. 79.

24. Cited in Clarkson, 1996, p. 15.

25. Cited in Wagenheim, 1996, p. 77.

26. The message of paternal responsibility was cleverly conveyed by one of the speakers at the Promise Keepers Jacksonville rally. Mr. Dennis Rainey, Executive Director of Family Life Today in Little Rock, Arkansas, used animal traps, in-

cluding one designed for bears, to symbolize the dangerous vices adolescents face today (e.g., drugs, alcohol, premarital sex). Mr. Rainey separated on either side of the stage a father and son pair who had volunteered for the demonstration. Mr. Rainey then positioned on the floor several rigged animal traps in the middle of the stage. The demonstration ended when Mr. Rainey asked the blindfolded boy to cross the stage but the father yelled at him to ignore the invitation. Blindfolded, the young boy negotiated the maze of "vices," but only after his father went to his side and led him across the stage. I am grateful to Andrew Cherlin for helping me formulate my point about liberal men and social agendas concerning procreation and fatherhood issues.

27. Swomley, 1996.

28. Swomley, 1996.

29. Levine and Pitt, 1995.

30. Paglia, 1992.

31. Griswold, 1993.

32. Griswold, 1993.

33. Griswold, 1993, pp. 261–262. My informal discussions with therapists and lawyers who work with men estranged from their children reinforce my sense that many of these fathers' have legitimate gripes about how their genuine efforts to be more involved in their children's lives are circumvented by others.

34. Bertoia and Drakich, 1995, p. 252.

35. Polikoff, 1983, p. 188.

36. Braver and Griffin, 1996.

37. Carrera, 1992; Forrest, Swanson, and Beckstein, 1989; see also Beckstein, 1987; and Danielson et al., 1988.

38. Schulte and Sonenstein, 1995.

39. Schulte and Sonenstein, 1995.

40. Schulte and Sonenstein, 1995.

41. Schulte and Sonenstein, 1995.

42. Mahler, 1996.

43. See Niego and Danielson (1996) for a summary of their *Reproductive Health Counseling for Young Men* program, developed and field tested between 1985 and 1987 on 1,200 males, aged 15 to 18. This program, organized in conjunction with the health maintenance organization called Northwest Region Kaiser Permanente, provided reproductive health education and counseling for young males in a primary-care setting.

44. Stone and Waszak, 1992.

45. Herek, 1987; Marsiglio, 1988b.

46. Louv, 1993.

47. Levine and Pitt, 1995.

48. Levine and Pitt, 1995.

49. Levine and Pitt, 1995.

50. National Urban League, 1987.

51. Levine and Pitt, 1995.

52. Levine and Pitt, 1995.

53. Westney, Cole, and Munford, 1988.

54. Shostak, McLouth, and Seng, 1984.

55. See Joffe, 1995, for an intriguing account of thirty-five male abortion providers' experiences (ten women were also interviewed) with the ethical, legal, medical, and professional issues associated with this area of reproduction and health care. Some of these "doctors of conscience," as Joffe refers to them, provided illegal abortions before *Roe v. Wade*. This work serves as a reminder that some male (and female) physicians are willing to risk professional marginalization and physical harm in order to protect women's reproductive freedoms.

56. While men were active in calling for the legalization of abortion, they have done little to demand that abortion clinics accommodate their participation in the clinic procedures.

57. Granberg, 1981; Luker, 1984; Maxwell and Jelen, 1995.

58. Ginsburg, 1993.

59. Planned Parenthood Federation of America has 151 affiliates in 49 states plus the District of Columbia (none in North Dakota). Many of these affiliates run more than one clinic site, for a total of nearly 1,000 Planned Parenthood Clinics in the United States. This information was provided by Lisa Radelet, Director of Public Affairs, Planned Parenthood of North Central Florida, Inc.

60. This figure is based on a document obtained from the National Right to Life Committee, Inc., that included a listing of the board of directors, one for every state.

61. Faludi, 1991; and Faux, 1990,

62. Ginsburg, 1993.

63. Faludi, 1991, pp. 401–402.

64. Maxwell and Jelen, 1995, pp. 126–127.

65. Luker, 1984.

66. Those readers interested in reviewing the literature that directly discusses the legal aspects of men's rights and obligations related to paternity, abortion, and child support should see Adams, 1991; Axelrod, 1990; Bentil, 1990; Diggins, 1989; Shifman, 1990; Shostak, McLouth and Seng, 1984; Stuart, 1990.

67. Additional permutations of the four versions of the PRCS contract might include terms that specified child custody and adoption concerns.

68. Shifman, 1990.

69. Shifman, 1990.

70. Institute of Medicine, 1995.

71. Scanzoni et al., 1989.

72. Studies should also examine whether recent and future efforts to enforce

tougher child support laws encourage men to be more responsible about practicing contraception effectively.

73. Marsiglio, 1995c.

74. Burke, 1980; 1991; Burke and Reitzes, 1991; see also Hogg, Terry, and White, 1995.

75. Amato, 1996.

76. Ron Mincy (1997) recently reported on one unique pattern found among some disadvantaged, inner-city African American men. Ethnographic evidence indicates that these young men sometimes intentionally get involved in repeat pregnancies because they are alienated from earlier paternity experiences where they were unable to establish a meaningful relationship with their offspring. In addition, some men who are fearful of dying young say that they sire children in order to ensure their legacy.

77. Callero, 1985; Thoits, 1991.

78. Pasley and Minton, 1997.

79. Cited in Maxwell and Jelen, 1995.

80. Schutz, 1970b.

References

Abbey, A., Andrews, F. M., and Halman, L. J. (1991). Gender's role in response to infertility. *Psychology of Women Quarterly, 15*, 295–316.

Achatz, M., and MacAllum, C. A. (1994). *Young unwed fathers: Report from the field*. Philadelphia: Public/Private Ventures.

Achilles, R. (1993). Protection from what? The secret life of donor insemination. *Politics and the Life Sciences, 12*, 171–172.

Adams, K. R. (1991). Uniform parentage act. *University of Dayton Law Review, 16*, 497–520.

Adebayo, Akin. (1990). Male attitudes toward abortion: An analysis of urban survey data. *Social Indicators Research, 22*, 213–228.

Adler, J. D., and Boxley, R. L. (1985). The psychological reactions to infertility: Sex roles and coping styles. *Sex Roles, 12*, 271–279.

Ahlburg, D. A., and De Vita, C. J. (1992). New realities of the American family. *Population Bulletin, 47*, 1–44. Washington, DC: Population Reference Bureau, Inc.

Akerlof, G. A., Yellen, J. L., and Katz, M. L. (1996). An analysis of out-of-wedlock childbearing in the United States. *Quarterly Journal of Economics, 111*, 277–317.

Althaus, F. (1995). Most vasectomies are performed in urology practices by physicians using ligation and local anesthesia. *Family Planning Perspectives, 27*, 220–221.

Amato, P. (1996). More than money? Men's contributions to their children's lives. Paper presented at the National Symposium on Men in Families. Pennsylvania State University, November 1.

Anderson, E. (1989). Sex codes and family life among poor inner city youths. *Annals of the American Academy of Political and Social Science, 501*, 59–78.

Anderson, E. (1990). *Streetwise: Race, class, and change in an urban community*. Chicago: University of Chicago.

Anderson, J. H. (1992). The functioning father: A unified approach to paternity determinations. *Journal of Family Law, 30(4)*, 847–873.

Anderson, J. E., Brackbill, R., and Mosher, W. D. (1996). Condom use for disease prevention among unmarried U.S. women. *Family Planning Perspectives, 28*, 25–28, 39.

Annie E. Casey Foundation (1995). *Kids count data book*. Baltimore, MD: Annie E. Casey Foundation.

Aron, L. Y., Barnow, B. S., and McNaught, W. (1988). *Paternity establishment among never-married mothers: Estimates from the 1986 Current Population Survey Alimony and Child Support Supplement*. Report prepared by Lewin/ICF for Office of Income and Security Policy, ASPE/DHHS, November.

Asch, R. H., and Marrs, R. P. (1992). *ART: Assisted reproductive technologies*. Norwell, MA: Serono Laboratories, Inc.

Axelrod, R. H. (1990). Whose womb is it anyway: Are paternal rights alive and well despite Danforth? *Cardozo Law Review II*, 685–711.

Bachrach, C. (1997). Why should we pay attention to male fertility and family formation? Paper presented at the Workshop for the Working Group on Male Fertility and Family Formation. Washington, DC, Urban Institute, January.

Bachu, A. (1996). *Fertility of American men*. Population Division Working Paper No. 14. Fertility Statistics Branch. Washington, DC: U.S. Bureau of the Census.

Back, K. W. (1989). *Family planning and population control: The challenges of a successful movement*. Boston: Twayne Publishers.

Bahr, H. M., and Bahr, K. S. (1996). A paradigm of family transcendence. *Journal of Marriage and the Family, 58*, 541–555.

Baldwin, W. H., and Nord, C. W. (1984). *Delayed childbearing in the U.S.: Facts and fictions*. Population Bulletin 39, No. 4. Washington, DC: Population Reference Bureau.

Balswick, J. O. (1972). Attitudes of lower class males toward taking a male birth control pill. *Family Coordinator, 21*, 195–199.

Baran, A., and Pannor, R. (1989). *Lethal secrets*. New York: Warner Books.

Barratt, C. L. R., Chauhan, M., and Cooke, I. D. (1990). Donor insemination—A look to the future. *Fertility and Sterility, 54*, 375–387.

Bauer, G. L. (Ed.) (1986). *The family: Preserving America's future*. White House working group on the family. Washington, DC, November.

Beck, W. W. (1984). Two hundred years of artificial insemination. *Fertility and Sterility, 41*, 193–195.

Beckstein, D. (1987). *Annotated guide to men's sexual and reproductive health resources*. Men's Reproductive Health, Capitola, CA.

Begley, S. (1995a). Nature plus nurture: Searching for how experience influences sexuality. *Newsweek, Nov. 13*, 72.

Begley, S. (1995b). The baby myth. *Newsweek, Sept. 4*, 38–41.

Belker, A. M., Thomas, A. J., Fuchs, E. F., Konnak, J. W., and Sharlip, I. (1991). Results of 1469 microsurgical vasectomy reversals by the basovasostomy study group. *Journal of Urology, 145*, 505–511.

Bellah, R. N., Madsen, R., Sullivan, W. M., Swidler, A., and Tipton, S. M. (1985).

Habits of the heart: Individualism and commitment in American life. Berkeley, CA: University of California Press.

Benditt, J. M. (1980). Current contraceptive research. *Family Planning Perspectives, 12,* 149–155.

Bentil, J. Kodowo. (1990). U.S. and Anglo-Australian decisions on a husband's right to prevent abortion. *Catholic Lawyer, 33,* 261–275.

Berg, B. J., Wilson, J. F., and Weingartner, P. J. (1991). Psychological sequelae of infertility treatment: The role of gender and sex-role identification. *Social Science and Medicine, 33,* 1071–1080.

Bernard, J. (1981). The good provider role: Its rise and fall. *American Psychologist, 36,* 1–12.

Berscheid, E. (1996). The "paradigm of family transcendence": Not a paradigm, questionably transcendent, but valuable, nonetheless. *Journal of Marriage and the Family, 58,* 556–564.

Bertoia, C. E., and Drakich, J. (1995). The fathers' rights movement: Contradictions in rhetoric and practice. In W. Marsiglio (Ed.), *Fatherhood: Contemporary theory, research, and social policy* (pp. 230–254). Thousand Oaks, CA: Sage.

Beutler, I. F., Burr, W. R., Bahr, K. S., and Herrin, D. A. (1989). The family realm: Theoretical contributions for understanding uniqueness. *Journal of Marriage and the Family, 51,* 805–816.

Bialy, G., and Patanelli, D. J. (1981). Potential use of male antifertility agents in developed countries. *Chemotherapy, 27,* 102–106.

Bielawska-Batorowicz, E. (1993). Not ready for openness: Donor insemination in Poland. *Politics and the Life Sciences, 12,* 173–174.

Blake, J. (1966). Ideal family size among White Americans: A quarter of a century's evidence. *Demography, 3,* 154–173.

Blake, J. (1974). Can we believe recent data on birth expectations in the United States? *Demography, 11,* 25–44.

Blankenhorn, D. (1995). *Fatherless America: Confronting our most urgent social problem.* New York: Basic Books.

Blankenship, K. M., Rushing, B., Onorato, S. A., and White, R. (1993). Reproductive technologies and the U.S. Courts. *Gender and Society, 7,* 8–31.

Blaser, A., Maloigne-Katz, B., and Gigon, U. (1988). Effect of artificial insemination with donor semen on the psyche of the husband. *Psychotherapy Psychosomatics, 49,* 17–21.

Bloom, D., and Trussell, J. (1984). What are the determinants of delayed childbearing and permanent childlessness in the United States? *Demography, 21,* 591–612.

Blumer, Herbert. (1969). *Symbolic interactionism.* Englewood Cliffs, NJ: Prentice-Hall.

Bogren, L. Y. (1984). The couvade syndrome: Background variables. *Acta Psychiatrica Scandinavica, 70*, 316–320.

Boswell, A., and Spade, J. (1996). Fraternities and collegiate rape culture: Why are some fraternities more dangerous places for women? *Gender and Society, 10*, 133–147.

Bowen, S. M., and Miller, B. C. (1980). Paternal attachment behavior as related to presence at delivery and preparenthood classes: A pilot study. *Nursing Research, 29*, 307–311.

Bradley, D. (1995). A new kind of family: Some gays, lesbians turn to artificial insemination. *Dallas Morning News* [online], *July 16*, 1–18. Available: NEXIS Library: NEWS File DALNWS.

Braithwaite, R. L. (1981). Interpersonal relations between black males and black females. In L. E. Gary (Ed.), *Black men*. Beverly Hills: Sage.

Braver, S. L., and Griffin, W. A. (1996). Involving fathers in the post-divorce family. Paper presented at Conference on Father Involvement, National Institute of Child Health and Human Development, Washington, D.C.

Bresnick, E., and Taymor, M. L. (1979). The role of counseling in infertility. *Fertility and Sterility, 32*, 154–156.

Brownlee, S., Wagner, B., Guttman, M., and Daniel, M. (1994). The baby chase. *U.S. News and World Report, 117*, 84.

Burfoot, A. (1993). DI or DIY (do it yourself)? Missing elements in the donor insemination secrecy/openness debate. *Politics and the Life Sciences, 12*, 174–176.

Burke, P. J. (1980). The self: Measurement requirements from an interactionist perspective. *Social Psychology Quarterly, 43*, 18–29.

Burke, P. J. (1991). Identity processes and social stress. *American Sociological Review, 56*, 836–849.

Burke, P. J., and Reitzes, D. C. (1981). The link between identity and role performance. *Social Psychology Quarterly, 44*, 83–92.

Burke, P. J., and Reitzes, D. C. (1991). An identity approach to commitment. *Social Psychology Quarterly, 54*, 280–286.

Bydgeman, M. (1989). Swedish law concerning insemination. *IPPF Medical Bulletin, 23*, 3–4.

Cale, A. R. J., Farouk, M., Prescott, R. J., and Wallace, I. W. J. (1990). Does vasectomy accelerate testicular tumour? Importance of testicular examinations before and after vasectomy. *British Medical Journal, 300*, 370.

Callero, P. (1985). Role-identity salience. *Social Psychology Quarterly, 48*, 203–215.

Carlsen, E., Giwercman, A., Keiding, N., and Skakkebaek, N. E. (1992). Evidence for decreasing quality of semen during past 50 years. *British Medical Journal, 305*, 609–613.

Carmeli, Y. S., and Birenbaum-Carmeli, D. (1994). The predicament of masculinity: Towards understanding the male's experience of infertility treatments. *Sex Roles, 30, 663–677.*

Carpenter, B. (1996). Investigating the next "silent spring"! *U.S. News and World Report, March 11,* 50–52.

Carrera, M. A. (1992). Involving adolescent males in pregnancy and STD prevention programs. *Adolescent Medicine: State of the Art Reviews, 3,* 269–281.

Chandra, A. (1995). His or hers: The choice of contraceptive sterilization among married couples in the U.S. Paper presented at the Annual Meeting of the Population Association of America, San Francisco, April.

Chauhan, M., Barratt, C. L. R., Cooke, S., and Cooke, I. D. (1988). A protocol for the recruitment and screening of semen donors for an artificial insemination by donor programme. *Human Reproduction, 3,* 873–876.

Child Support Report. (1990). Involved from the start: In-hospital paternity establishment. *Child Support XII, 7,* Publication of the National Child Support Enforcement Reference Center MS OCSE/RC, 370 L'Enfant Promenade, S.W., Washington, DC.

Child Support Report. (1996). Record collections from federal income tax refund offset. *Child Support XVIII, 12,* Publication of the National Child Support Enforcement Reference Center, MS OCSE/RC, 370 L'Enfant Promenade, S.W., Washington, DC.

Cicero, T. J. (1994). Effects of paternal exposure to alcohol on offspring development. *Alcohol Health and Research World, 18,* 37–41.

Clark, S. D. (1981). An examination of the sperm content of human pre-ejaculatory fluid. Master's thesis, Johns Hopkins University, Baltimore, MD.

Clarkson, F. (1996). Righteous brothers. *In These Times, August 5,* 14–17.

Clatterbaugh, K. (1997). *Contemporary perspectives on masculinity: Men, women, and politics in modern society.* 2d ed. Boulder, CO: Westview Press.

Clinton, J. (1987). Physical and emotional responses of expectant fathers throughout pregnancy and the early postpartum period. *International Journal of Nursing Studies, 24,* 59–68.

Collins, A., Freeman, E. W., Boxer, A. S., and Tureck, R. (1992). Perceptions of infertility and treatment stress in females as compared with males entering in vitro fertilization treatment. *Fertility and Sterility, 57,* 350–356.

Coltrane, S. (1995). The future of fatherhood: Social, demographic, and economic influences on men's family involvements. In W. Marsiglio (Ed.), *Fatherhood: Contemporary theory, research, and social policy* (pp. 255–274). Thousand Oaks, CA: Sage.

Coltrane, S. (1996). *Family man: Fatherhood, housework, and gender equity.* New York: Oxford University Press.

Coltrane, S., and Hickman, N. (1992). The rhetoric of rights and needs: Moral discourse in the reform of child custody and child support laws. *Social Problems, 39,* 401–420.

Comhaire, F. H. (1994). Male contraception: Hormonal, mechanical, and other. *Human Reproduction, 9,* 586–590.

Conner, G. K., and Denson, V. (1990). Expectant fathers' response to pregnancy: Review of literature and implications for research in high-risk pregnancy. *Journal of Perinatal and Neonatal Nursing, 4,* 22–42.

Contraceptive Technology Update (CTU) (1993). Researchers find no sperm in pre-ejaculate fluid. *Vol. 14, no. 10.* Atlanta, GA: American Health Consultants.

Cooke, C. (1986). *The best baby shower book: A complete guide for party planners.* Deephaven, MN: Meadowbrook Creations.

Cooke, I. D. (1993). Secrecy, openness, and DI in the UK. *Politics and the Life Sciences, 12,* 176–177.

Cooley, C. H. (1902). *Human nature and the social order.* New York: Scribner.

Corney, R. H. (1990). Sex differences in general practice attendance and help seeking for minor illnesses. *Journal of Psychosomatic Research, 34,* 525–534.

Crain Communications, Inc. (1994). AIDS driving condom sales. *Rubber and Plastics News, February 14,* 10.

Crowe, C. (1985). Women want it: In vitro fertilization and women's motivation for participation. *Women's Studies International Forum, 8,* 47–52.

Crowell, N. A., and Leeper, E. M. (1994). *America's fathers and public policy: Report of a workshop.* Washington, D.C.: National Academy Press.

Curie-Cohen, M., Luttrell, L., and Shapiro, S. (1979). Current practice of artificial insemination by donor in the United States. *New England Journal of Medicine, 300,* 585–590.

Curtis, J. L. (1955). A psychiatric study of 55 expectant fathers. *U.S. Armed Forces Medical Journal, 6,* 937–950.

Curtis v. School Committee of Falmouth, 652 N.E. 2d 580 (Mass. 1995).

Cutright, P. (1986). Child support and responsible male procreative behavior. *Sociological Focus, 19,* 27–45.

Daniels, K. R. (1987). Semen donors in New Zealand: Their characteristics and attitudes. *Clinical Reproduction and Fertility, 5,* 177–190.

Daniels, K. R. (1989). Semen donors: Their motivations and attitudes to their offspring. *Journal of Reproductive and Infant Psychology, 7,* 121–127.

Daniels, K. R. (1993). Moving towards openness in donor insemination: Variations on a theme. *Politics and the Life Sciences, 12,* 200–203.

Daniels, K. R., and Taylor, K. (1993a). Secrecy and openness in donor insemination. *Politics and the Life Sciences, 12,* 155–170.

Daniels, K. R., and Taylor, K. (1993b). Moving towards openness in donor insemination: Variations on a theme. *Politics and the Life Sciences, 12,* 200–203.

Danielson, R., Marcy, S., Plunkett, A., Wiest, W., and Greenlick, M. R. (1990). Reproductive health counseling for young men: What does it do? *Family Planning Perspectives, 22,* 115–121.

Danielson, R., McNally, K., Swanson, J., Plunkett, A., and Klausmeier, W. (1988). Title X and family planning services for men. *Family Planning Perspectives, 20,* 234–237.

Da Vanzo, J., and Rahman, M. O. (1993). American families: Trends and correlates. *Population Index, 59,* 350–386.

Davis, K. (1987). Low fertility in evolutionary perspective. In K. Davis, M. S. Berstam, and R. Ricardo-Campbell (Eds.), *Below replacement fertility in industrialized societies* (pp. 48–65). Cambridge: Cambridge University Press.

Davis, M. S. (1983). *Smut: Erotic reality/obscene ideology.* Chicago: University of Chicago Press.

Dawson, W. (1929). *The custom of couvade.* Manchester: University Press.

De Cherney, A. H. (1990). Male infertility. In N. G. Kase, B. Weingold, and D. M. Gerson (Eds.), *Principles and practice of clinical gynecology* (pp. 419–424). New York: Churchill Livingston.

DeCrow, K. (1982). Letter to the editor. *New York Times Magazine, May 9,* 108.

DeGarmo, R., and Davidson, K. (1978). Psychological effects of pregnancy on the mother, father, marriage and family. In L. McNall and J. Calleener (Eds.), *Current practice in ob-gyn nursing.* Vol. 2 (pp. 24–44). St. Louis: C. V. Mosby.

Delaisi de Parseval, G., and Hurstel, F. (1987). Paternity "à la Francaise." In M. E. Lamb (Ed.), *The father's role: Cross-cultural perspectives* (pp. 59–87). Hillsdale, NJ: Lawrence Erlbaum.

DeLamater, J. (1987). Gender differences in sexual scenarios. In K. Kelly (Ed.), *Females, males and sexuality: Theories and research* (pp. 127–139). Albany: State University of New York Press.

DeVault, M. (1987). Doing housework: Feeding and family life. In N. Gerstel and H. E. Gross (Eds.), *Families and work* (pp. 178–191). Philadelphia: Temple University Press.

Diggins, M. (1989). Paternal interests in the abortion decision: Does the father have a say? *University of Chicago Legal Forum, 1989,* 377–398.

Djerassi, C. (1980). *The politics of contraception.* New York: Norton.

Djerassi, C. (1981). Birth control in the year 2001. *Bulletin of the Atomic Scientists, 37,* 24–28.

Djerassi, C., and Leibo, S. P. (1994). A new look at male contraception. *Nature, 370,* 11–12.

Dobkin, P. L., Tremblay, R. E., Desmaraisgervais, L., and Depelteau, L. (1994). Is having an alcoholic father hazardous for children's physical health? *Addition, 89,* 1619–1627.

Edwards, J. N. (1989). The family realm: A future paradigm or failed nostalgia? *Journal of Marriage and the Family, 51,* 816–818.

Edwards, J. N. (1991). New conceptions: Biosocial innovations and the family. *Journal of Marriage and the Family, 53,* 349–360.

Edwards, S. (1994). The role of men in contraceptive decision-making: Current knowledge and future implications. *Family Planning Perspectives, 26,* 77–82.

Ehrenreich, B. (1983). *The hearts of men: American dreams and the flight from commitment.* New York: Anchor.

Ellingboe, D. A. (1994). Sex, lies, and genetic tests: Challenging the marital presumption of paternity under the Minnesota Parentage Act. *Minnesota Law Review, 78,* 1013–1044.

Engels, F. (1972 [1884]). *The origin of the family, private property, and the state* [introduction and notes by Eleanor Burke Leacock]. New York: International Publishers.

Engle, P., and Leonard, A. (1995). Fathers as parenting partners. In J. Bruce, C. Lloyd, and A. Leonard (Eds.). *Families in focus—New perspectives on mothers, fathers, and children* (pp. 49–64). New York: Population Council.

Ernst, S. (1975). *Father participation guide.* Rochester, NY: International Childbirth Education Association.

Espenshade, T. J. (1984). *Investing in children: New estimates of parental expenditures.* Washington, DC: Urban Institute.

Evans, T. (1994). Spiritual purity. In A. Janssen and L. K. Weeden (Eds.), *Seven promises of a promise keeper* (pp. 73–81). Colorado Springs: Promise Keepers.

Faludi, S. (1991). *Backlash: The undeclared war against American women.* New York: Crown.

Family Impact Seminar. (1990). *Encouraging fathers to be responsible: Paternity establishment, child support and JOBS strategies.* Background Briefing Report. Washington, DC: The AAMFT Research and Education Foundation.

Faux, M. (1990). *Crusaders' voices from the abortion front.* New York: Birch Lane Press.

Figueira-McDonough, J. (1989). Men and women as interest groups in the abortion debate in the United States. *Women's Studies International Forum, 12,* 539–550.

Filhiol, C. (1990). *Michael H. v. Gerald D.:* Upholding the marital presumption against a dual paternity claim. *Louisiana Law Review, 50,* 1015–1037.

Fisher, H. E. (1982). *The sex contract: The evolution of human behavior.* New York: William Morrow and Company.

Fletcher, J. (1988). *The ethics of genetic control.* Buffalo, NY: Prometheus Books.

Forrest, K. A., Swanson, J. M., and Beckstein, D. E. (1989). The availability of educational and training materials on men's reproductive health. *Family Planning Perspectives, 21,* 120–122.

Forste, R., Tanfer, K., and Tedrow, L. (1995). Sterilization among currently married men in the United States, 1991. *Family Planning Perspectives, 27,* 100–107, 122.

Fox, J. S. (1993). *Affording your infertility.* Norwell, MA: Serono Laboratories, Inc.

Francoeur, R. T. (1983). Religious reactions to alternative life styles. In E. D.

Macklin and R. H. Rubin (Eds.), *Contemporary families and alternative lifestyles* (pp. 379–399). Beverly Hills: Sage.

Frankel, M. (1976). Human-semen banking: Social policy issues. *Man and Medicine, 1*, 289.

Franklin, C. W., II. (1984). *The changing definition of masculinity*. New York: Plenum Press.

Free, M. J., and Alexander, N. J. (1976). Male contraception without prescription: A reevaluation of the condom and coitus interrupts. *Public Health Reports 91, 5*, 556–562.

Freud, S. (1927). *Totem and taboo. Resemblances between the psychic lives of savages and neurotics*. New York: New Republic.

Furstenberg, F. F., Jr. (1988). Good dads—bad dads: Two faces of fatherhood. In A. J. Cherlin (Ed.), *The changing American family and public policy* (pp. 193–218). Washington, DC: Urban Institute.

Furstenberg, F. F., Jr. (1995). Fathering in the inner city: Paternal participation and public policy. In W. Marsiglio (Ed.), *Fatherhood: Contemporary theory, research, and social policy* (pp. 119–147). Thousand Oaks, CA: Sage.

Furstenberg, F. F., Jr., and Cherlin, A. J. (1991). *Divided families: What happens to children when parents part*. Cambridge, MA: Harvard University Press.

Gagnon, J. and Simon, W. (1973). *Sexual conduct: The social sources of sexuality*. Chicago: Aldine.

Gaines, J. (1990). A scandal of artificial insemination. *New York Times, October 7, 23.*

Gallop Report. (1986). *Gallup report: Political, social, and economic trends*. Princeton, NJ: Trenton Publishing.

Gaylin, W. (1992). *The male ego*. New York: Penguin Books.

Gerson, K. (1993). *No man's land: Men's changing commitments to family and work*. New York: Basic Books.

Gertner, N. (1989). Position paper: Interference with reproductive choice. In S. Cohen and N. Taub (Eds.), *Reproductive laws for the 1900s*. Clifton, NJ: Humana Press.

Gerzi, S., and Berman, E. (1981). Emotional reactions of expectant fathers to their wives' first pregnancy. *British Journal of Medical Psychology, 54*, 259–265.

Gilder, G. (1981). *Wealth and poverty*. New York: Basic Books.

Gilder, G. (1986). *Men and marriage*. Gretna: Pelican Publishing Company.

Gilbreath, E. (1995). Manhood's great awakening: Promise keeper's ambitious agenda. *Christianity Today, 39*, 20–28.

Gilmore, D. D. (1990). *Manhood in the making: Cultural concepts of masculinity*. New Haven, CT: Yale University Press.

Gilmore, S., DeLamater, J., and Wagstaff, D. (1995). *Sexual decision-making by inner-city black adolescent males*. CDE Working Paper 95–04, Center for Demography and Ecology. Madison: University of Wisconsin-Madison.

Gimenez, M. E. (1991). The mode of reproduction in transition. A Marxist-Feminist analysis of the effects of reproductive technologies. *Gender and Society,* 5, 334–350.

Ginsburg, F. (1993). Saving America's souls: Operation Rescue's crusade against abortion. In M. E. Marty and R. S. Appleby (Eds.), *Fundamentalisms and the state* (pp. 557–588). Chicago: University of Chicago Press.

Glick, P. (1989). Remarried families, stepfamilies, and stepchildren: A brief demographic analysis. *Family Relations, 38,* 24–27.

Gough, H. G. (1979). Some factors related to men's stated willingness to use a male contraceptive pill. *Journal of Sex Research, 15,* 27–37.

Grady, W. R., Klepinger, D. H., Billy, J. O. G., and Tanfer, K. (1993). Condom characteristics: The perceptions and preferences of men in the United States. *Family Planning Perspectives, 25,* 67–73.

Grady, W. R., Tanfer, K., Billy, J. O. G., and Lincoln-Hanson, J. (1996). Men's perceptions of their roles and responsibilities regarding sex, contraception and childbearing. *Family Planning Perspectives, 28,* 221–226.

Granberg, D. (1981). Comparison of members of pro- and anti-abortion organizations in Missouri. *Social Biology, 28,* 239–252.

Graves, R. (1955). *The Greek myths* (vol. 1). Harmondsworth, Middlesex, U.K.: Pelican Books.

Green, P. (1995). Condom companies in U.S. eye sales growth abroad. *The Journal of Commerce* [online], *March 28.*

Greene, A. D., Emig, C., and Hearn, G. (1996). *Improving federal data on fathers: A summary of the Town Meeting on Fathering and Male Fertility.* Report prepared for the NICHD Family and Child Well-Being Research Network, May. Bethesda, MD: NICHD.

Greene, A. D., and Emig, C. (1997). *Conference of father involvement: A summary report.* Report prepared for the NICHD Family and Child Well-Being Research Network. Washington, DC: Child Trends, Inc.

Greene, A. D., Hearn, G., and Emig, C. (1996). *Developmental, ethnographic, and demographic perspectives on fatherhood: Summary report of the conference.* Report prepared for the NICHD Family and Child Well-Being Research Network, September. Bethesda, MD: NICHD.

Greil, A. L. (1991). *Not yet pregnant: Infertile couples in contemporary America.* New Brunswick, NJ: Rutgers University Press.

Greil, A. L., Leitko, T. A., and Porter, K. L. (1988). Infertility: His and hers. *Gender and Society, 2,* 172–199.

Griffin, P. D., and Waites, G. M. H. (1993). The 1993 Annual Report of Task Force on Methods for the Regulation of Male Fertility. World Health Organization, Geneva, Switzerland, unpublished.

Griswold, R. L. (1993). *Fatherhood in America: A history.* New York: Basic Books.

Guess, H. A. (1990). Invited commentary: Vasectomy and prostate cancer. *American Journal of Epidemiology, 132,* 1062–1065.

Guttman, M. C. (1996). *The meanings of macho: Being a man in Mexico City.* Berkeley, CA: University of California Press.

Hackett, D. G. (1996). Wild men and Promise Keepers: Men and American Protestantism in historical perspective. Paper presented at the American Academy of Religion Annual Meeting, New Orleans, November.

Haimes, E. (1993). Secrecy and openness in donor insemination: A sociological comment on Daniels and Taylor. *Politics and the Life Sciences, 12,* 178–179.

Hall, E., and Ferree, M. M. (1986). Racial differences in abortion attitudes. *Public Opinion Quarterly, 50,* 193–207.

Harris, G. (1986). Fathers and fetuses, *Ethics, 96,* 594–603.

Harrison, K. L., Callan, V. J., and Hennessy, J. F. (1987). Stress and semen quality in an in vitro fertilization program. *Fertility and Sterility, 48,* 633–636.

Hawkins, A. J., Christiansen, S. L., Sargent, K. P., and Hill, E. J. (1995). Rethinking fathers' involvement in child care: A developmental perspective. In W. Marsiglio (Ed.), *Fatherhood: Contemporary theory, research, and social policy* (pp. 41–56). Thousand Oaks, CA: Sage.

Hawkins, A. J., and Dollahite, D. C. (1997). *Generative fathering: Beyond deficit perspectives.* Thousand Oaks, CA: Sage.

Healy, B. J. (1993). Letter to the editor. *Journal of American Medical Association, 269,* 2620.

Heggenhougen, H. (1980). Father and childbirth: An anthropological perspective. *Journal of Nurse-Midwifery, 25,* 21–25.

Heinowitz, J. (1982). *Pregnant fathers—how fathers can enjoy and share the experiences of pregnancy and childbirth.* Englewood Cliffs, NJ: Prentice Hall.

Henshaw, S. K. (1991). The accessibility of abortion services in the United States. *Family Planning Perspectives, 23,* 246–252, 263.

Henshaw, S. K. (1992). Abortion trends in 1987 and 1988. *Family Planning Perspectives, 24,* 85–86 and 96.

Henshaw, S. K., Forrest, J. D., and Blaine, E. (1984). Abortion services in the United States, 1981 and 1982. *Family Planning Perspectives, 16,* 119–127.

Henshaw, S. K., and O'Reilly, D. (1983). Characteristics of abortion patients in the United States, 1979 and 1980. *Family Planning Perspectives, 19,* 63–70.

Henshaw, S. K., and Van Vort, J. (1990). Abortion services in the United States, 1987 and 1988. *Family Planning Perspectives, 12,* 102–108, 142.

Herek, G. M. (1987). On heterosexual masculinity: Some psychical consequences of the social construction of gender and sexuality. In M. S. Kimmel (Ed.), *Changing men: New directions in research on men and masculinity* (pp. 68–82). Newbury Park, CA: Sage.

Hernandez, D. J. (1988). The demographics of divorce and remarriage. In E. M. Hetherington and J. D. Arasteh (Eds.), *Impact of divorce, single parenting, and stepparenting on children* (pp. 3–22). Hillsdale, NJ: Lawrence Erlbaum.

Herzog, J. M. (1982). Patterns of expectant fatherhood: A study of fathers of premature infants. In S. H. Cath, A. R. Gurwitt, and J. M. Ross (Eds.), *Father and child: Development and clinical perspectives* (pp. 301–314). Boston: Little, Brown.

Hill, D. (1992). Doing business at the sperm bank—How to deposit, how to withdraw. *Cosmopolitan, February*, 208–211.

Hill, R., Stycos, J. M., and Bach, K. W. (1959). *The family and population control: A Puerto Rican experiment in social change.* Chapel Hill: University of North Carolina Press.

Hinnant, T. M. (1990). Lovers' triangle turns Bermuda Triangle: The natural father's right to rebut the marital presumption: *Michael H. v. Gerald D. Wake Forest Law Review*, 14, 259–270.

Hinting, A., Comhaire, F., Vermeulen, L., Dhont, M., Vermeulen, A., and Vandekerckhove, D. (1990). Possibilities and limitations of techniques of assisted reproduction for the treatment of male infertility. *Human Reproduction, 5*, 544–548.

Hirczy, W. (1993). A new twist in divorce: Paternity tests as Solomon's sword. *Journal of Divorce and Remarriage, 20*, 85–104.

HMSO. (1990). Human Fertilisation and Embryology Bill. Standing Committee B Hansard, HMSO, London.

Hochschild, A. (1979). Emotion work, feeling rules, and social structure. *American Journal of Sociology, 85*, 551–575.

Hochschild, A. (1989). *The second shift: Working parents and the revolution at home.* New York: Viking.

Hogg, M. A., Terry, D. J., and White, K. M. (1995). A tale of two theories: A critical comparison of identity theory with social identity theory. *Social Psychology Quarterly, 58*, 255–269.

Holbrook, S. M. (1990). Adoption, infertility, and the new reproductive technologies: Problems and prospects for social work and welfare policy. *Social Work, 35*, 333–337.

Hollander, D. (1996). Nonmarital childbearing in the United States: A government report. *Family Planning Perspectives, 28*, 29–32, 41.

Holmes, H. B. (1993). Openness, fatherhood, and responsibility: A feminist analysis. *Politics and the Life Sciences, 12*, 180–182.

Hood, J. (1983). *Becoming a two-job family.* New York: Praeger.

Horbay, G. L., Cowell, C. A., and Casper, R. F. (1991). Multiple follicular recruitment and intrauterine insemination outcomes compared by age and diagnosis. *Human Reproduction, 6*, 947–952.

Howe, R.-A. W. (1993). Legal rights and obligations: An uneven evolution. In R. I. Lerman and T. J. Ooms (Eds.), *Young unwed fathers: Changing roles and emerging policies* (pp. 141–169). Philadelphia: Temple University Press.

Humphrey, M., and Humphrey, H. (1988). *Families with a difference: Varieties of surrogate parenthood.* London: Routledge.

Humphrey, M., and Humphrey, H. (1993). Vasectomy as a reason for donor insemination. Social *Science and Medicine, 37,* 263–266.

Ihinger-Tallman, M., Pasley, K., and Buehler, C. (1995). Developing a middle-range theory of father involvement postdivorce. In W. Marsiglio (Ed.), *Fatherhood: Contemporary theory, research, and social policy* (pp. 57–77). Thousand Oaks, CA: Sage.

Iizuka, R., Sawada, Y., Nichina, N., and Ohi, M. (1968). The physical and mental development of children born following artificial insemination. *International Journal of Fertility, 13,* 24–32.

Ilaria, G., Jacobs, J. L., Polsky, B., Koll, B., Baron, P., MacLow, C., and Armstrong, D. (1992). Detection of HIV-1 DNA sequences in pre-ejaculatory fluid. *Lancet 340,* 1, 469.

Institute of Medicine. (1995). *The best intentions: Unintended pregnancy and the well-being of children and families.* S. Brown and L. Eisenberg (Eds.). Washington, D. C. National Academy Press.

Issacs, S. L., and Holt, R. J. (1987). Redefining procreation: Facing the issues. *Population Bulletin, 42,* 3–37.

Jaccard, J., Hand, D., Ku, L., Richardson, K., and Abella, R. (1981). Attitudes toward male oral contraceptives: Implications for models of the relationship between beliefs and attitudes. *Journal of Applied Social Psychology, 11,* 181–191.

Jacobs, M. (1995). The wish to become a father: How do men decide in favour of parenthood? In M. C. P. van Dongen, G. A. B. Frinking, and M. J. G. Jacobs (Eds.), *Changing fatherhood: An interdisciplinary perspective* (pp. 67–83). Amsterdam, The Netherlands: Thesis Publishers.

Jackson, D. (1989). DNA fingerprinting and proof of paternity. *Family Law Reporter, 15(2), May 16,* 3007–3013.

James, P. D. (1992). *The children of men.* London: Faber and Faber.

Jencks, C. (1992). *Rethinking social policy.* Cambridge: Harvard University Press.

Jequier, A. M. (1990). Andrology: A new sub-specialty. *British Journal of Obstetrics and Gynecology, 97,* 969–972.

Joffe, C. (1995). *Doctors of conscience: The struggle to provide abortion before and after* Roe v. Wade. Boston: Beacon Press.

Johnson, C., and Sum, A. (1987). *Declining earnings of young men: Their relation to poverty, teen pregnancy, and family formation.* Adolescent Pregnancy Prevention Clearinghouse Report. Washington, DC: Children's Defense Fund.

Jurich, J. (1989). The family realm: Expanding its parameters. *Journal of Marriage and the Family, 51,* 819–822.

Kanter, R. de (1994). Psychic consequences of artificial insemination and the consequences on the experience of parenthood. Paper presented at the Conference for Changing Fatherhood, Tilburg University, May.

Kaplan, H. S., Lancaster, J. B., and Anderson, K. G. (1996). Human parental investment and fertility: The life histories of men in Albuquerque. Paper presented at the National Symposium on Men in Families, Pennsylvania State University, October 31.

Kapp, M. B. (1982). The father's (lack of) rights and responsibilities in the abortion decisions: An examination of legal-ethical implications. *Ohio Northern University Law Review,* 9, 369–383.

Kaufman, G. (1995). Men's attitudes toward fatherhood. Paper presented at the Annual Meeting of the Population Association of America, San Francisco, April.

Keiding, N., and Skakkebaek, N E. (1995). Sperm decline—real or artifact? *Fertility and Sterility,* 65, 450–451.

Kentenich, H., Schmiady, H., Radke, E., Stief, G., and Blankau, A. (1992). The male IVF patient—psychosomatic considerations. *Human Reproduction,* 7, 13–18.

Keoun, B. (1996). Sperm: Still alive and kicking. *Gainesville Sun, May 7.*

Kimmel, M. S., and Kaufman, M. (1994). Weekend warriors: The new men's movement. In H. Broad and M. Kaufman (Eds.), *Theorizing masculinities* (pp. 259–288). Thousand Oaks, CA: Sage.

Kinjn, T. (1995). Towards post-paternalism? Social and theoretical changes in fatherhood. In M. C. P. van Dongen, G. A. B. Frinking, and M. J. G. Jacobs (Eds.), *Changing fatherhood: An interdisciplinary perspective* (pp. 1–20). Amsterdam, The Netherlands: Thesis Publishers.

Kirby, D., Harvey, P. D., Claussenius, D., and Novar, M. (1989). A direct mailing to teenage males about condom use: Its impact on knowledge, attitudes and sexual behavior. *Family Planning Perspectives,* 21, 12–18.

Kirshenbaum, J. (1989). Special report, an American disgrace: A violent and unprecedented lawlessness has arisen among college athletes in all parts of the country. *Sports Illustrated, February 27,* 16–19.

Kiselica, M. S. (1995). *Multicultural counseling with teenage fathers: A practical guide.* Thousand Oaks, CA: Sage.

Klein, H. (1991). Couvade syndrome: Male counterpart to pregnancy. *International Journal of Psychiatry in Medicine,* 21, 57–69.

Klinman, D. G., Sanders, J. H., Rosen, J. L., and Longo, K. R. (1986). The teen father collaboration: A demonstration and research model. In A. B. Elster and M. E. Lamb (Eds.), *Adolescent fatherhood* (pp. 155–170). Hillsdale, NJ: Lawrence Earlbaum.

Klitsch, M. (1995). Still waiting for the contraceptive revolution. *Family Planning Perspectives,* 27 (6), 246–253.

Klock, S. C., and Maier, D. (1991). Psychological factors related to donor insemination. *Fertility and Sterility, 56,* 489–495.

Knijn, T. (1995). Towards post-paternalism? Social and theoretical changes in fatherhood. In M. C. P. van Dongen, G. Frinking, and M. Jacobs (Eds.), *Changing fatherhood: A multidisciplinary perspective.* Amsterdam, The Netherlands: Thesis Publishers.

Knoppers, B. M. (1993). Donor insemination: Children as *in concreto* or *in abstracto* subjects of rights? *Politics and the Life Sciences, 12,* 182–185.

Koman, J. J., III. (1991). An inventory to measure contact with medical health care professionals. *Psychological Reports, 69,* 43–49.

Kovacs, G. T., Clayton, C. E., and McGovern, P. (1983). The attitudes of semen donors. *Clinical Reproduction and Fertility,* 73–75.

Kraemer, S. (1991). The origins of fatherhood: An ancient family process. *Family Process, 30,* 377–392.

Ku, L., Sonenstein, F. L., and Pleck, J. H. (1992). Patterns of HIV risk and preventive behaviors among teenage men. *Public Health Reports, 107,* 131–138.

Ku, L., Sonenstein, F. L., and Pleck, J. H. (1994). The dynamics of young men's condom use during and across relationships. *Family Planning Perspectives, 26,* 246–251.

Laborie, F. (1988). New reproductive technologies: News from France and elsewhere. *Reproductive and Genetic Engineering, 1,* 77–85.

Lacay, R. (1992). Abortion: The future is already here. *Time, May 4,* 29.

Laird, J. (1994). A male pill? Gender differences in contraceptive commitment. *Feminism and Psychology, 4,* 458–468.

Lamb, M. E. (1987). *Introduction: The emergent American father.* In M. E. Lamb (Ed.), The father's role: Cross-cultural perspectives (pp. 3–25). Hillsdale, NJ: Lawrence Erlbaum.

Lamb, M. E. (1997). Fathers and child development: An introductory overview and guide. In M. E. Lamb (ed.), *The role of the father in child development (3d edition).* New York: Wiley.

Lamb, M. E., Pleck, J. H., Charnov, E. L., and Levine, J. A. (1987). A biosocial perspective on paternal behavior and involvement. In J. B. Lancaster, J. Altmann, A. S. Rossi, and L. R. Sherrod (Eds.), *Parenting across the life span* (pp. 111–142). New York: Aldine de Gruyter.

Landry, D. J., and Camelo T. M. (1994). Young unmarried men and women discuss men's role in contraceptive practice. *Family Planning Perspectives, 26,* 222–227.

Langer, L. M., Zimmerman, R. S., and Katz, J. A. (1994). Which is more important to high school students: Preventing pregnancy or preventing AIDS? *Family Planning Perspectives, 26,* 154–159.

Lansac, J. (1993). One father only: Donor insemination and CECOS in France. *Politics and the Life Sciences, 12,* 185–186.

LaRossa, R. (1988). Fatherhood and social change. *Family Relations, 37*, 451–458.

LaRossa, R. (1997). *The modernization of fatherhood: A social and political history*. Chicago: University of Chicago Press.

Larson, J. (1992). Understanding stepfamilies. *American Demographics, July*, 36–40.

Lasker, J. N. (1993). Doctors and donors: A comment on secrecy and openness in donor insemination. *Politics and the Life Sciences, 12*, 186–188.

Laumann, E., Gagnon, J., Michael, R., and Michaels, S. (1994). *The social organization of sexuality: Sexual practices in the United States*. Chicago: University of Chicago Press.

Lauritzen, P. (1993). DI's dirty little secret. *Politics and the Life Sciences, 12*, 188–189.

Leigh, B. C., Temple, M. T., and Trocki, K. (1993). The sexual behavior of U.S. adults: Results from a national survey. *American Journal of Public Health, 83*, 1400–1408.

Leigh, B. C., Morrison, D. M., Trocki, K., and Temple, M. T. (1994). Sexual behavior of American adolescents: Results from a U.S. national survey. *Journal of Adolescent Health, 15*, 117–125.

Lemonick, M. D. (1996). What's wrong with our sperm? *Time, March 18*, 78–79.

Leonard, L. (1977). The father's side. *Canadian Nurse, 73*, 16–20.

Lerner, G. (1986). *The creation of patriarchy*. New York: Oxford University Press.

Lethbridge, D. J. (1990). The use of contraception by women of high socio-economic status. *Heath Care for Women International, 11*, 305–318.

Levine, J. A., and Pitt, E. W. (1995). *New expectations: Community strategies for responsible fatherhood*. New York: Families and Work Institute.

Lewis, R. A. (1986). Men's changing roles in marriage and the family. In R. A. Lewis and M. B. Sussman (Eds.), *Men's changing roles in the family*. Marriage and Family Review, 9 (pp. 1–10). New York: Haworth.

Lichter, D. T., McLaughlin, D. K., Kephart, G., and Landry, D. J. (1992). Race and the retreat from marriage: A shortage of marriageable men? *American Sociological Review, 57*, 781–799.

Lindbohm, M., Hemminski, M., Bonhomme, M. G., Anttila, A., Rantala, K., Heikkila, P., and Rosenberg, M. J. (1991). Effects of paternal occupational exposure on spontaneous abortion. *American Journal of Public Health, 81*, 1029–1033.

Link, P. W., and Darling, C. A. (1986). Couples undergoing treatment for infertility: Dimensions of life satisfaction. *Journal of Sex and Marital Therapy, 12*, 46–59.

Lipkin, M., and Lamb, M. (1982). The couvade syndrome: An epidemiologic study. *Annals of Internal Medicine, 96*, 509–511.

Liskin, L., Benoit, E., and Blackburn, R. (1992). *Vasectomy: New opportunities.* Population Reports, Series D, No. 5. Baltimore: Johns Hopkins University, Population Information Program.

Lissner, E. A. (1992). New nonhormonal contraceptive methods for men. *Changing Men, Summer/Fall,* 24–25.

Lissner, E. A. (1994). Frontiers in nonhormonal male contraception: A call for research. Male Contraceptive Information Project, P.O. Box 3674, Stanford, CA, unpublished.

Louv, R. (1993). *Father love: What we need, what we seek, what we must create.* New York: Pocket Books.

Luker, K. (1984). *Abortion and the politics of motherhood.* Berkeley, CA: University of California Press.

Lynxwiler, J., and Gay, D. (1994). Reconsidering race differences in abortion attitudes. *Social Science Quarterly, 75,* 67–84.

Lynxwiler, J., and Gay, D. (1995). The abortion attitudes of African American and white males. *Masculinities, 3,* 66–75.

Lynxwiler, J., and Gay, D. (1996). The abortion attitudes of black women: 1972–1991. *Journal of Black Studies, 27,* 260–277.

Mackey, W. C., White, U., and Day, R. (1992). Reasons American men become fathers: Men's divulgences, women's perceptions. *Journal of Genetic Psychology, 153,* 435–445.

Macklin, R. (1991). Artificial means of reproduction and our understanding of family. *Hastings Center Report, 21,* 5–11.

MacNair, R., Derr, M. K., and Naranjo-Huebl, L. (1996). *Prolife feminism: Yesterday and Today.* New York: Sulzburger and Graham.

Mahler, K. (1996). Condom availability in the schools: Lessons from the courtroom. *Family Planning Perspectives, 28,* 75–77.

Mahlstedt, P. P. (1994). Psychological issues of infertility and assisted reproductive technology. *Urologic Clinics of North America, 21,* 557–566.

Mahlstedt, P. P., and Probasco, K. (1991). Sperm donors: Their attitudes toward providing medical and psychosocial information for recipient couples and donor offspring. *Fertility and Sterility, 56,* 747–753.

Major, B., Cozzarelli, C., and Testa, M. (1992). Male partners' appraisals of undesired pregnancy and abortion: Implications for women's adjustment to abortion. *Journal of Applied Social Psychology, 22,* 599–614.

Majors, R., and Billson, J. M. (1992). *Cool Pose: The dilemmas of black manhood in America.* New York: Lexington Books.

Malinowski, B. (1966). *The father in primitive psychology.* New York: Norton Library.

Mallon, D. A. (1989). Paternity: Standing to sue and presumptions of legitimacy. [Selected developments in Massachusetts law]. *Boston College Law Review, 30,* 671–679.

Manion, J. (1977). A study of fathers and infant caretaking. *Birth Family Journal, 4,* 174–179.

March, K. (1995). Perception of adoption as social stigma: Motivation for search and reunion. *Journal of Marriage and the Family, 57,* 653–660.

Mare, R. D., and Winship, C. (1991). Socioeconomic change and the decline of marriage for whites and blacks. In C. Jencks and P. E. Peterson (Eds.), *The urban underclass.* Washington, DC: Brookings Institute.

Marín, B. V. O., Goméz, C. A., and Hearst, N. (1993). Multiple heterosexual partners and condom use among Hispanics and non-Hispanic Whites. *Family Planning Perspectives, 25,* 170–174.

Marks, S. R. (1996). The problem and politics of wholeness in family studies. *Journal of Marriage and the Family, 58,* 565–571.

Marshall, J. F. (1980). Acceptability of drugs for male fertility regulation: A prospectus and some preliminary data. *Contraception, 21,* 121–134.

Marsiglio, W. (1985). Husbands' sex-role preferences and contraceptive intentions: The case of the male pill. *Sex Roles, 12,* 655–663.

Marsiglio, W. (1987). Adolescent fathers in the United States: Their initial living arrangements, marital experience, and educational outcomes. *Family Planning Perspectives, 19,* 240–251.

Marsiglio, W. (1988a). Commitment to social fatherhood: Predicting adolescent males' intentions to live with their child and partner. *Journal of Marriage and the Family, 50,* 427–441.

Marsiglio, W. (1988b). Adolescent male sexuality and heterosexual masculinity: A conceptual model and review. *Journal of Adolescent Research, 3,* 285–303.

Marsiglio, W. (1989). Adolescent males' pregnancy resolution preferences and family formation intentions: Does family background make a difference for blacks and whites? *Journal of Adolescent Research, 4,* 214–237.

Marsiglio, W. (1991). Male procreative consciousness and responsibility: A conceptual analysis and research agenda. *Journal of Family Issues, 12,* 268–290.

Marsiglio, W. (1992). Stepfathers with minor children living at home: Parenting perceptions and relationship quality. *Journal of Family Issues, 13,* 195–214.

Marsiglio, W. (1993). Adolescent males' orientation toward paternity and contraception. *Family Planning Perspectives, 25,* 22–31.

Marsiglio, W. (Ed.) (1995a). *Fatherhood: Contemporary theory, research, and social policy.* Thousand Oaks, CA: Sage.

Marsiglio, W. (1995b). Young nonresident biological fathers. *Marriage and Family Review, 20(3/4),* 325–348.

Marsiglio, W. (1995c). Fathers' diverse life course patterns and roles: Theory and social interventions. In W. Marsiglio (Ed.), *Fatherhood Contemporary theory, research, and social policy* (pp. 78–101). Thousand Oaks, CA: Sage.

Marsiglio, W., and Menaghan, E. (1987). Couples and the male birth control pill:

A future alternative in contraceptive selection. *Journal of Sex Research, 23,* 34–49.

Marsiglio, W., and Menaghan, E. (1990). Pregnancy resolution and family formation: Understanding gender differences in adolescents' preferences and beliefs. *Journal of Family Issues, 11,* 313–333.

Marsiglio, W., and Shehan, C. (1993). Adolescent males' abortion attitudes: Data from a national survey. *Family Planning Perspectives, 25,* 162–169.

Martin, P. Y., and Hummer, R. A. (1989). Fraternities and rape on campus. *Gender and Society, 3,* 457–473.

Mastroianni, L., Jr., Donaldson, P. J., and Kane, T. T. (Eds.) (1990). *Developing new contraceptives: Obstacles and opportunities.* Washington, DC: National Academy Press.

Maxwell, C. J. C. and Jelen, T. G. (1995). Commandos for Christ: Narratives of male pro-life activists. *Review of Religious Research, 37,* 117–129.

May, K. A. (1980). A typology of detachment/involvement styles adopted during pregnancy by first-time fathers. *Western Journal of Nursing Research, 2,* 445–453.

May, K. A. and Perrin, S. P. (1985). Prelude: Pregnancy and birth. In S. M. H. Hanson and F. W. Bozett (Eds.), *Dimensions of fatherhood* (pp. 64–91). Beverly Hills, CA: Sage.

McDonald, S. W. (1990). Vasectomy and the human testis. *British Medical Journal, 301,* 618–619.

McDonough, P. G. (1995). Editorial comment: Sperm decline—real or artifact? *Fertility and Sterility, 65,* 453.

McEwan, K. L., Costello, C. G., and Taylor, P. J. (1987). Adjustment to infertility. *Journal of Abnormal Psychology, 96,* 108–116.

McGrade, J. J., and Tolor, A. (1981). The reaction to infertility and the infertility investigation: A comparison of the responses of men and women. *Infertility, 4,* 7–27.

McLanahan, S., and Sandefur, G. (1994). *Growing up with a single parent: What hurts, what helps.* Cambridge, MA: Harvard University Press.

McLaren, A. (1990). *A history of contraception: From antiquity to the present day.* Cambridge, MA: Basil Blackwell.

McNeil, M. (1990). Reproductive technologies: A new terrain for the sociology of technology. In M. McNeil, I. Varcoe, and S. Yearley (Eds.), *The new reproductive technologies* (pp. 1–26). New York: St. Martin's Press.

McNeil, M., Varcoe, I. and Yearley, S. (Eds.) (1990). *The new reproductive technologies.* New York: St. Martin's Press.

McWhinnie, A. M. (1993). Doubts and realities in DI family relationships. *Politics and the Life Sciences, 12,* 189–191.

Meacham, R. B., and Lipschultz, L. I. (1991). Assisted reproductive technologies for male factor infertility. *Current Opinion in Obstetrics and Gynecology, 3,* 656–661.

Medical Journal of Australia. (1981). Recent advances in contraception. *Medical Journal of Australia, January,* 55–57.

Meerabeau, L. (1991). Husbands' participation in fertility treatment: They also serve who only stand and wait. *Sociology of Health and Illness, 11,* 396–410.

Meigs, A. S. (1976). Male pregnancy and the reduction of sexual opposition in a New Guinea Highlands society. *Ethnology, 15,* 393–407.

Menaghan, E. G. (1989). Escaping from the family realm: Reasons to resist claims for its uniqueness. *Journal of Marriage and the Family, 51,* 822–825.

Menning, B. E., Wentz, A. C., and Garner, C. H. (1993). *Insights into infertility.* Norwell, MA: Serono Laboratories, Inc.

Meyer, D. R. (1992). Paternity and public policy. *Focus, 14,* 1–14.

Meyers, M. (1994). Sperm donors could be liable for child support. *Star Tribune* [online], *Jan. 10,* 1–6. Available: NEXIS Library: NEWS File STRIB.

Miall, C. E. (1986). The stigma of involuntary childlessness. *Social Problems, 33,* 268–282.

Michael H. v. Gerald D., 491 U.S. 110 (1989).

Miller, W. B. (1992). Personality traits and developmental experiences as antecedents of childbearing motivation. *Demography, 29,* 265–285.

Miller, W. B., and Pasta, D. J. (1995). Behavioral intentions: Which ones predict fertility behavior in married couples? *Journal of Applied Social Psychology, 25,* 530–55.

Mincy, R. (1997). Personal communication. Workshop for the Working Group on Male Fertility and Family Formation, Urban Institute, Washington, DC, January.

Mintz, S. (1996). From patriarchy to androgyny and other myths: Placing men's family roles in historical perspective. Paper presented at the National Symposium on Men in Families, Pennsylvania State University, October.

Mitchell, S. (1996). *The official guide to American attitudes: Who thinks what about the issues that shape our lives.* Ithaca, NY: New Strategist Publications.

Moir, A., and Jessel, D. (1989). *Brain sex: The real difference between men and women.* London: Michael Joseph.

Moore, K. (1994). *Facts at a glance.* Washington, DC: Child Trends, Inc.

Moore, K. (1987). Policy-relevant research on teenage childbearing: Potential topics. Paper presented at the National Council on Family Relations meetings, Atlanta, GA, November.

Moran, J. S., Janes, H. R., Peterman, T. A., and Stone, K. M. (1990). Increase in condom sales following AIDS education and publicity, United States. *American Journal of Public Health, 80,* 607–609.

Morse, K. G. (1995/96). National Center for Men, Internet transmissions, MEN@DCS.ST-AND.AC.UK.

Mosher, W. D., and Pratt, W. F. (1990). *Fecundity and infertility in the United States, 1965–88.* Advance Data, 192, 1–12.

Mott, F. L. (1983). *Fertility-related data in the 1982 National Longitudinal Surveys of Work Experience of Youth: An evaluation of data quality and some preliminary analytical results.* Columbus: Ohio State University, Center for Human Resource Research.

Mott, F. L. (1990). When is a father really gone? Parental-child conduct in father-absent homes. *Demography, 27,* 499–517.

Munroe, R. L., and Munroe, R. H. (1971). Male pregnancy symptoms and cross-sex identity in three societies. *Journal of Social Psychology, 84,* 11–25.

Munroe, R. L., and Munroe, R. H. (1973). Psychological interpretation of male initiation rites: The case of male pregnancy symptoms. *Ethos, 1,* 490–498.

Munroe, R. L., Munroe, R. H., and Nerlove, S. B. (1973). Male pregnancy symptoms and cross-sex identity: Two replications. *Journal of Social Psychology, 89,* 147–148.

Murchison, W. (1996). Promises are for keeps. *Human Life Review, 22,* 5–12.

Myers, B. J. (1982). Early intervention using Brazelton training with middle-class mothers and fathers of newborns. *Child Development, 53,* 462–471.

Nachtigall, R. D., Becker, G., and Wozny, M. (1992). The effects of gender-specific diagnosis on men's and women's response to infertility. *Fertility and Sterility, 57,* 113–121.

National Adoption Information Clearinghouse. (1995). *Adoption Statistics.* 5640 Nicholson Lane, Ste. 300, Rockville, MD 20852.

National Center for Men. (1996). Reproductive rights affidavit. P.O. Box 317, Brooklyn, NY 11240.

National Urban League. (1987). *Adolescent male responsibility: Pregnancy prevention and parenting program.* New York: National Urban League.

Neal, A. G., Groat, H. T., and Wicks, J. W. (1989). Attitudes about having children: A study of 600 couples in the early years of marriage. *Journal of Marriage and the Family, 51,* 313–327.

Nevid, J. S., Fichner-Rathus, L., and Rathus, S. A. (1995). *Human sexuality in a world of diversity.* 2d ed. Needham Heights, MA: Allyn and Bacon.

Newman, R. (1987). His sexuality, her reproductive rights. *Changing Men, 47,* 2–4.

Newton, C. R., Hearn, M. T., Yuzpe, A. A., and Houle, M. (1992). Motives for parenthood and response to failed in vitro fertilization: Implications for counseling. *Journal of Assisted Reproduction and Genetics, 9,* 24–31.

Nicholas, M. K., and Tyler, J. P. P. (1983). Characteristics, attitudes and personalities of AI donors. *Clinical Reproduction and Fertility, 2,* 389–396.

Nicholas-Casebolt, A., and Garfinkel, I. (1991). Trends in paternity adjudications and child support awards. *Social Science Quarterly, 72,* 83–97.

Niego, S., and Danielson, R. (1996). Reproductive health counseling for young men. *PSAY Network Newsletter, 4,* 5–6.

Nieschlag, E., Wickings, E. J., and Breuer, H. (1981). Chemical methods for male fertility control: Expert consultation of the European Medical Research Council Advisory Subgroup on Human Reproduction. *Contraception, 23,* 1–10.

Nieschalg, E., Behre, H. M., and Weinbauer, G. F. (1992). Hormonal male contraception: A real chance? In E. Nieschlag and U. F. Halbernicht (Eds.), *Spermatogenesis—fertilization—contraception: Molecular, cellular and endocrine events in male reproduction* (pp. 477–501). Heidelberg: Springer Verlag.

Noble, E. (1987). *Having your child by donor insemination.* Boston: Houghton Mifflin Company.

Nock, S. L. (1987). The symbolic meaning of childbearing. *Journal of Family Issues, 8,* 373–393.

Novosad, N. (1996). God squad: The Promise Keepers fight for a man's world. *Progressive, August,* 24–29.

O'Brien, M. (1981). *The politics of reproduction.* Boston: Routledge and Kegan Paul.

O'Campo, P., Faden, R. R., Gielen, A. C., Kass, N., and Anderson, J. (1993). Contraceptive and sexual practices among single women with an unplanned pregnancy: Partner influences. *Family Planning Perspectives, 25,* 215–219.

O'Connell, M. (1993). *Where's papa: Fathers' role in child care.* Washington, DC: Population Reference Bureau.

O'Connell, M., and Rogers, C. C. (1984). Out-of-wedlock births, premarital pregnancies and their effect on family formation and dissolution. *Family Planning Perspectives, 16,* 157–162.

Office of Population Census and Surveys. (1990). *General Household Survey: Preliminary Results for 1989.* Table 17. HMSO, London.

Office of Technology Assessment. (1988). *Artificial insemination practice in the United States: Summary of a 1987 survey.* Washington, DC: U.S. Government Printing Office.

Olsen, G. W., Ross, C. E., Bodner, K. M., and Lipshultz, L. I. (1995). Reply to the authors. *Fertility and Sterility, 65,* 451–453.

Olsen, G. W., Ross, C. E., Bodner, K. M., Lipshultz, L. I., and Ramlow, J. M. (1995). Have sperm counts been reduced 50 percent in 50 years? A statistical model revisited. *Fertility and Sterility, 63,* 887–892.

Overall, C. (1987). *Ethics and human reproduction: A feminist analysis.* Boston: Allen and Unwin.

Paglia, C. (1992). *Sex, art, and American culture.* New York. Vintage Books.

Paige, K. E., and Paige, J. M. (1973). The politics of birth practices: A strategic analysis. *American Sociological Review, 38,* 663–676.

Pangkahila, W. (1991). Reversible azoospermia by androgen—progestin combination regimen in Indonesian men. *International Journal of Androl., 14,* 248–256.

Parke, R. (1996). *Fatherhood.* Cambridge, MA: Harvard University Press.

Partridge-Brown, M. (1993). *In vitro fertilization clinics: A North American directory of programs and services.* Jefferson, NC: McFarland and Company.

Pasley, K., and Minton, C. (1997). Generative fathering after divorce and remarriage: Beyond the "disappearing dad." In A. J. Hawkins and D. C. Dollahite (Eds.), *Generative fathering: Beyond deficit perspectives* (pp. 118–133). Thousand Oaks, CA: Sage.

People in the Interest of S.P.B., Colo., 651 p. 2d 1213 (1982).

Perry, S., and Dawson, J. (1985). *Nightmare: Women and the Dalkon Shield.* Old Tappan, NJ: Macmillan.

Petchesky, R. P. (1980). Reproductive freedom: Beyond a woman's right to choose. In C. R. Stimpson and E. S. Person (Eds.), *Women: Sex and sexuality.* Chicago: University of Chicago Press.

Peterson, G. H., Mehl, L. E., and Leiderman, P. H. (1979). The role of some birth related variables in fathers' attachment. *American Journal of Orthopsychiatry, 49,* 330–338.

Peterson, L. S. (1995). *Contraceptive use in the United States: 1982–90.* Advance data from vital and health statistics, no. 260. Hyattsville, MD: National Center for Health Statistics.

Pinchbeck, D. (1996). Downward motility. *Esquire, January,* 79–84.

Pirog-Good, M. A. (1993). In-kind contributions as child support: The teen alternative parenting program. In R. L. Lerman and T. J. Ooms (Eds.), *Young unwed fathers: Changing roles and emerging policies* (pp. 251–266). Philadelphia: Temple University Press.

Planned Parenthood of Central Missouri v. Danforth, 428 U.S. 52 (1976).

Planned Parenthood of Southeastern Pennsylvania v. Casey, 505 U.S. 833, 112 S. Ct. 2791, 120 L. Ed. 2d 674 (1992).

Pleck, J. H. (1985). *Working wives/working husbands.* Beverly Hills, CA: Sage.

Pleck, J. H. (1987). American fathering in historical perspective. In M. S. Kimmel (Ed.), *Changing men: New directions in research on men and masculinity* (pp. 83–97). Newbury Park, CA: Sage.

Pleck, J. H. (1994). Are "family-supportive" employer policies relevant to men? In J. C. Hood (Ed.), *Men, work, and family* (pp. 217–237). Thousand Oaks, CA: Sage.

Pleck, J. H. (1997). Paternal involvement: Levels, sources, and consequences. In M. E. Lamb (Ed.), *The role of the father in child development* (pp. 66–103, 325–332. New York: Wiley.

Pleck, J. H., Sonenstein, F., and Ku, L. (1990). Contraceptive attitudes and intention to use condoms in sexually experienced and inexperienced adolescent males. *Journal of Family Issues, 11,* 294–312.

Pleck, J. H., Sonenstein, F., and Ku, L. (1991). Adolescent males' condom use: Relationships between perceived cost-benefits and consistency. *Journal of Marriage and the Family, 53*, 733–745.

Pleck, J. H., Sonenstein, F., and Ku, L. (1993). Changes in adolescent males' use of and attitudes toward condoms, 1988–1991. *Family Planning Perspectives, 25*, 106–109, 117.

Pleck, J. H., Sonenstein, F., and Ku, L. (1996). Effects of pregnancy experience on young males' subsequent fertility behavior. Unpublished manuscript.

Pleck, J. H., Sonenstein, F., and Swain, S. O. (1988). Adolescent males' sexual behavior and contraceptive use: Implications for male responsibility. *Journal of Adolescent Research, 3*, 275–284.

Polikoff, N. D. (1983). Gender and child-custody determinations: Exploding the myths. In I. Diamond (Ed.), *Families, politics, and public policy: A feminist dialogue on women and the state* (pp. 183–202). New York: Longman.

Popenoe, D. (1996). *Life without father*. New York: Free Press.

Potts, D. M. (1985). Coitus interruptus. In S. L. Corson, R. J. Derman, and L. B. Tyrer (Eds.), *Fertility Control* (pp. 299–305). Boston: Little, Brown.

Poynor, R. (1996). Personal communication. Associate Professor of Art History, University of Florida.

Pudney, J., Oneta, M., Mayer, K., Seage, G., III, and Anderson, D. (1992). Pre-ejaculatory fluid as a potential vector for sexual transmission of HIV-1. *Lancet, 340, 1*, 470.

Purdie, A., Peek, J. C., Adair, V., Graham, F., and Fisher, R. (1994). Attitudes of parents of young children to sperm donation—implications for donor recruitment. *Human Reproduction, 9*, 1355–1358.

Pyke, K. (1994). Women's employment as a gift or burden? *Gender and Society, 8*, 73–91.

Quill, T. E., Lipkin, M., and Lamb, G. S. (1984). Health-care seeking by men in their spouse's pregnancy. *Psychosomatic Medicine, 46*, 277–283.

Raboy, B. (1993). Secrecy and openness in donor insemination: A new paradigm. *Politics and the Life Sciences, 12*, 191–192.

Ragoné, H. (1994). *Surrogate motherhood: Conception in the heart*. Boulder, CO: Westview Press.

Reiss, I. (1986). *Journey into sexuality: An exploratory voyage.* Englewood Cliffs, NJ: Prentice-Hall.

Rickert, V. I., Jay, M. S., Hill, C. A., and Bridges, C. (1989). Females' attitudes and behaviors toward condom purchase and use. *Journal of Adolescent Health Care, 10*, 313–316.

Ringheim, K. (1993). Factors that determine prevalence of use of contraceptive methods for men. *Studies in Family Planning, 24*, 87–99.

Ringheim, K. (1995). Evidence for the acceptability of an injectable hormonal method for men. *Family Planning Perspectives, 27*, 123–128.

Robinson, C. (1993). Surrogate motherhood: Implications for the mother-fetus relationship. In J. C. Merrick and R. H. Blank (Eds.), *The politics of pregnancy: Policy dilemmas in the maternal-fetal relationship* (pp. 203–224). New York: Haworth Press.

Robinson, J. N., Forman, R. G., Clark, A. M., Egan, D. M., Chapman, M. G., and Barlow, D. H. (1991). Attitudes of donors and recipients to gamete donation. *Human Reproduction, 6,* 307–309.

Rodholm, M. (1981). Effects of father-infant postpartum contact on their interaction 3 months after birth. *Early Human Development, 5,* 79–85.

Roe v. Wade, 410 U.S. 133 (1973).

Rogow, D., and Horowitz, S. (1995). Withdrawal: A review of the literature and an agenda for research. *Studies in Family Planning, 26,* 140–153.

Rosenwasser, S. M., Wright, L. S., and Barber, R. B. (1987). The rights and responsibilities of men in abortion situations. *Journal of Sex Research, 23,* 97–105.

Ross, J. A. (1992). Sterilization: Past, present, future. *Studies in Family Planning, 23,* 187–198.

Rossi, A. S. (1987). Parenthood in transition: From lineage to child in self-orientation. In A. Lancaster and A. S. Rossi (Eds.), *Parenting across the life span* (pp. 31–81). New York: Aldine de Gruyter.

Rothman, B. K. (1986). *The tentative pregnancy: Prenatal diagnosis and the future of motherhood.* New York: Viking.

Rothman, B. K. (1989). *Recreating motherhood: Ideology and technology in a patriarchal society.* New York: Norton.

Rotundo, E. A. (1985). American fatherhood: A historical perspective. *American Behavioral Scientist, 29,* 7–25.

Rowland, R. (1983). Attitudes and opinions of donors on an artificial insemination by donor (AID) programme. *Clinical Reproduction and Fertility, 2,* 249–259.

Rowland, R. (1993). Donor insemination to *in vitro* fertilization: The confusion grows. *Politics and the Life Sciences, 12,* 192–193.

Rowland, R., and Ruffin, C. (1983). Community attitudes to artificial insemination by husband or donor, in vitro fertilisation and adoption. *Journal of Clinical Reproduction and Fertility, 2,* 195–206.

Rue, V. (1986). *Forgotten fathers: Men and abortion.* Lewiston, NY: Life Cycle Books.

Runner, B. J. (1989–90). Protecting a husband's parental rights when his wife disputes the presumption of legitimacy. *Journal of Family Law. University of Louisville School of Law, 28,* 115–131.

Ryan, B., and Plutzer, E. (1989). When married women have abortions: Spousal notification and marital interaction. *Journal of Marriage and the Family, 51,* 41–50.

Ryder, N. B. (1979). The future of American fertility. *Social Problems, 26,* 359–370.

Sable, M. R., Stockbauer, J. W., Schramm, W. F., and Land, G. H. (1990). Differentiating the barriers to adequate prenatal care in Missouri, 1987–1988. *Public Health Reports, 105,* 549–555.

Sanday, P. R. (1990). *Fraternity gang rape: Sex, brotherhood, and privilege on campus.* New York: New York University Press.

Savage, B. D. (1987). *Child support and teen parents.* Washington, DC: Children's Defense Fund, Adolescent Pregnancy Prevention Clearinghouse.

Savitz, D. A., and Chen, J. (1994). Influence of paternal age, smoking, and alcohol consumption on congenital abnormalities. *Teratology, 44,* 429–440.

Scanzoni, J. (1989). Alternative images for public policy: Family structure versus families struggling. *Policy Studies Review, 8,* 599–609.

Scanzoni, J. (1996). Personal communication. Professor of Sociology, University of Florida.

Scanzoni, J., and Marsiglio, W. (1991). Wider families as primary relationships. *Marriage and Family Review, 17(1/2),* 117–133.

Scanzoni, J., and Marsiglio, W. (1993). New action theory and contemporary families. *Journal of Family Issues, 14,* 105–132.

Scanzoni, J., Polonko, K., Teachman, J., and Thompson, L. (1989). *The sexual bond: Rethinking families and close relationships.* Beverly Hills, CA: Sage.

Schearer, B. S. (1978). Current efforts to develop male hormonal contraception. Studies in Family Planning. *Population Council, 9,* 229–231.

Schulte, M. M., and Sonenstein, F. L. (1995). Men at family planning clinics: The new patients? *Family Planning Perspectives, 27 (5),* 212–216, 225.

Schutz, A. (1970a). *On phenomenology and social relations.* Chicago: University of Chicago Press.

Schutz, A. (1970b). *Reflections on the problem of relevance.* New Haven, CT: Yale University Press.

Schutz, A., and Luckmann, T. (1973). *The structures of the life-world.* Evanston, IL: Northwestern University Press.

Seaman, B. (1972). *Free and female.* New York: Coward, McCann and Geoghegan.

Seccombe, K. (1991). Assessing the costs and benefits of children: Gender comparisons among childfree husbands and wives. *Journal of Marriage and the Family, 53,* 191–202.

Secor, G. A. (1990). *Michael H. v. Gerald D.*: Due process and equal protection rights of unwed fathers. *Hastings Constitutional Law Quarterly, 17,* 759–790.

Segal, S. J. (1972). Contraceptive research: A male chauvinist plot? *Family Planning Perspectives, 4,* 21–25.

Seligman, J. (1990). Variations on a theme: The 21st century family. *Newsweek, Special Issue, Winter/Spring,* 20–24.

Seltzer, J. A., and Brandreth, Y. (1995). What fathers say about involvement with children after separation. In W. Marsiglio (Ed.), *Fatherhood: Contemporary theory, research, and social policy* (pp. 166–192). Thousand Oaks, CA: Sage.

Service, R. F. (1994). Barriers hold back new contraception strategies. *Science,* 266, 1489.

Shalev, C. (1989). *Birth power: The case of surrogacy.* New Haven, CT: Yale University Press.

Sherwen, L. N. (1987). The pregnant man. In L. N. Sherwen (Ed.), *Psychosocial dimensions of the pregnant family* (pp. 157–176). New York: Springer.

Shifman, P. (1990). Involuntary parenthood: Misrepresentation as to the use of contraceptives. *International Journal of Law and the Family,* 4, 279–296.

Shoop, J. G. (1993). `Nonbiological' fathers win paternity rights. *Trial,* 29, 14, 16.

Shostak, A. B., McLouth, G., and Seng, L. (1984). *Men and abortion. Lessons, losses, and love.* New York: Praeger.

Siegel, A. B. (1982). Pregnant dreams: Developmental processes in the manifest dreams of expectant fathers. Doctoral dissertation, California School of Professional Psychology. Ann Arbor, University Microfilms International.

Sigman, M. (1991). Assisted reproductive techniques for the treatment of male factor infertility. *Rhode Island Medical Journal,* 74, 591–596.

Simon, W., and Gagnon, J. H. (1986). Sexual scripts: Permanence and change. *Archives of Sexual Behavior,* 15, 97–120.

Smith, J. B., Potts, D. M., and Fortney, J. A. (1991). Political constraints on contraceptive development in the United States. *NCMJ,* 51, 484–488.

Snowden, R. (1993). Sharing information about DI in the UK. *Politics and the Life Sciences,* 12, 194–195.

Snowden, R., Mitchell, G. D., and Snowden, E. M. (1983). *Artificial reproduction: A social investigation.* London: Allen and Unwin.

Society for Assisted Reproductive Technology (SART). (1994). Personal communication. Birmingham, AL, May 16.

Sonenstein, F. L., Holcomb, P. A., and Seefeldt, K. S. (1993). What works best in improving paternity rates? *Public Welfare, Fall,* 26–43.

Sonenstein, F. L., Pleck, J. H., and Ku, L. (1989). Sexual activity, condom use and AIDS awareness in a national sample of adolescent males. *Family Planning Perspectives,* 21, 152–158.

Soule, B., Stanley, K., and Copans, S. (1979). Father identity. *Psychiatry,* 42, 255–263.

Stetson, D. M. (1991). *Women's rights in the U.S.A.: Policy debates and gender roles.* Pacific Grove, CA: Brooks/Cole Publishing Company.

Stewart, F. H. (1997). Expectations about men's role and responsibility. Paper presented at Another Gender Gap? Men's Role in Preventing Pregnancy, a briefing for journalists, New York City, March.

Stokes, B. (1980). *Men and family planning*. Worldwatch paper 41. Washington, DC: Worldwatch Institute.

Stolcke, V. (1988). New reproductive technologies: The old quest for fatherhood. *Reproductive and Genetic Engineering, 1,* 5–19.

Stone, R., and Waszak, C. (1992). Adolescent knowledge and attitudes about abortion. *Family Planning Perspectives, 24,* 52–57.

Stranger, K. (1989). *J. W. F. v. Schoolcraft*: The husband's rights to his wife's illegitimate child under Utah law [Case note]. *Brigham Young University Law Review,* 955–976.

Straub v. B.M.T. (1994). No. 10A04-9302-JV-53. Court of Appeals of Indiana, Fourth District.

Strikland, O. L. (1987). The occurrence of symptoms in expectant fathers. *Nursing Research, 36,* 184–189.

Stringfellow, T. (1994). Gender differences in young college students' condom purchases and use. Master's thesis, University of Florida.

Stryker, S. (1980). *Symbolic interactionism: A social structural version*. Palo Alto: Benjamin/Cummings.

Stryker, S. (1987). Identity theory: Developments and extensions. In K. Yardley and T. Honess (Eds.), *Self and Identity* (pp. 89–104). New York: Wiley.

Stryker, S., and Serpe, R. T. (1982). Commitment, identity salience, and role behavior. In W. Ickes and E. S. Knowles (Eds.), *Personality, roles, and social behavior* (pp. 199–218). New York: Springer-Verlag.

Stuart, J. (1990). Unmarried fathers and gendered justice. *Men's Studies Review, 7,* 1, 3–8.

Stycos, J. M. (1996). Men, couples, and family planning: A retrospective look. Population and Development Program Working Paper No. 96.12. Ithaca, NY: Cornell University.

Sugland, B. W., Wilder, K. J., and Chandra, A. (1996). Sex, pregnancy, and contraception: A report of focus group discussions with adolescents. Unpublished paper. Child Trends, Washington, DC.

Suitor, J. J. (1981). Husbands' participation in childbirth: A nineteenth-century phenomenon. *Journal of Family History, Fall,* 278–293.

Sullivan, M. (1989). Absent fathers in the inner city. *Annals of the American Academy of Political and Social Science, 501,* 48–58.

Sullivan, M. (1995). Teenage males' beliefs and practices about contraception: Findings from comparative ethnographic research in high-risk neighborhoods. Paper presented at the Annual Meetings of the Population Association of America, San Francisco, April.

Sundaram, K., Kumar, N., and Bardin, C. W. (1993). 7 _-methyl-nortestosterone (MENT): The optimal androgen for male contraception. *Annals of Medicine, 25,* 199–205.

Swanson, H. S. W. (1993). Donor anonymity in artificial insemination: Is it still necessary? *Columbia Journal of Law and Social Problems, 27,* 151–190.

Swanson, J. M. (1985). Men and family planning. In S. M. H. Hanson and F. W. Bozett (Eds.), *Dimensions of fatherhood* (pp. 21–28). Beverly Hills, CA: Sage.

Swerdloff, R. S., Wang, C., and Bhasin, S. (1989). Male contraception: 1988 and beyond. In H. Burger and D. de Krester (Eds.), *The testis.* 2d ed. (pp. 547–568). New York: Raven Press.

Swidler, A. (1986). Culture in action: Symbols and strategies. *American Sociological Review, 51,* 273–286.

Swomley, J. (1996). Promises we *don't* want kept. *Humanist, 56,* 35–36.

Sylvain, J. C. (1990). *Michael H. v. Gerald D.:* The presumption of paternity. *Catholic University Law Review, 39,* 831–858.

Tanfer, K., Grady, W. R., Klepinger, D. H., and Billy, J. O. G. (1993). Condom use among U.S. men, 1991. *Family Planning Perspectives, 25,* 61–66.

Tang, G. H., Zhong, Y. H., Ma, Y. M., et al. (1988). Vasectomy and health: Cardiovascular and other diseases following vasectomy in Sichuan Province, People's Republic of China. *International Journal of Epidemiology, 17,* 608–617.

Tannahill, R. (1980). *Sex in history.* New York: Stein and Day.

Thoits, P. A. (1991). On merging identity theory an stress research. *Social Psychology Quarterly, 54,* 101–112.

Thompson, L. (1991). Family work: Women's sense of fairness. *Journal of Family Issues, 12,* 181–196.

Thornton, A. (1989). Changing attitudes toward family issues in the United States. *Journal of Marriage and the Family, 51,* 873–893.

Thornton, A. (1995). Attitudes, values, and norms related to nonmarital fertility. In *Report to Congress on out-of-wedlock childbearing,* Department of Health and Human Services Publication no. (PHS) 95–1257. Washington, DC: Government Printing Office.

Tournaye, H., Camus, M., Khan, I., Staeaaen, C., Van Steireghem, A. C., and Devroery, P. (1991). In vitro fertilization, gamete or zygote intrafallopian transfer for the treatment of male infertility. *Human Reproduction, 6,* 263–266.

Trethowan, W. H. (1968). The couvade syndrome—some further observations. *Journal of Psychosomatic Research, 12,* 107–115.

Trethowan, W. H., and Colon, M. F. (1965). The couvade syndrome. *British Journal of Psychiatry, 111,* 57–66.

Triseliotis, J. (1993). Donor insemination and the child. *Politics and the Life Sciences, 12,* 195–197.

Tse, F. L. S. (1980). Current concepts in birth control methods. *NARD,* February, 441–444.

Turner, C. (1993). A call for openness in donor insemination. *Politics and the Life Sciences, 12,* 197–199.

Udry, R. (1988). Biological predispositions and social control in adolescent sexual behavior. *American Sociological Review, 53*, 709–722.

Uniform Parentage Act, 9B U.L.A. (1973).

U.S. House of Representatives. (1990). Hearings before the Subcommittee on Health and the Environment of the Committee on Energy and Commerce. No. 101-141. Washington, DC: U.S. Government Printing Office.

Velde, E. te (1994). The impact of some biomedical advances on reproduction and parenthood. Paper presented at the Conference on Changing Fatherhood, Tilburg University, The Netherlands, May.

Venohr, J. C., Williams, R. G., and Baxter, D. E. (1996). *Results from the Massachusetts paternity acknowledgment program: Final quarterly report.* Denver: Policy Studies, Inc.

Ventura, S. J., Taffel, S. M., Mosher, W. D., et al. (1995). *Trends in pregnancies and pregnancy rates: Estimates for the United States, 1980–1992.* Monthly Vital Statistics Report, vol. 43, no. 11, supp. Hyattsville, MD: National Center for Health Statistics.

Ventura, S. J., Martin, J. A., Taffel, S. M., Mathews, T. J., and Clarke, S. C. (1995). *Advanced report of final natality statistics, 1993.* Monthly vital statistics report, vol. 44, no. 3, supp. Hyattsville, MD: National Center for Health Statistics.

Wagenheim, J. (1996). Among the Promise Keepers: An inside look at the evangelical men's movement. *Utne Reader, 73*, 74–77.

Waites, G. M. H. (1993). Male fertility regulation: The challenges for the year 2000. *British Medical Bulletin, 49*, 210–221.

Walker, A., Gregson, S., and McLaughlin, E. (1987). Attitudes towards donor insemination—a post-Warnock survey. *Human Reproduction, 2*, 745–750.

Walters, M. F. (1989). Who decides? The next abortion issue: A discussion of fathers' rights. *West Virginia Law Review, 91*, 165–191.

Walzer, S. (1996). Thinking about the baby: Gender and divisions of infant care. *Social Problems, 43*, 219–234.

Wattenberg, E. (1993). Paternity actions and young fatherhood. In R. I. Lerman and T. J. Ooms (Eds.), *Young, unwed fathers: Changing roles and emerging policies* (pp. 213–234). Philadelphia: Temple University Press.

Weaver, R., and Cranley, M. (1983). An exploration of paternal-fetal attachment behavior. *Nursing Research, 32*, 68–72.

Webb, R. B. (1976). *The presence of the past: John Dewey and Alfred Schutz on the genesis and organization of experience.* Gainesville: University Presses of Florida.

Weisman, C. S., Plichta, S., Nathanson, C. A., Ensminger, M., and Robinson, C. (1991). Consistency of condom use for disease prevention among adolescent users of oral contraceptives. *Family Planning Perspectives, 23*, 71–74.

Weltzien, J. (1984). *A study of the psychological fathers associated with infertil-*

ity: Depression, locus of control, quality of marital interaction. Dissertation Abstracts International, 44, 2910-B.

Westney, O. E., Cole, O. J., and Munford, T. L. (1988). The effects of prenatal education intervention on unwed prospective adolescent fathers. *Journal of Adolescent Health Care, 9*, 214–218.

Westoff, C. F., and Jones, E. F. (1979). *Patterns of aggregate and individual changes in contraceptive practice: United States, 1965–1975.* Series 3, no. 7. Washington, DC: U.S. Department of Health, Education, and Welfare.

Westreich, R., Spector-Dunsky, L., Klein, M., Papageorgiou, A., Kramer, M., and Gelfand, M. (1991). The influence of birth setting on the fathers' behavior toward his partner and infant. *Birth, 18*, 198–202.

Whicker, M. L., and Kronenfeld, J. J. (1986). Men and women together: The impact of birth control technology on male-female relationships. *International Journal of Sociology of the Family, 16*, 61–81.

Whiteford, L. M. (1989). Commercial surrogacy: Social issues behind the controversy. In L. M. Whiteford and M. L. Poland (Eds.), *New approaches to human reproduction: Social and ethical dimensions* (pp. 145–169). Boulder, CO: Westview Press.

Whitehead, B. Dafoe (1996). Women and the future of fatherhood. *Wilson Quarterly, 20*, 30–34.

Wilson, M. D., Kastrinakis, M., and D'Angelo, L. J. (1994). Attitudes, knowledge, and behavior regarding condom use in urban black adolescent males. *Adolescence, 29*, 13–26.

Wilson, W. J. (1987). *The truly disadvantaged.* Chicago: University of Chicago Press.

Wolinsky, H. (1994). The father factor: Technology allows infertile men to reproduce. *Chicago Sun-Times* [online], *June 19*, 1–10. Available: NEXIS Library: NEWS File CHISUN.

Wood, R. G. (1995). Marriage rates and marriageable men: A test of the Wilson hypothesis. *Journal of Human Resources, 30*, 163–193.

Woodward, K. L., and Keene-Osborn, S. (1994). The gospel of guyhood. *Newsweek, August 29*, 60–61.

World Health Organization (WHO) Task Force on Psychological Research in Family Planning. (1982). Hormonal contraception for men: Acceptability and effects on sexuality. *Studies in Family Planning, 13*, 328–342.

World Health Organization (WHO) Task Force on Psychological Research in Family Planning. (1990). Contraceptive efficacy of testosterone-induced azoospermia in normal men. *Lancet, October 20*, 955–959.

World Health Organization (WHO) (1992), *Annual Technical Report, Special Programme of Research, Development and Research Training in Human Reproduction.* Geneva.

World Health Organization (WHO) Task Force on Methods for the Regulation of Male Fertility. (1995). Rates of testosterone-induced suppression to severe oligozoospermia or azoospermia in two multinational clinical studies. *International Journal of Andrology, 18*, 157–165.

Working Group on Conceptualizing Male Parenting. (1997). Social fatherhood and paternal involvement: Conceptual, data, and policy issues. Report prepared for the Conference on Fathering and Male Fertility: Improving Data and Research, Washington, DC, March.

Working Group on Male Fertility and Family Formation. (1997). Report prepared for the Conference on Fathering and Male Fertility: Improving Data and Research, Washington, DC, March.

Wright, L. (1996). Silent sperm. *New Yorker, January 15*, pp. 42–55.

Wright, J., Duchesne, C., Sabourin, S., Bissonnette, F., Benoit, J., and Girard, Y. (1991). Psychosocial distress and infertility: Men and women respond differently. *Fertility and Sterility, 55*, 100–108.

Zayas, L. H. (1988). Thematic features in the manifest dreams of expectant fathers. *Clinical Social Work Journal, 16*, 282–296.

Zelles, P. (1984). Feedback from 521 waiting room males. In A. B. Shostak, G. McLouth, and L. Seng (Eds.), *Men and abortion: Lessons, losses, and love* (pp. 299–304). New York: Praeger.

Zelnick, M., Kantner, J. F., and Ford, K. (1981). *Sex and pregnancy in adolescence*. Beverly Hills, CA: Sage Publications.

Zilbergeld, B. (1992). *The new male sexuality*. New York: Bantam Books.

Index

differences, 153; dreams, 188; drive, 34; experiences with, 49; as a form of leverage, 39; men's participation in, 112; outside of marriage, 39, 165; ratio, 87; talk about, 58

Sex-based differences, 155

Sex education, 169, 170

Sexist ideology, 81, 155

Sex-symbol, 56

Sexual: ability, 54, 55; abuse, 162; acts, 35; arousal, 54; behavior, 169, 170, 180, 185; beings, 152; climax, 50, 54; consciousness, 59; contract, 33; decisions, 151; double standard, 49; encounter, 50; episode, 50, 52, 70, 115; experiences, 32, 182; fidelity, 133; gratification, 65; history, 179; identity, 58, 59; involvement, 177; issues, 168; liaisons, 151; men, 167; partner, 34, 71, 87, 99, 112, 138, 144, 175, 179; pleasures, 34, 38, 54–56, 69; prowess, 20, 22, 54–56; realm, 51, 115, 175, 184; relations, 118; relationship, 179, 181; relations without marriage, 39; responsibility, 20; revolution, 39; sphere, 73; union, 112; vigor, 55

Sexual intercourse, 10, 22, 32, 35, 39, 69, 101, 104, 106, 117, 118, 144, 145; abstinence from, 38, 81; fathering a child through, 117; risky behavior and, 22

Sexuality, 19, 49, 54, 101, 120, 148, 169, 170, 174, 179, 182; female, 56; men's, 169; within a patriarchal society, 50; progressive view of, 181; traditional view of, 182; women's, 56

Sexually active, 18, 66, 70, 169; couple, 25

Sexually based: procreation, 106; relationship, 29; reproduction, 50

Shotgun marriages, 39

Shug, 76. *See* Silicone vas deferens plug

Silicone vas deferens plug, 52, 76. *See also* Injectable vas deferens plug

Single female household, 150

Single men, 98, 165; condom use and, 189

Single motherhood, 27. *See also* Mothers

Single-parenthood issues, 66

Single women: children born to, 135

Social activists, 191

Social bond, 6, 7

Social change, 147, 156

Social class, 89, 180, 184

Social constructionist, 152, 155

Social context, 148, 174

Social conventions, 61

Social customs, 138

Social developments, 37

Social expectations, 1, 10, 11

Social factors, 9, 15, 20, 79

Social forces, 20, 63, 154

Social initiatives, 147

Social institutions, 32, 36, 90, 96

Social interactions, 8

Socialization, 8

Social kinship, 33, 34

Social life, 5, 11, 37, 38, 152, 153, 155, 188, 190; prehistoric, 36

Socially constructed relationships, 38

Social movement, 164, 187

Social organization, 32, 33

Social paternal gesture, 7

Social patterns, 57; gendered, 62

Social policies, 21, 24, 90, 96, 97, 180

Social policymakers, 1, 43, 95

Social policy perspective, 4